The Society for Old Testament Study

BOOK LIST
1992

Printed for the Society

ISSN 0309 0892

ISBN 0 905495 11 X

© THE SOCIETY FOR OLD TESTAMENT STUDY 1992

PRINTED BY W. S. MANEY AND SON LTD HUDSON ROAD LEEDS LS9 7DL

Contents

	Page
Preface	5
1. General	7
2. Archaeology and Epigraphy	25
3. History and Geography	40
4. Text and Versions	44
5. Exegesis and Modern Translations	48
6. Literary Criticism and Introduction (including History of Interpretation, Canon, and Special Studies)	60
7. Law, Religion, and Theology	97
8. The Life and Thought of the Surrounding Peoples	115
9. Apocrypha and Post-Biblical Studies	122
10. Philology and Grammar	133
Books received too late for notice in 1992	143
Index of Authors	147

One copy of the *Book List* is supplied free to all members of the Society.

Copies of the *Book List* for 1992 may also be obtained from M. E. J. Richardson, Esq., Department of Middle Eastern Studies, University of Manchester, Manchester M13 9PL, England. Back numbers of the *Book List* are also available from Mr Richardson. Orders should not be accompanied by payment; an invoice will be sent. The price of these is £15.00 including postage or $30.00, for a single copy. Payment should be made by cheque in sterling or U.S. dollars payable to the Society for Old Testament Study, or direct to Post Office Giro Account No. 50 450 4002.

Review copies of books for the *Book List* should be sent to the new Editor:

Dr Lester L. Grabbe
Department of Theology
University of Hull
Hull HU6 7RX
England

PREFACE

With the publication of the present number I retire from the Editorship of the *Book List*. It is my first pleasant task to offer my warmest good wishes to my successor, Dr L. L. Grabbe of the University of Hull. I have appreciated over six and a half years the cooperation of several overseas scholars; this year the 'support group' of Professor B. Albrektson, Professor H. Cazelles, Dr F. Garcia Martínez, Dr K. Jeppesen, Professor G. L. Prato, and Professor A. S. van der Woude has been joined by Dr D. T. Tsumura from Tokyo; and I have had advice also from Dr A. Abela and Professor G. Fohrer. Among colleagues closer to home, Professor G. W. Anderson, Dr S. P. Brock, Professor R. P. Carroll, Mr R. J. Coggins, Dr P. R Davies, Mr A. R. Millard, Dr S. C. Reif, Dr W. G. E. Watson, Professor R. N. Whybray, and Dr N. Wyatt have drawn books to my attention or supplied reviews from personal copies. To them as to the many members of the Society who are regular reviewers or recent recruits my warmest thanks. I am grateful too to my Edinburgh Faculty colleague, Professor D. B. Forrester, who contributed a review. During my editorship I have dealt with well over three hundred publishers large and very small, and with many the relationship has been particularly cordial. Our printers, Messrs W. S. Maney and Son, have continued the excellent support all my predecessors have enjoyed. I have benefited greatly from the ready help of Mr Derek Brown in Leeds. Recently too Maneys have been playing a larger part in the sale and distribution of the *Book List*.

The following abbreviations and symbols are employed as in earlier issues:

B.L.	=	*Book List*
Eleven Years	=	*Eleven Years of Bible Bibliography* 1957
Decade	=	*A Decade of Bible Bibliography*
Bible Bibliog.	=	*Bible Bibliography 1967–1973:*
		Old Testament (1974)

NEW COLLEGE EDINBURGH   A. GRAEME AULD

CORRECTION to *Book List* 1991, p. 43:

The full review by Professor Knibb of J. C. VanderKam's critical text and translation of Jubilees was marred in its final paragraph as it appeared last year by two substantial omissions. The complete text is printed below:

VanderKam, like Charles, regards BL Orient. 485 as the best manuscript, and he expresses the hope that he has reproduced its readings more fully and accurately than Charles did. (Baars and Zuurmond quite properly drew attention to serious omissions and inaccuracies in Charles's edition.) A test collation indicated that VanderKam's text does follow that of BL Orient. 485 accurately *except* that he does not always reproduce the orthography of the manuscript (thus there are instances where *s* is used for *š* or *ḥ* for *h*, or where first-order vowels are used with gutturals where the manuscript has fourth order vowels), and unfortunately he does not discuss in detail the way he has treated the manuscript. The same considerations apply to VanderKam's apparatus, but with the addition that here a check against BL Orient. 485 and Ṭānāsee 9 indicated a number of minor omissions and inaccuracies. Finally, it is no doubt arguable whether the sixteenth-century BL Orient. 485 or the fifteenth-century Ṭānāsee 9 (=Kebrān 9) should have been used as the base text; Zuurmond has argued for the priority of Ṭānāsee 9 and Berger based his translation above all on this manuscript and on Pontifical Biblical Institute A.2.12 of the fourteenth/fifteenth century. However, VanderKam's view that a group of seventeenth- and eighteenth-century manuscripts are to be ranked in second place after BL Orient. 485, and before such manuscripts as Ṭānāsee 9 and Pontifical Biblical Institute A.2.12, as representing 'the oldest form of the text that can now be attained' seems on the face of it implausible. VanderKam base his view on a statistical analysis of two samples of variants; but while he gives us the results of his analysis, he does not list even a proportion of the variants on which the results are based, and it is difficult to know how far the variants he used really are significant.

GENERAL

1. GENERAL

ATTRIDGE, H. W., COLLINS, J. J., and TOBIN, T. H. (eds): *Of Scribes and Scrolls: Studies on the Hebrew Bible, Intertestamental Judaism, and Christian Origins, presented to John Strugnell on the occasion of his sixtieth birthday* (College Theology Society Resources in Religion 5). 1990. Pp. vii, 289. (University Press of America, Lanham, New York and London. Price: $32.50; paperback price: $19.95. ISBN 0 8191 7902 7; 0 8191 7903 5 (pbk))

As its subtitle implies, the brief but detailed and suggestive studies in this Festschrift are gathered under three headings. Seven are on the Hebrew Bible and its text. J. R. Davila writes on new Qumran readings for Genesis 1 in three Qumran manuscripts (4QGen$^{g, h, k}$), S. A. White concludes that 4QDeut^n is an excerpted text rather than a 'true biblical manuscript', and E. C. Ulrich provides a detailed comparative study of the orthography and text of 4QDan^a, 4QDan^b and the MT. Some Qumran evidence also features in R. Fuller's proposal that the two readings for the last word of Zech. 2:12 are both ancient, and in J. H. Charlesworth's study of the use of the *beth essentiae* in 1QH 8:4–5 and of the permissive hiphil in Ps. 155:11 and other texts. There are also two studies on Wisdom material: E. Tov concludes that the translator of LXX Proverbs used a Hebrew text different from that of the MT, and L. M. Wills discusses how wisdom traditions in court narratives should be identified and defined.

Ten studies cover matters of second temple Judaism. E. Puech proposes a new reconstruction for the Hebrew of Ms. B of Ben Sira 48:11, J. J. Collins demonstrates that there is variety in the use of *qṣ* in Daniel 7–12, R. Doran suggests that 2 Macc. 4:9–17 is directed primarily against Jason's educational reforms, and F. J. Murphy provides an exegesis of Korah's rebellion in Pseudo–Philo 16. There are four Qumran studies, a lively comparative rhetorical analysis of 1QS 7:15–25 and 1QH 5:20–27:5 by C. A. Newsom, a description of blessing formulae in Qumran texts by E. Schuller, a consideration of 4 Q185 in relation to Jewish wisdom literature by T. H. Tobin, and two notes on the Aramaic Levi document (involving 4QTestLevi^a and *mebaqqer*) by J. C. Greenfield and M. E. Stone. B. J. Brooten argues convincingly that Jael in the principal Jewish inscription from Aphrodisias is a feminine name, and R. A. Kraft asks for a reevaluation of Philo's later life and literary career through the juxtaposition of *De Somniis* 2:110–54 and some passages in Josephus.

In the final section on early Christianity and its environment, three of the eight studies may be of interest to readers of the *Book List*. A. Y. Collins asserts forcefully that Dan. 7:13 lies behind Jesus' use of Son of Man, K. E. McVey proposes that the polemic in Ephrem's *Hymns on the Nativity* is best understood against a background of the lack of acceptance of rabbinic prescriptions in fourth century Mesopotamian Jewish communities, and G. W. E. Nickelsburg examines the possible significance for the better understanding of Egyptian Christianity of the placing of I Enoch with other particular texts in Codex Panopolitanus and Chester Beatty Biblical Papyrus XII. The remaining studies in this valuable collection are by D. J. Harrington, J. C. VanderKam, J. G. Gager, H. W. Attridge and D. Levenson.

G. J. BROOKE

AVIRAM, J., and SHACHAR, A. (eds): *David Amiran Volume* (Eretz-Israel. Archaeological, Historical and Geographical Studies, 22). 1991. Pp. 41, 226(Hebrew). (Israel Exploration Society, in cooperation with the Department of Geography, The Hebrew University of Jerusalem. Price: $40.00)

The Israel Exploration Society has properly honoured Ruth and David Amiran in successive volumes of *Eretz Israel* (see below p. 11). An

8   GENERAL

introduction sketches the life-time in study of the Land of Israel of the founder of the Department of Geography in the Hebrew University. Most of the very varied twenty-three Hebrew and three English papers in this volume relate to contemporary or at least recent geographical issues. And perhaps only R. Rubin's Hebrew study of 'Original Maps and their Copies: Cartogenealogy of the Early Maps of Jerusalem, from the fifteenth to the eighteenth Century' overlaps with the interests of this *Book List*. Eight map families are reconstructed from some three hundred maps of Jerusalem created in that period. Many readers would be interested to see this piece in English.

A. G. AULD

Bibelen i Norge. 1991. Pp. 384, with many illustrations in the text. (Det Norske Bibelskap, Oslo. ISBN 82 541 0314 3)

This handsome volume has been published to mark the 175th anniversary of the founding of the Norwegian Bible Society, the chairman of whose executive committee, Bishop A. Aarflot, contributes a brief foreword. The seventeen essays in the book are concerned, not with the history of the Society, but with the influence of the Bible in Norwegian life, literature, and art. In an introductory article M. Saebø surveys the entire field, emphasizing the perenially renewed and developing influences of Scripture. J. Schumacher writes on the interpretation of the Bible in the Middle Ages and the varying ways in which its message permeated national life. O. Jensen describes the increased influence brought about by the Lutheran Reformation and its impact on ecclesiastical and political life. Å. Holter traces subsequent developments in the translation of the Bible in language which was eventually freed from Danish influence and more truly Norwegian. A. B. Amundsen analyses the treatment of death in funeral sermons from the sixteenth, seventeenth, and eighteenth centuries. Å. Haavik discusses the use of the Bible in the work of the great Norwegian hymn writers. S. Christie considers the impact of the Reformation on art in church buildings and the expression through art of biblical teaching. The place of the Bible in schools is described by B. Haraldsø. D. Kullerud evaluates the impact of newer views concerning the Bible towards the end of the nineteenth century. Ø. Hodne deals with biblical elements in Norwegian legends and folk tradition. The place of biblical motifs in contemporary Norwegian art is described by G. Danbolt. Four essays (by D. G. Myhren, I. Hauge, C. F. Engelstad, and J. I. Sørbø) are devoted to the place and influence of the Bible in the work of various Norwegian authors in the nineteenth and twentieth centuries. In a concluding essay, 'the people's book and the source of faith', O. Chr. M. Kvarme outlines ways in which a revived use of the Bible could bring about the renewal of culture, community life, and the Church. The value of this impressive volume is increased by extensive annotation and bibliographies.

G. W. ANDERSON

BORG, V. (ed.): *Veterum Exempla. Essays in honour of Mgr Prof. Emeritus Joseph Lupi* (Melita Theologica Supplementary Series, 1). 1991. Pp. 194. (Faculty of Theology, University of Malta)

This 'Festschrift' in honour of a patristic scholar who has served the Catholic diocese of Malta for more than fifty years, opens a series of publications attached to the review of the Faculty of Theology, *Melita Theologica*.

The present volume contains six contributions 'covering various aspects of the theological sciences'. Readers of the *Book List* will mostly be interested in the contribution by Anthony Abela, 'Redactional Structuring within the

GENERAL 9

Abraham Narratice in Genesis' (pp. 35–82), in which the author argues that Gen. 12–25 is held together by a global structure which consists of two parallel panels (B 12:10–13:1; 13:2–18; 14:1–24; 15:1–21 and B' 20:1–18; 21:1–21; 21:22–34; 22:1–19) and a central element C (16:1–16; 17:1–27; 18:1–33; 19:1–28; 19:29–38) wedged in between the two panels. Outflanking B/B' we find A(11:27–12:9) which is meant to introduce the Abraham narrative and A' (22:20–25:18) which brings the narrative to its natural ending.

A. G. AULD

BOTTERWECK, G. J., and RINGGREN, H. (eds): *Theological Dictionary of the Old Testament*. Vol. vi. Translated by David E. Green, 1990. Pp. xx, 491. (Eerdmans, Grand Rapids MI; distributed by SCM, London. Price: $35.95; £20.00. ISBN 0 8028 2330 0)

The speed of publication of the parts of this English translation of the *Theologisches Wörterbuch zum Alten Testament*, now edited by H.-J. Fabry and H. Ringgren, has somewhat improved: the interval between this and the previous volume is only four years. There is still a long way to go to catch up the German original, which is itself still incomplete: this volume covers *yōbēl* to *yātar* (the arrangement of the articles is according to the Hebrew diction-ary), which takes it as far as the end of volume three of the German edition which has reached its seventh volume with *rāṣāh*. The translation, again by David E. Green, is of a high standard, and the technical improvements noted in the review of volume five (*B.L.* 1987, p. 8) are retained. On the individual contributions, many of which are by distinguished scholars, see *B.L.* 1983, pp. 8–9. Although the price inevitably puts it beyond the range of most individuals, the usefulness of this authoritative work for all students and teachers of the Old Testament cannot be overstated.

R. N. WHYBRAY

BRIEND, J., and COTHENET, E. (eds): *Supplément au Dictionnaire de la Bible*. Vol. xi. Fasc. 63–64A (*Salut-Samuel [Livres de]*). 1990. Cols. 737–1056. (Letouzey & Ané, Paris. Price: Fr. 350.00 (subscr). ISBN 2 7063 0161 9 (series); 2 7063 0116 3 (vol. xi))

Apart from the last few columns of the article on salvation repeated from the previous fascicle and the initial few columns of that on the Books of Samuel by A. Cacquot with which it concludes, this fascicle is entirely concerned with matters Samaritan. J. Briend writes on the city of Samaria — name, history, archaeology (with a plan); A. Lemaire on the Samaria ostraca; J. Margain on the Samaritan Pentateuch. The remainder of the fascicle — 275 columns — is devoted to the article on the Samaritan sect by M. Baillet. Here, after an introductory section briefly describing the present community, its beliefs and practices and Samaritan history and literature, there follows an immense documentation (142 columns) of sources and bibliography covering both internal and external and both ancient and modern sources, scholarly literature and archaeological data. The remainder of the article deals in detail with chronological problems, the history of the sect together with its own historical traditions and the question of its identity and origins. The arrange-ment of the article, as will be seen from the above description, involves a good deal of repetition, and the interweaving of historical fact and sectarian tradition in the section entitled 'history and traditions' is somewhat confusing. But the material here assembled, not least the bibliography, makes this a major study which will be indispensable to Samaritan scholars. It is to be hoped that the article, like some earlier ones from the *Supplément*, will be reprinted as a separate work.

R. N. WHYBRAY

10 GENERAL

CLEMENTS, R. E. (ed.): *The World of Ancient Israel: Sociological, anthropological and political perspectives*. Essays by Members of the Society for Old Testament Study. 1989; 1991 (pbk). Pp. xi, 436. (Cambridge University Press. Price: £15.95 ($19.95). ISBN 0 521 42392 9)

This is a paperback edition of the original work (also reprinted in 1991 in hardback) noted in *B.L.* 1990, p. 13.

N. WYATT

COGAN, M., and EPH'AL, I. (eds): *Ah, Assyria . . .: Studies in Assyrian History and Ancient Near Eastern Historiography presented to Hayim Tadmor* (Scripta Hierosolymitana, XXXIII). 1991. Pp. 347. (Magnes, Jerusalem. Price: $33.00. ISSN 0080 8369)

Most of the thirty essays in this worthy Festschrift appropriately centre on Neo-Assyrian historiography and literature, many with direct reference and application to Old Testament studies. Among these I. M. Diakonoff interprets 'the cities of the Medes' (2 Kings 17:5–6) as the Kar-Kašši district settled after 716 BC; while I. Eph'al examines all references to Samaria(ns) in Assyrian sources. Not all were Israelites. B. Oded discusses 'the command of the God' as the authority for (holy) war and N. Na'aman the part played by forced alliances during Assyria's western campaigns with special reference to Israel's relations with Damascus. F. M. Fales argues for ideological factors alongside facts in Sargon's 714 BC campaign and M. Cogan defends the royal scribes against charges of rewriting history (e.g. to emphasize victories) and shows a balance of the divine and human in a dual causality in the events recorded. He considers the Assyrian annals as highly developed historiography and no less objective than Babylonian Chronicles. A. R. Millard studies all large numbers in Assyrian Royal inscriptions to show a balanced use of round numbers and estimates alongside accurate accounting. W. W. Hallo examines accounts of the death of kings and suggests that the Bible may reflect a distrust of kingship. Interesting comparative studies include T. Ishida on the Succession Narrative (1 Kgs 1–2) and Esarhaddon's Apology and S. N. Kramer on 'Solomon and Sulgi' portraying both as ideal kings noted for fame, wisdom and music yet diverging over temple-building and economic reforms. M. Liverani writes on the trade network of Tyre in Ezek. 27, M. Greenberg the Babylonian use of omens to determine the direction of Nebuchadnezzar's advance in Ezek. 21:26–27 and M. Elat Phoenician overland trade in the Neo-Babylonian period. Altogether a valuable volume.

D. J. WISEMAN

COHN-SHERBOK, D. (ed.): *A Traditional Quest. Essays in Honour of Louis Jacobs* (Journal for the Study of the Old Testament Supplement Series 114). 1991. Pp. 233. (JSOT Press, Sheffield. Price: £35.00 ($60.00). ISBN 1 85075 279 6; ISSN 0309 0787)

As inspired teacher, controversial rabbi and prolific author of books on Jewish theology, mysticism and talmudic logic, Louis Jacobs well deserves the honour of these thirteen essays by British and American scholars. The dominant theme is Jewish thought (including admiration and criticism of his own); but there are also treatments of Byzantine Jewish culture, talmudic medicine, a eulogy for Menasseh ben Israel, and challenging biblical passages. A. Cunningham argues the value of a psychoanalytic approach to biblical narrative as long as one is careful to distinguish individual from humanity, literal and symbolic, and exegesis from application; and demonstrates how the method can identify and explain the basic motifs and themes in the Eden story. J. Magonet characterizes the legislation of the 'Book of the Covenant' as relating to ownership and conflicts of interest as well as to non-owners and God who represents them. He includes Exodus 23:4–5

GENERAL

among numerous 'pairs' of laws and tentatively suggests that these verses teach the need for a human solidarity that transcends the issue of ownership conflicts.

S. C. REIF

DAVIES, P. R. (ed.): *Second Temple Studies*. 1. *Persian Period* (JSOT Supplement Series 117). 1991. Pp. 192. (JSOT Press, Sheffield. Price: £22.50 ($39.50); sub. price: £18.75 ($29.50). ISBN 1 85075 315 6; ISSN 0309 0787)

This collection is focused on the society of Achaemenid Yehud, the place of the Temple in that society, the policies of the Persian administration, and the relationships between the returned exiles and the 'remainees'. J. Blenkinsopp refines J. Weinberg's *Bürger-Tempel-Gemeinde* thesis; the new community is controlled by the Babylonian immigrants, who imposed their own social structures (p. 53), regaining the land lost to them during the exile and rebuilding and controlling the temple. P. R. Redford (pp. 154–62) questions Blenkinsopp's assumption that the Jerusalem temple was necessarily comparable with other Achaemenid regional cult centres, and asks pertinent questions about the legal authority in Judah and the real-estate holdings of such a *Gemeinde*. D. L. Smith also emphasises the influence of the returned exilic community on post-exilic society. K. Hogland, however, sees Judah's society in the context of the Achaemenid policy of turning the Jews into a collective economic unit by developing rural settlements and commerce, and establishing military garrisons. R. A. Horsley responds that the Persian policy was to restore and strengthen, not to break down, the traditional patterns of society in Judah (pp. 171–72). J. M. Halligan's critique analyses the economic crisis described in Neh. 5; Nehemiah's solution to it 'defies reality' (p. 152). R. P. Carroll relates the story of Jeremiah the landowner (Jer. 32), the inheritance laws of Lev. 25, and the story of Naboth's murder to Second Temple society; D. Jobling criticises him for methodological inconsistency, and firmly insists that 'The biblical text does not want us to know about the sociology of the second Temple' (p. 182). L. Grabbe undermines much scholarly reconstruction by casting serious doubts on the authenticity of the 'Aramaic documents' in Ezra and of the 'Ezra memoir' itself. D. L. Petersen analyses the varied understanding of the significance of the temple in post-exilic prophetic works. In his introductory essay, P. R. Davies questions the assumption that the pre-exilic society is necessarily to be seen as the direct predecessor of the post-exilic (p. 16 f.), but the following contributions suggest continuity rather than a new beginning. The papers are 'an attempt to juxtapose literary, sociological and archaeological data, and seek some synthesis' (p. 15). But synthesis is not achieved. The literary problems of Ezra-Nehemiah remain intractable; 'the gap between texts and the real world remains as unbridgeable as ever' (Carroll, p. 124); the archaeology of the period remains sketchy; and the sociology (central to this collection) remains based on inadequate data. These papers, however, mark an important advance in our approach to the Persian period.

J. R. BARTLETT

EITAN, A., GOPHNA, R., and KOCHAVI, M. (eds): *Ruth Amiran Volume* (Eretz-Israel. Archaeological, Historical and Geographical Studies, 21). 1990. Pp. viii, 110, 258 (Hebrew). (Israel Exploration Society, Jerusalem. Price: $60.00)

Forty-eight authors honour the *doyenne* of Israeli archaeologists with twenty-four Hebrew and fourteen English articles. About half the essays concern aspects of the Early Bronze Age, ranging from studies of individual objects such as 'A Stamp Seal and a Seal Impression from Tel Gerar' (A. Ben-Tor), and local matters like 'The Question of Early Arad's Population' (Y. Govrin, arguing for a complete break between Chalcolithic and Early

12 GENERAL

Bronze Age cultures at the site due to greater aridity) to continuing discussion of international connections in P. R. S. Moorey's 'From Gulf to Delta ... The Syrian Connection', which stresses the 'enterprise of Uruk' in the light of recent discoveries at Buto in Egypt. While Ruth Amiran's interests have focused on this period through her energetic programme of excavations at Arad, her range is much wider, and many essays reflect that, coming closer to biblical studies. M. Bietak considers 'The Concept of Eternity in Ancient Egypt and the Bronze Age World', concluding from evidence of burials and miniature vessels that it was alien to Canaan; J. Bourriau describes 'Canaanite Jars Memphis, Kom Rabbi'a' and P. O. Harper 'A Bronze Head' probably part of a supporting figure of Achaemenid date. In Hebrew, D. Ussishkin argues that one revetment wall at Hazor was actually a foundation for a Middle Bronze Age platform, while another, in Area G, was the basis for an Iron Age tower, and A. Biran reports on 'The Middle Bronze II Ramparts of Tel Dan'. Other Middle Bronze Age topics are nomadism and settlement in northern Sinai (E. Oren, Y. Yikutieli), burials at Geshur (Y. Garfinkel, R. Bonfil), and Tell el-Yahudiyah juglets from Afula (U. Zevulun). In the Late Bronze Age there were foundation deposits of a lamp enclosed in two bowls, apparently inspired by Egyptian customs (S. Bunimowitz, O. Zimhoni) and metal-working in the Jordan Valley which O. Negbi believes was not influenced by the Sea Peoples and was not connected with Hiram's metallurgical aid to Solomon, *contra* J. Tubb. Piecing together scattered and forgotten notes of finds made over a century, G. Barkay suggests an Egyptian temple stood north of Jerusalem in the area of the Ecole biblique. 'A Figurine from Tel Ira' is the only Iron Age object treated, a rare hermaphroditic tambourine player, according to P. Beck, with transjordanian associations. However, Iron Age lamps receive special notice in V. Sussman's 'Pottery Vessels versus Lamps: Identity of Fashioning' when the heavy disc bases appear. A. Mazar's review of excavations at Tel Beth-Shean in 1989 and 1990 reveals a new Late Bronze Age temple under the Level IX courtyard and a destruction level from the late eleventh century BC, perhaps David's work.

There is a brief appreciation of Ruth Amiran and a bibliography of her writings.

A. R. MILLARD

ERIKSEN, E. O.: *Holy Land Explorers*. 1989. Pp. 171. (Franciscan Printing Press, Jerusalem)

Much of this book consists of popular articles about three early expeditions which navigated the Dead Sea (those of Costigin in 1835, Molyneux in 1847 and Lynch in 1848), based on extracts from contemporary sources, which are reproduced in part. The remainder makes no attempt to be comprehensive, concentrating on visits to the Dead Sea and the Jordan River. The narratives make interesting reading and the bibliographies are of some value, but there is much unnecessary repetition and some carelessness. More scholarly treatments of the subject can be found elsewhere (see, for example, Y. Ben-Arieh, *The rediscovery of the Holy Land in the nineteenth century* (Jerusalem, 1979)).

G. I. DAVIES

FABRY, H.-J., and RINGGREN, H. (eds): *Theologisches Wörterbuch zum Alten Testament*. Band VII, Lfg 3/5 (cols. 257–640). 1990. (Kohlhammer, Stuttgart. Price: DM 138.00. ISBN 3 17 011553 7)

This triple fascicle begins with the final columns of rā'āh (H. F. Fuhs) and concludes with the initial column of rāṣāh (with rāṣōn — H. Barstad). It contains forty-eight complete articles. rā'āh, with over forty columns in all, is the longest article, followed by rûaḥ (S. Tengström and Fabry), rab and cognates (E. Blum and Fabry, disproportionately long) and r'' (C. Dohmen

GENERAL

with a brief section on Qumran by Rick). Other important words discussed, in some cases too briefly, include *rō'š* ('head' — W. A. M. Beuken and U. Dahmen; *rī'šōn* has a separate article by H. D. Preuss), *rē'šīt* (S. Rattray and J. Milgrom), *rūm* (Firmage, J. Milgrom and Dahmen; *t'rūmāh* will have a separate article), *rwš* with *rāš*, *rīš* etc. (M. Saebø), *rāhab* (with *rahab* — U. Rüterswörden; too brief), *reḥem* (T. Kronholm; *rḥm* has a separate article by H. Simian-Yofré and Dahmen), *rîb* with *m'rîbāh*, Ringgren — too short with only seven columns), *rā'āh* (I, = 'graze', G. Wallis) and *r'pā'îm* (R. Liwak). *rāḥab* (R. Bartelmus) hardly needs ten columns in a theological dictionary. *rāmaś* (with *remés*, R. E. Clements) is mainly of sociological rather than theological interest.

R. N. WHYBRAY

FOHRER, G.: *Studien zum Alten Testament (1966–1988) mitsamt Bibliographie Georg Fohrer (1991)* (Beihefte zur Zeitschrift für die alttestamentliche Wissenschaft 196). 1991. Pp. 186. (De Gruyter, Berlin. Price: DM 104.00. ISBN 3 11 012819 5; ISSN 0934 2575)

This is the fifth volume of Georg Fohrer's collected essays; previous collections contained his studies on prophecy (1949–65), theology and history (1949–66), the book of Job (1956–79) and texts and themes (1966–72). Although the title of the present volume is more general than those chosen for his other collections, the essays included in it fall into two main groups, the first containing exegetical studies and the second more theological studies; this is therefore a second volume of 'texts and themes'. Among the exegetical studies are: two on sections of Jeremiah, one on Job, one on Habakkuk's prayer and one on the Day of the Lord passages. Three of the theological studies are in English and have been grouped together under the general title of 'Basic Structures of Biblical Faith'.

Because most of these essays have appeared in various Festschriften and collected essays, their publication in this volume has made them more readily available to a wider circle of students. They are fittingly accompanied by a bibliography of Fohrer's publications between 1959 and 1991.

G. H. JONES

GAMMIE, J. G. and PERDUE, L. G. (eds): *The Sage in Israel and the Ancient Near East*. 1990. Pp. xiv, 545. (Eisenbrauns, Winona Lake IN. Price: $42.50. ISBN 0 931464 46 3)

Many distinguished contributors here provide thirty-six essays on the sage, ranging from Sumerian times down to rabbis and Romans. About half of the essays deal with the Old Testament, while the rest examine relevant neighbouring cultures and later developments, such as the sage in Hellenistic literature and Jesus as sage. It was an attractive idea to focus on the person of 'the sage', but alas, it is often an elusive figure in the sources. Definition of 'sage', as indeed of 'wisdom', is a persistent difficulty, and many a brave contributor has to write about a form of sagedom on which his source is not in the least forthcoming. It is not surprising that contributors sometimes contradict one another. Nevertheless, this is a useful, readable and informative volume, contributing from many angles to the interpretation of literature, thought and society in the ancient Near East.

J. H. EATON

GARRONE, D. and ISRAEL, F. (eds): *Storia e tradizioni di Israele. Scritti in onore di J. Alberto Soggin*. 1991. Pp. xlvi, 310. (Paideia Editrice, Brescia. Price: Lire 80,000. ISBN 88 394 0467 8)

After a brief introduction by S. Moscati, a *tabula gratulatoria*, and a bibliography of Soggin's writings extending to twenty-six pages, this

14   GENERAL

Festschrift contains twenty-four articles, all of which are directly relevant to
Old Testament Study. Eleven articles are in English, five in French, and four
each in German and Italian. They vary in length from four to twenty-seven
pages. Malamat's contribution consists of two sections of a longer study, the
two previous sections of which have been published separately in a French
Assyriological journal. Eleven articles are studies of particular passages of the
Old Testament, three of them from Amos. Four address wider literary
questions in the Old Testament, and one the citation of Old Testament
passages in the New Testament. The remaining eight studies are concerned
with questions relating to the history of Israel. The essays thus reflect the
interests of the honorand, and the distinguished list of contributors guaran-
tees the quality of this Festschrift, which is a worthy tribute to our newly
elected honorary member.
                                                                    A. GELSTON

GESE, H.: *Alttestamentliche Studien*. 1991. Pp. 307. (Mohr, Tübingen.
Price: DM 59.00. ISBN 3 16 145699 8 (brosch); 3 16 145739 0 (gewebe)))

The first collection of Professor Gese's essays appeared in 1974 under the
title *Vom Sinai zum Zion*; it is now being followed by another collection of
which all but one of the essays have been published elsewhere between 1977
and 1987. Among the variety of topics under discussion are: the Abraham
narrative; the Samson narrative; Ezekiel 20:25f; Hosea 12:3–14; Amos (two
studies); Jonah; Psalms (two studies); Job; Daniel (two studies). Other essays
have been devoted to more general studies, such as hermeneutics and biblical
exegesis, and again the implications of Brevard Childs's canon studies.

It is useful to have these essays collected into one volume and made
accessible to those who may have missed them when they were first published.

                                                                    G. H. JONES

GOODRICK, E. W. and KOHLENBERGER, J. R. III: *The NIV Exhaustive
Concordance*. 1990. Pp. xxii, 1853. (Zondervan, Grand Rapids MI: Price:
$49.95. ISBN 0 310 43690 7)

KOHLENBERGER. J. R.: *The NRSV Concordance Unabridged*. Including
the Apocryphal/Deuterocanonical Books. 1991. Pp. xiv, 1483, 76, 53, 76.
(Zondervan, Grand Rapids MI. Price: $39.95. ISBN 0 310 53910 2)

The Goodrick/Kohlenberger Concordance to the New International
Version (NIV) of the Bible provided the model for the Kohlenberger
Concordance to the New Revised Standard Version (NRSV), so allowing its
production in a very much shorter time. Both should prove very useful, and
relatively straightforward to use. The NIV Concordance relates only to the
Protestant canon of the Bible, while that on the NRSV handles the Apocrypha as well. Both include a listing of all words used in the King James Version
but not in the version in question, with a cross-reference to the word or words
or indeed fresh spelling or transliteration now preferred. Because NIV is
available in an Anglicized as well as the parent North American version,
Goodrick/Kohlenberger provide cross-references also for the substantial
variants within modern English in 227 verses from 'assistant' to 'aide', 'ears of
corn' to 'heads of grain', and 'cock' to 'rooster', to offer just three examples.
Yet the impression gained that North American farming language must have
developed faster than British is diminished when one finds in NRSV that
Joseph's corn still has ears and that Peter did not require a rooster to remind
him of his betrayal. Bidcar (2 Kgs 9:25) survives the transition from RSV to
NRSV as the solitary 'aide' in that version, but is regraded to 'chariot officer'
in NIV; his role-label is taken there by the more famous Joshua and an
underling of Sanballat.

GENERAL

A typical entry in each is headed first by the summary total of occurrences, then by cross-references to relates entries: 'leading' and 'led' both refer to 'lead', for example, while 'lead' refers across to all of 'leader', 'leader's', 'leaders', 'leaders'', 'leadership', 'leading', 'leads', 'led', 'ringleader' — and also to the adjective 'leaden' in the case of the NRSV volume. The entries under 'lead', of course, also illustrate an important difference between these Concordances and Analytical Concordances such as the classic by Cruden or the recent Eerdmans volume on the RSV (see *B.L.* 1989, p. 24): homonyms such as 'ark', 'lead', and 'will' are not distinguished — and that means, among other things, that statistics of usage have to be handled with great care. Each biblical use of the word in question is listed on its own line, in English Bible order, with reference and immediate context. In the case of the NIV Concordance only, the line ends with the code-number of the Hebrew, Aramaic, or Greek word in the parent text. All words are fully listed in both Concordances, the commonest articles, conjunctions, particles, prepositions, and pronouns being listed by chapter and verse, but without context provided, in a separate Index following the main body of the work; different editorial decisions have been taken over selection: 'also', 'could', and 'even' are just the first examples of a small set of words handled more summarily by the NRSV volume than the other. Some (theologically) significant selections of references to these commonest words do appear in the main concordance section of each volume. Among the examples are 'will' where that is deliberate and not simply future and some cases of the pairing 'I am'. This helps, but only so far: since Hebrew *'hyh* is translated different ways, the invitation to compare Exodus 3 and Judges 6 is never delivered.

It is in their closing section that the two Concordances go their own ways. The NIV volume offers three Index-Lexicons from each of Hebrew, Aramaic, and Greek to English. Each entry is headed by code-number, word, transliteration, and total of occurrences. Each on its own line below follow the varied translations of this parent word, sorted first by order of frequency and then alphabetically. And this Concordance ends with an index correlating its code numbers with those in Strong's Exhaustive Concordance to the King James Version. The NRSV volume ends with an Index to NRSV footnotes; and, this time compiled by V. D. Verbrugge, a Topical Index to the NRSV.

A lot can be learned about translation, about the biblical languages, and even about the Bible itself from sampling these volumes — and even more from comparing them. And if some of the resultant questions send the reader back to the parent texts for an answer, that will be gain rather than loss. I wonder repeatedly whether the translators of these versions would have made all the decisions they did, had they had these concordances available to them. Till we can all make our own concordances from user-friendly programmes loaded on computers on our own desks, we are greatly indebted to Zondervan and to John Kohlenberger and his colleagues. A. G. AULD

GREISCH, J. and KEARNEY, R. (eds): *Actes du colloque de Cerisy-la-Salle 1er-11 août 1988: Paul Ricœur. Les Métamorphoses de la Raison Herméneutique.* 1991. Pp. 413. (Cerf, Paris. Price: Fr 175.00. ISBN 2 204 04308 7; ISSN 0298 9972)

This volume contains the papers given at a colloquium in Cerisy-la-Salle on Paul Ricoeur's work in August (1–11) 1988. Ricoeur is one of the most formidable continental philosophers of contemporary phenomenological metaphysics, whose work has had some direct influence on modern theology. Some of his work has also touched on biblical studies, especially his writings on metaphor and narrative. His *oeuvre* — already considerable and growing all the time — is something all biblical scholars should be familiar with and this volume will give considerable assistance to anybody wishing to find out

16 GENERAL

something of the background and structure of his work. It is divided into four parts: part I looks at the historical and intellectual traditions behind Ricoeur's work (especially that of Husserl, Heidegger, Nabert, Schleiermacher, Bultmann, and Dilthey). Monique Schneider's piece 'Éros tragique' (pp. 51–64) caught my eye as a very useful contribution here to Ricoeur's thought, especially her account of Spinoza's influence on Ricoeur. Part II focuses on Ricoeur's epistemology and hermeneutics. Part III looks at the hermeneutics of Ricoeur's *oeuvre*. Part IV looks at 'horizons' of his work and includes a piece by Ricoeur himself 'L'attestation: entre phénoménologie et ontologie' (pp. 381–403).

Reading commentary is a very poor substitute for reading texts, but if reading this volume (entirely in French) will encourage members of the Guild to start reading Ricoeur for themselves then it is to be commended. There is certainly a wealth of informed discussion of Ricoeur's own work in it and a great deal of the background material necessary to appreciating the influences on his work. Ricoeur's range of thought is phenomenal, so this volume makes a most useful introduction to or commentary on that wide-ranging *oeuvre*. Biblical scholars will find the contribution by Anne-Marie Pelletier entitled 'L'exégèse biblique sous l'inspiration de l'herméneutique: un accès réouvert à la temporalité biblique' (pp. 297–309) directly relevant to their own work. Twenty-four contributions (plus Ricoeur's piece) make this a very representative volume (but impossible to review or even to list all the contributions) on the work of Ricoeur. In particular I enjoyed Richard Kearney's treatment of the hermeneutic imagination and postmodernism (pp. 357–71), but that's just a personal point of view. A book well worth reading by any scholar interested in hermeneutics.

R. P. CARROLL

HAIK-VANTOURA, S.: *The Music of the Bible Revealed. The Deciphering of a Millenary Notation*. Translated from French by D. Weber. Edited by J. Wheeler. 1991. Pp. xviii, 557. (Bibal Press, Berkeley CA; King David's Harp, San Francisco CA. Price: $29.95. ISBN 0 941037 10 x)

Translator and editor are to be congratulated on giving us this English version of the French work first published in 1976 and revised in 1978 (*La Musique de la Bible révélée*). The author has engaged for many years with the question of the musical meaning of the Massoretic accents, the *ṭe'amim*, and has evolved a comprehensive explanation which she expounds with inspirational conviction. She believes the signs represent the hand-signals of musical directors, a system of chironomy like that represented by Egyptian artists and well-attested in Greek tradition. Her decipherment reveals the signs beneath the letters as fixed degrees of the scale, while those above have a value dependent on the adjacent sign below. Two systems, one for the prose and one for the poetical books, cover the entire Hebrew Bible, and preserve the musical chant which was inherent in the composition from the start, whether from the First or Second Temple.

It may seem incredible that the signs which are only attested in manuscripts from about the tenth century CE should preserve for every syllable its musical rendering from biblical times, but the author can argue the lack of a convincing alternative explanation of the signs and that they were always claimed to be of biblical origin. She is also justified in finding a great importance in chironomy. Her book will certainly stimulate fresh interest in the work of the Massoretes and in the history of music in the ancient Near East. She has done well to make cassettes of her reconstructed music available. Difficult as the Massoretic and musical history fields are, especially in correlation, it is to be hoped that there will be some who can sympathetically test and further this bold exploration.

J. H. EATON

GENERAL

IMHOF, P. (ed.): *Gottes Nähe: Religiöse Erfahrung in Mystik und Offenbarung. Festschrift zum 65. Geburtstag von Josef Sudbrack SJ.* 1990. Pp. 451 (Echter, Würzburg. Price: DM 48.00. ISBN 3 429 01295 3)

Of specific interest to *Book List* readers will be Norbert Lohfink's essay, 'Das Böse im Herzen und Gottes Gerechtigkeit in der weiten Welt. Gedanken zu Psalm 36' (pp. 327–41) in the section on 'The Presence of the Eternal in World-Religions'; his exegesis leads him to conclude that, paradoxically, the 'nearness' of God, for the psalmist, is in the 'distance' of Creation.

J. M. DINES

LANG, B. (ed.): *Internationale Zeitschriftenschau für Bibelwissenschaft und Grenzgebiete*, Bd xxxvi 1988–1990. 1991. Pp. xiv, 507. (Patmos, Düsseldorf. Price: DM 158.00. ISSN 0074 9745)

After the shorter Vol. xxxv 1987/88 (*B. L.* 1991, p. 19), this new volume relating to a longer period has returned to the length of its predecessors. Changes in the sub-headings within the concluding list of contents sometimes appear to relate to trends in the disciplines related to biblical studies: many more introductory items are reviewed this year; and myth, intertextuality, and rhetorical criticism appear among the categories isolated. On the other hand, while there are many more items also within archaeology and geography, these are listed under fewer sub-headings. Lang and his slightly enlarged band of collaborators again deserve our thanks.

A. G. AULD

LAWTON, D.: *Faith, Text and History. The Bible in English.* 1990. Pp. x, 203. (Harvester Wheatsheaf, New York. Price: £35.00. ISBN 0 7450 0569 1; 0 7450 1033 4 (pbk))

The dustjacket bills this as 'an important, even a brilliant book' (Stephen Prickett), as 'uniformly lucid and clear-headed' (Northrop Frye). I was not so enthusiastic. The aim of the book seems to be to 'disturb the polarisation of religious and literary uses of the Bible' (dustjacket again), and its major theme appears to be the way literary concerns and non-literal interpretation have always formed an important strand in Biblical interpretation, both ancient and modern. The author, an English literary critic, certainly knows his way around current Biblical scholarship, and has a good eye for the curious or telling quotation, whether from Origen or Ronald Reagan. But the writing is rather discursive and it is hard to tell what argument is going on at any point. Chapters on words and languages, on the history of Biblical interpretation, on narrative in Genesis, Ruth and Job, on belief and interpretation in the Gospels, on metaphor and literality in the Song of Songs and Revelation are interestingly written essays, free of jargon and pretentiousness, but their intended audience must be the general reader who has only a hazy knowledge of the Bible text and none of Biblical scholarship.

D. J. A. CLINES

LLOYD JONES, G.: *Robert Wakefield [1524] On The Three Languages* (Medieval and Renaissance Texts and Studies 68 Renaissance Text Series 13). 1989. Pp. xii, 260. (Binghampton, New York. Price: $40.00)

In reprinting, translating, and editing Wakefield's *De laudibus et utilitate trium linguarum* (sc. Arabic, Aramaic, and Hebrew) Lloyd Jones might have appositely added *et neglegentia quartae*: it is the indictment of ourselves, as teachers, that we have condoned the growth of an educational climate that has consigned to near-oblivion what was, until relatively recently, the *lingua franca* of west European intellectualism. He has done a first class job in tracing Wakefield's biography, sources, and scholarly apparatus, and the

18 GENERAL

result, significant for the history of biblical scholarship, is even more important for students of the sixteenth-century English renaissance, revealing as it does Wakefield's enquiring mind and scholarly competence. He not only refers to the standard mediaeval Jewish commentators and grammarians (the Qimḥis, Solomon Farḥon, David b. Yaḥya etc.) and utilizes their Christian followers (Lyre, Paul of Burgos, Reuchlin) but cites *inter alios* Megasthenes' *Indica* (this *via* Eusebius), the ninth-century Persian astronomer Abu Mashʿar, and, of his near contemporaries, Elio Antonio of Nebrija, who worked at Alcalá on the Complutensian Polyglot. It must be confessed that Wakefield's tract makes turgid reading (not so the editor's introduction and notes): and if his inaugural lecture was in fact delivered as printed, his audience (and perhaps Henry VIII, to whom it was dedicated) will have had to evince no less patience than the modern editor himself has done.

R. LOEWE

LONGMAN, T. III: *Old Testament Commentary Survey*. 1991. Pp. 160. (Baker Book House, Grand Rapids MI. Price: $10.95. ISBN 0 8010 5670 5)

Which of us has not known some sinking of the spirit when asked by a zealous student or dedicated layperson for a list of the best commentaries on the books of the Bible? Longman, like some faithful servant, has suffered vicariously the burdens of others by working on just such a list, a task he tells us which has taken him many years. In this work, not only commentaries, but theologies, histories, dictionaries, and concordances have all been rated on a one to five star system, like a list of hotels in an AA Guide. Unfortunately, the results are literally eclectic, for the comments on each are too brief to be informative, and the principle of choice too individualistic to be universal. Longman warns us that he is a conservative evangelical and the result is that, all other things being equal, those whose views coincide with Longman's get the higher ratings, rather like a loaded roulette wheel which, while it appears to be turning dispassionately, has the ball finishing up too often for comfort on a number favourable to the casino proprietor. I fear this is not the oracular answer to my *Klagelied* next time I am asked for a list of the 'best' commentaries.

R. A. MASON

MCCREESH, T. P. (ed.): *Old Testament Abstracts*. Vol. 13, No. 3; Vol. 14, Nos. 1, 2. 1990; 1991. Pp. 219–364; 1–239. (Catholic University of America, Washington D.C. Price: $14.00 per volume. ISSN 0364 8591)

Old Testament Abstracts continues to provide a helpful and up-to-date source of information concerning both articles and books on the Old Testament and related subjects.

M. A. KNIBB

MÜLLER, G. (ed.): *Theologische Realenzyklopädie (TRE)*, Bd. 20: *Kreuzzüge-Leo XIII*. 1990. Pp. 793. (De Gruyter, Berlin. Price: DM 396.00. ISBN 3 11 012655 9)

The only article in this volume entirely devoted to matters of special interest to readers of the *Book List* is that on Lachish (V. Fritz). But several articles contain substantial relevant sections: those on War (J. A. Soggin), Life (H. Seebass on the Old Testament, G. A. Wewers on Judaism), Body (H.-H. Schrey), Suffering (J. Scharbert on the Old Testament, S. Lauer on Judaism). Cross-references indicate the location of information in other articles on such subjects as the War Scroll, the Ark, Lamech, Tabernacles and Leah. There are biographical articles on A. Kuenen (J. Hahn), Paul de Lagarde (R. Heiligenthal) and Lambert of Avignon, 1487–1530 (Müller).

GENERAL 19

Other articles of at least peripheral interest to *Book List* readers include those on Criticism and Critical Theory, Art and Religion, and Culture. Finally, the articles on three universities (Lausanne, Leiden and Leipzig) mention their contributions to Old Testament scholarship.

R. N. WHYBRAY

MÜLLER, H.-P.: *Mythos — Kerygma — Wahrheit. Gesammelte Aufsätze zum Alten Testament in seiner Umwelt und zur Biblischen Theologie* (Beihefte zur Zeitschrift für die alttestamentliche Wissenschaft 200). 1991. Pp. xiv, 319. (De Gruyter, Berlin. Price: DM 132.00. ISBN 3 11 012865 3; ISSN 0934 2575)

This volume contains twelve essays by the author, eleven of which have already appeared elsewhere: the twelfth, on the correlation between language and perceptions of reality, is published for the first time. The book is in two sections. The first comprises seven exegetical studies of Old Testament texts with reference to parallel ancient New Eastern material, five dealing with aspects of the creation narratives and the flood in Genesis one on cuneiform parallels to Job and one on myth in lyric form in the Song of Songs. Throughout these discussions, however, the author is concerned with the wider implications they raise for the understanding of myth, its hermeneutical function, its understanding of reality and the justification for mythical speech, and this leads on to the second and more theological part of the work. Here, two of the five contributions are directly on Old Testament topics, one dealing with some theological implications of the concept of blessing, the other discussing new aspects of Job's questions to God. The remainder consist of an essay on myth, irony, and the standpoint of faith as elements in the phenomenology of Biblical religion, a discussion of anthropological and theological features in the relationship between myth and kerygma in the light of the *Entmythologisierung* debate, and the final essay mentioned above, which makes extensive use of the methods and conclusions of modern linguistic studies. It is useful to have these various articles collected together in a single volume: they are all thought-provoking and merit the careful attention of scholars concerned with the question of myth or the Bible and the ancient Near East or with Biblical theology in general.

J. R. PORTER

MURAOKA, T. (ed.): *Abr-Nahrain XXIX (1991)*. 1991. Pp. vii, 146. (Peeters, Leuven. Price: c.BF 1200)

Friends of this University of Melbourne annual will note that Professor Takamitsu Muraoka is continuing as editor despite his move to Leiden. As for the present volume, the coverage remains wide and the articles are for the most part of interest to scholars involved in Biblical and related studies. 'The Proto-alphabetic Inscriptions of Canaan' by B. E. Colless (pp. 18–66) continues the author's earlier studies in the same periodical (1988 and 1990), applying his insights into the proto-alphabetic script to the inscriptions from Canaan. Conclusions about values of letters are compared with those of B. Sass (on whose book see *B.L.* 1990, pp. 35–36). There is much that is uncertain. M. Florentin writes on 'The Object Suffixes in Samaritan Aramaic and the Modes of their Attachment to the Verb' (pp. 67–82). This is followed by 'Qᵊtûl Nouns in Classical Hebrew' by C. W. Gordon (pp. 83–86), an interesting note linking the $q^\partial t\hat{u}l$ nouns with Arabic broken plurals of the *qutûl* type (though it states misleadingly that 'broken plurals are treated as fem. sg. in Arabic', whereas the normal rule is that *all* plurals, broken *and* sound, which refer to inanimate objects and irrational beings — *mulûk*, 'kings', which is cited, does not qualify — are treated as feminine singular). 'Tūr Abdīn through the Ages' by R. Macuch (pp. 87–105) is in fact a (quite favourable) review-article commenting on aspects of A. Palmer's *Monk and mason on the Tigris frontier — The early history of the Tūr Abdīn*, 1990, and

20 GENERAL

related matters. The volume also contains a further instalment in the work of T. Muraoka and Z. Shavitsky on 'Abraham Ibn Ezra's Biblical Lexicon', continuing the Minor Prophets from the 1990 volume (pp. 106–28), and, as usual, reviews.

J. F. HEALEY

MURPHY-O'CONNOR, J.: *Le Nouveau Testament. Cent ans d'Exégèse à l'École Biblique* (Cahiers de la Revue Biblique 27). 1990. Pp. 217. (Gabalda, Paris. Price: Fr 340.00. ISBN 2 85021 045 5; ISSN 0575 0741)

VESCO, J.-L.: *L'Ancien Testament. Cent Ans d'Exégèse à l'École Biblique* (Cahiers de la Revue Biblique 28). 1990. Pp. 220. (Gabalda, Paris. Price: Fr 320.00. ISBN 2 85021 046 3; ISSN 0575 0741)

LAGRANGE, M.-J., OP: *Exégète à Jérusalem. Nouveaux Mélanges d'Histoire Religieuse (1890–1939)* (Cahiers de la Revue Biblique 29). 1991. Pp. 258. (Gabalda, Paris. Price: Fr 370.00. ISBN 2 85021 047 1)

These three supplements to the *Revue Biblique* are a fitting tribute to the record and contribution of the institution whose centenary they celebrate, and of its rightly celebrated founder. Murphy-O'Connor's survey of a hundred years of New Testament exegesis at the École Bible is introduced by the present Director, Jean-Luc Vesco who briefly sets the École Pratique d'Études Bibliques in its 1890 context as the first Catholic school created exclusively to specialise in biblical studies and also the first modern 'Institution universitaire' established in Jerusalem. M.-O'C.'s account offers a short report on the beginnings of a tradition, then moves to handle, chapter by chapter, the careers of the founder M.-J. Lagrange, Pierre Benoit, M.-E. Boismard, J. Murphy-O'Connor (this chapter being contributed by J. Taylor), F.-P. Dreyfus, and the new generation consisting of B. T. Viviano, J. Taylor, and of F. Refoulé and J.-L. Vesco, the two most recent Directors, both recruited from outwith the Professors of the School and both having published on New Testament themes. A 'Last Word' attractively sketches a definition of the 'School', and is followed by classified bibliographies of all the professors discussed.

The parallel account of a century of exegesis of the Old Testament, edited by Vesco himself, includes contributions by many of the present staff, and is organized topically. The first part reviews studies of the biblical 'milieu': geography, with special mention of F.-M. Abel; ethnography; Assyriology, with special mention of P. (E.) Dhorme, R. J. Tournay, and R. M. Sigrist; and semitic philology. The second part reviews studies of history before and after the exile. The third part occupies half the volume and reviews studies on the books of the Old Testament with chapters on Pentateuch (especially Lagrange and R. de Vaux), prophets before and after the world war, and poetic and wisdom books (noting particularly the contributions of Lagrange and R. J. Tournay). The fourth part, 'Intertestament', relates to studies of pre-Christian Judaism, Qumran, and Flavius Josephus.

It is not unfitting that the third celebratory volume under review should be edited by an outsider to the Dominican order, the Jesuit Maurice Gilbert. He has collected fourteen studies which had escaped F.-M. Braun's attentions when collecting Lagrange's works for publications in 1935 and 1943. Five relate to archaeology and topography, four to the history of the ancient Near East, and five to biblical exegesis (of both Testaments). Gilbert offers in a four-page preface his appreciation of the founder's 'oeuvre'. Lagrange's contribution is of course assessed more fully in the other two volumes just discussed. However, reading these essays which had eluded an earlier collector confirms that the laudatory assessments of Père Lagrange, O.P., are not over-generous; and helps to explain just how the great institution which has nourished many of us at first hand and all of us through its publications could

GENERAL   21

have developed to what we know from inauspicious beginnings in November 1890 in a former Ottoman abattoir lit only by its open door. In 1992, we should also salute the Révue Biblique, launched by the same giant one hundred years ago.

A. G. AULD

NORTH, R. (ed.): *Elenchus of Biblica 1988* (Elenchus of Biblical Bibliography, 4). 1991. Pp. 1056. (Biblical Institute Press, Rome. ISBN 88 7653 594 2)

The distilled riches of this annual never fail to impress. Father North's Preface of December 1990 opens with a remembrance of his predecessor Father Nober who had died ten years earlier. A few of the changes introduced in the 1980s are sketched, including the rearrangement of the editorial programme for the volume under review which permitted earlier reporting of the most recent exegetical studies. The interval between materials cited and time of publication has been reduced to two years. As in an earlier Preface, the Editor remarks that 'the future of the *Elenchus* must lie along the lines of greater computerization, now being studied'. We wish our Roman colleagues well.

A. G. AULD

O'NEILL, J. C.: *The Bible's Authority. A Portrait Gallery of Thinkers from Lessing to Bultmann.* 1991. Pp. ix, 323. (T. & T. Clark, Edinburgh. Price: £12.50. ISBN 0 567 29189 8)

This collection of brief essays on twenty-one writers and biblical scholars who have influenced biblical scholarship since the mid-eighteenth century is based upon lectures originally given in Cambridge. Given that the author is a New Testament scholar it is understandable that most space is given over to New Testament scholars, and that the New Testament agenda dominates the treatment of Old Testament scholars. Thus, Ewald and Wellhausen are considered primarily from this perspective although their Old Testament work is not ignored. Each chapter consists of a brief introduction to the life of each scholar, and the author has a keen eye for interesting reminiscences and 'gossip'. It will be a useful way of introducing students to some of the great figures of modern theology.

J. W. ROGERSON

OTTO, E. and UHLIG, S.: *Bibel und Christentum im Orient. Studien zur Einführung der Reihe "Orientalia Biblica et Christiana"* (Orientalia Biblica et Christiana, 1). 1991. Pp. 87. (J. J. Augustin, Glückstadt. Price: DM 48.00. ISBN 3 87030 150 3)

This is the first volume of a new series that embraces within its purview two broad, but interrelated, fields of study, on the one hand the Old Testament and its environment, including Palestinian archaeology, on the other the so-called Christian Orient. The two editors of the series planned it while they were colleagues at the University of Osnabrück, and they themselves have contributed the three studies contained in this volume, which are representative of the concerns of the series, and of the titles of the further volumes in the series that have so far been announced. Siegbert Uhlig publishes the text of his inaugural lecture at the University of Hamburg as Professor of African Languages and Cultures with special reference to Ethiopian Studies; in it he discusses the circumstances surrounding the publication in 1540 by the Portuguese humanist Damian de Gois of the 'confession of faith' of the Ethiopian envoy Saga za-Ab, a work which was for a long time of fundamental importance for European knowledge of Ethiopia. Eckart Otto prèsents the text of a lecture given at Rostock, in which he

22 GENERAL

outlines some of the major changes that have occurred in Old Testament research over the last two decades and considers some of the implications of these changes for the future of the study of the Old Testament as a theological discipline. Otto also contributes an article on 'The Birth of Moral Consciousness: The Ethics of the Hebrew Bible'.

M. A. KNIBB

OTTOSSON, M. (ed.): *Svensk exegetisk årsbok, 56*. 1991. Pp. 152. (Uppsala; Graphic Systems, Göteborg. ISSN 1100 2298)

J. R. Lundbom's Fulbright Lecture (in English), 'Jeremiah and the Break-away from Authority Preaching' is the only Old Testament contribution to this volume. Having presented the contrast between authority based and dialogical rhetoric and argued that the former is characteristic of the eighth and seventh century prophets, Lundbom contends that, while authority preaching is found in Jeremiah, dialogical rhetoric is also present. It is seen in the dialogues between Yahweh and Jeremiah and in Jeremiah's reasoned address to his audience, in which Lundbom finds parallels to classical rhetoric. There are four articles on New Testament subjects. B. Gerhardsson contributes a Swedish translation of his Presidential Address to the 45th general conference of the SNTS: a consideration of the synoptic parables as they have been transmitted in their contexts. W. Übelacker discusses Luke-Acts in relation to Mark (Swedish). A. J. Hultgren writes on 'The Self-Definition of Paul and His Communities' (English). W. A. Meeks submits a hermeneutical meditation on Romans 9–11 (Swedish). There are also some thirty-three pages of reviews. Under its new editor the annual maintains the high standard of previous years.

G. W. ANDERSON

PROPP, W. H., HALPERN, B. and FREEDMAN, D. N. (eds): *The Hebrew Bible and its Interpreters* (Biblical and Judaic Studies from the University of California, I). 1990. Pp. vi, 225. (Eisenbrauns, Winona Lake IN. Price: $25.00. ISBN 0 931464 52 8)

Six of the essays in this stimulating and wide-ranging volume were first presented at the Fourth Conversation in Biblical Studies held at the University of California, San Diego, in 1986. The others were contributed by the editors. Though this volume inaugurates a series, the three previous conversations did lead to publications (only *The Poet and the Historian*, edited by R. E. Friedman, was noted in *B.L.* 1985, pp. 78f). J. J. Collins asks 'Is a Critical Biblical Theology Possible?', and answers that historical criticism is compatible with open-ended enquiry into the meaning and function of God-language. M. D. Coogan, in 'Archaeology and Biblical Studies: The Book of Joshua', offers a careful review of some archaeological evidence which seems to him to support the thesis of seventh-century Deuteronomistic authorship of Joshua. D. N. Freedman probes interestingly the unity of 'The Book of Job', and especially the relationship of prose tale and poetic dialogues. W. Randall Garr, 'Interpreting Orthography', provides an impressive account of the vowel system in Biblical Hebrew. Baruch Halpern offers 'A Historiographic Commentary on Ezra 1–6: Achronological Narrative and Dual Chronology in Israelite Historiography', concluding that Ezra 1–6 was not by the Chronicler though it may possibly have been used by him as the source for 1 Esdras. Writing on 'The Bible in the University', J. L. Kugel underlines the fundamentally Protestant ethos of biblical criticism, and proposes a fresh shape for courses in Biblical Introduction. C. A. Newsom's '"Sectually Explicit" Literature from Qumran' proposes 'good reasons for assuming that the documents recovered from the eleven caves near Khirbet Qumran are indeed the remains of the library of the sect described in the

GENERAL 23

Serek ha-Yahad'. In 'Eden Sketches', W. H. Propp explores eleven problematic features of what he holds to be 'doubtless the best studied passage in the Hebrew Bible', Genesis 2:4b–3:24. Finally, J. C. Vander Kam's 'People and High Priesthood in Early Maccabean Times' reviews the usage of 'people' referring to the army and uses passages in the Habakkuk *pesher* to develop the suggestion of Stegemann and Murphy-O'Connor that the Teacher of Righteousness had been ousted by Jonathan from the High Priest's position in 152.

A. G. AULD

REVENTLOW, H. Graf: *Epochen der Bibelauslegung*. Band I: *Vom Alten Testament bis Origenes*. 1990. Pp. 224. (Beck, München. Price: DM 48.00. ISBN 3 406 34663 4)

This is the first volume in a new series which offers for the general reader a survey of biblical interpretation from the beginnings to the present-day. Reventlow's succinct yet meaty account starts with relatively brief chapters on 'inner-biblical exegesis' and developments in the intertestamental period (including a section on the classical interpretation of Homer and Hesiod as necessary background to making sense of much early patristic exegesis). The bulk of the book deals with interpretation of the Old Testament in the New, and with developments (Jewish as well as Christian) up to the middle of the third century CE, by which time, with Origen, the main ground-rules for patristic exegesis have been established. There are no footnotes, but primary sources are used wherever possible in the text itself; while a select and up-to-date bibliography (including an appreciable amount of material in English) encourages further reading.

J. M. DINES

ROBERTSON, E.: *Makers of the English Bible*. 1990. Pp. 222. (Lutterworth, Cambridge. Price: £7.95. ISBN 0 7188 2774 0)

As the title indicates, this book is not primarily concerned with the characteristics of various English versions of the Bible, though it does occasionally touch on them, but with the lives and work of many of the translators. Somewhat surprisingly, the first chapter deals with Jerome, who is described as the 'patron saint' of English translators of the Bible. Subsequent chapters are devoted to Wycliffe. Tyndale and the later 16th-century translators, the King James Version and some of those who worked on it, notably Lancelot Andrewes. An account is given of the Douai Version and its subsequent vicissitudes. In the chapter on the Revised Version, special attention is given to the work of Scrivener, Westcott, and Hort. Translators (Roman Catholic and Protestant) into modern English are then discussed, a separate chapter being devoted to C. H. Dodd and J. B. Phillips. As a brief Epilogue indicates, much recent work has had to be omitted. The book presents a mass of information in readable style.

G. W. ANDERSON

SMEND, R.: *Epochen der Bibelkritik. Gesammelte Studien* Band 3 (Beiträge zur evangelischen Theologie 109). 1991. Pp. 254. (Kaiser, München. Price: DM 98.00. ISBN 3 459 01885 2)

Smend's third volume of collected essays and lectures (for the two very different earlier volumes see *B.L.* 1987, p. 91 and 1988, p. 42) comprises a relatively coherent group of fourteen articles written over more than thirty years on aspects of the history of Old Testament scholarship from the eighteenth to the twentieth centuries. The first, hitherto unpublished, article justifies the title of the collection that there *are* such epochs discernible in the

24   GENERAL

history of biblical (including New Testament) criticism: he treats of four in particular, the first three of which he finds marked by the precise dates 30 March 1787, 28 August 1805 and 13 January 1902 (answers on pp. 18 and 25!); the fourth period of the 1960s and 70s is tactfully not focused so specifically (why not 18 December 1968?). Thereafter he offers studies on J. G. Carpzov, R. Lowth, J. D. Michaelis, G. E. Lessing (two), J. P. Gabler, universalism and particularism in nineteenth-century Old Testament theology, F. Schleiermacher, W. M. L. de Wette, H. Ewald, J. Wellhausen (two, of which one was published in English in *Semeia* 25, 1983) and K. Barth. Of these latter, only that on Lowth has not been published before; it is of particular interest to members of the Society not only because of its subject (the impact of Lowth's work on J. D. Michaelis, J. G. Herder and the German nineteenth-century commentaries on Isaiah) but also because it was read in abbreviated form at the Oxford meeting of the Society in July 1988. This collection provides a valuable complement to H.-J. Kraus's well-known *Geschichte der historisch-kritischen Erforschung* (appropriately Smend's article on Michaelis was published in the Kraus *Festschrift*).

W. JOHNSTONE

SUCUPIRA, L. (ed.): *Revista Bíblica Brasileira. Ano 7, 4; 8, 1–3*. 1990; 1991. Pp. 213–304; 1–240. (Nova Jerusalém, Fortaleza CE. Brazil. Price: $25.00 p.a.)

Ano 7, 4 concludes the study of 'Q' in the New Testament, lists journals received in exchange, and provides the index for 1990. Year 8 launches a new venture, for which years 1–7 have been the preparation: a Theology of the whole (Christian) Bible, deemed both possible and desirable. Old and New Testaments are seen as cohering in a tripartite dialectic, according to which the pre-exilic period provides the thesis (Covenant established), the Exile the antithesis (Covenant broken) and the New Testament the synthesis (Covenant renewed). The aim is to put critical study at the service of evangelization by an approach which transcends localized 'political' readings: hence, the presuppositions and methods of Liberation Theology are largely rejected, in what is clearly a parting of the ways (pp. 82–88; the debt to Hegel is acknowledged on p. 90). Padre Minette de Tillesse also engages in what he labels (perhaps regrettably!) 'The War of the Pentateuch' by means of (1) a translation of Fanuli's review-article of Whybray's 'The Making of the Pentateuch' (*B.L.* 1988:97) (both Fanuli and Minette de Tillesse uphold the validity of the Documentary Hypothesis), pp. 21–46; (2) a lengthy (and useful) review section on recent work on the Pentateuch, pp. 47–72, and (3) an attempt to date 'the Yahwist' from Gen. 2:10–14, which, it is argued, evokes the boundaries of the Solomonic Empire, pp. 95–104. 8, 1 contains a brief introduction to the theology project in French (p. 4), and 8, 2 a loose-leaf apologia for the RBB in English.

J. M. DINES

TÖKEI, F.: *Acta Orientalia Academiae Scientiarum Hungaricae*. Tom. XLII, Fasc. 2–3; Tom. XLIII, Fasc. 1. 1988; 1989. Pp. 161–416; 1–144. (Akadémiai Kiadó, Budapest. HU ISSN 0001 6446)

Neither of these issues contains any articles relevant to the study of the Old Testament.

J. A. EMERTON

TREVES, M.: *Conjectures sur la Bible*. 1990. Pp. 350. (Privately printed by L'Imprimerie Pinson, 85100 Les Sables-d'Olonne, France)

The late Marco Treves contributed over a number of years many articles to a variety of journals including *Vetus Testamentum*, the *Journal of Biblical*

GENERAL

Literature and the *Revue de Qoumran*. This volume is a comprehensive collection of his articles, of which roughly half are on Old Testament subjects, the remainder on the Apocrypha, the New Testament, Qumran and the origins of Christianity. Almost all are in French, a few in Italian. Most will be unfamiliar to readers of the *B.L.* Many of the Old Testament contributions present the author's view that much of the Old Testament is to be dated very late, in the Hellenistic or Maccabean periods. While Treves's views will be unlikely to convince the majority of readers today, the volume is a fitting memorial to an original and consistent scholar.

R. N. WHYBRAY

VIVIAN, A. (ed.): *Biblische und Judaistische Studien. Festschrift fur Paolo Sacchi* (Judentum und Umwelt 29). 1990. Pp. xxvi, 709. (Lang, Frankfurt (Main)–Bern–New York–Paris. Price: SwFr 64.00. ISBN 3 631 43180 5)

Thirty-five essays in Italian, German, French, English, and Spanish on themes including ancient Israel, textual criticism, pseudepigrapha, rabbinics and medieval Judaism. Of especial interest to Old Testament scholars are J. Maier's 'Torah und Pentateuch, Gesetz und Moral', J. A. Soggin's 'Appunti per lo studio della religione d'Israele in epoca preesilica', F. Parente on the Nazirate, P. G. Borbone on the textual transmission of Hosea, G. Miletto on *Kethib-Qere*, A. Rofé on 2 Sam. 24, 1 Chron. 21 and 4QSamᵃ, C. Dell'Aversano on Qoh. 11:9c, C. Kraus Reggiani on Wisdom 6:17–20, G. Boccaccini on Pseudo-Aristeas, L. Rosso Ubigli on the *Apocalypse of Moses*, and G. Stemberger on apocalyptic in the rabbinic literature, A. Pinero on 1QH and Pseudo-Philo and F. García Martínez on 4QSecEzekiel. Most contributions are quite brief: however, the editor permitted himself sixty-five pages (and the editor of the series, J. Maier, fifty-four pages!)

P. R. DAVIES

ZATELLI, I. (ed.): *La Bibbia a stampa da Gutenberg a Bodoni*. (Catalogue of an exhibition in the Biblioteca Medicea Laurenziana, Florence, 8 October–23 November 1991). 1991. Pp. 1–222. (Centro Di, Firenze. ISBN 88 7038 2141)

This is the commemorative catalogue of an exhibition of printed bibles, biblical books and commentaries, from the Gutenberg Bible (1455–56) to the period of the great Italian typographer G. Bodoni (1740–1813), which was held in the Biblioteca Laurenziana, Florence in the autumn of 1991, the exhibits representing many libraries and collections. It is a beautifully printed volume, containing seven introductory essays on aspects of biblical printing and illustration, documented descriptions of all the 171 exhibited items and an excellent bibliography, with six colour plates (and a seventh on the cover) and well over 100 half-tone illustrations. There are nearly twenty Hebrew items, a number of polyglots, and many ancient and modern languages (including a Ladino bible) are represented. This is a book to treasure.

R. P. R. MURRAY

2. ARCHAEOLOGY AND EPIGRAPHY

AUFRECHT, W. E.: *A Corpus of Ammonite Inscriptions*. (Ancient Near Eastern Texts and Studies, 4). 1989. Pp. xxxix, 516. (Edwin Mellen, Lewiston NY and Lampeter, Wales. Price: $89.95. ISBN 0 88946 089 2)

It is a pleasure to welcome the publication of two new collections of Semitic inscriptions, this one of Ammonite inscriptions and that edited by G. I. Davies of Hebrew, reviewed below. It is a matter of regret that neither

26 ARCHAEOLOGY AND EPIGRAPHY

ancient Israel nor Ammon has produced many texts of any length, but this lack is at least partially compensated for by the very considerable quantity of smaller inscribed objects like seals and stamps which have been found in both countries. Aufrecht's volume contains the text of four inscriptions, a dozen ostraca, a couple of stamps and over 120 seals which have been claimed by their first editors or some subsequent scholars to be Ammonite. As much information as possible about the provenance and physical appearance of each text is given along with a translation, notes and detailed bibliography of studies and even of short notices. Aufrecht does not impose his own views on the material but is content to record the opinions of others, gently sorting them into the more or less likely. This is a wise policy for a Corpus which is intended to make available to other scholars and to students texts, few of which were known a mere generation ago and many of which are ill-preserved and difficult to interpret. Photographs, most of them quite excellent, are given of all the texts. With this volume a people long known to us from the Old Testament but not given there a very good press is now beginning to emerge from the mists of history to tell us their side of the story in their language. Like Davies' volume on the Hebrew inscriptions, though by the nature of the subject matter in a more preliminary and tentative way, it is a fine example of primary scholarship.

J. C. L. GIBSON

BERNAL, M.: *Cadmean Letters. The Transmission of the Alphabet to the Aegean and Further West before 1400 B.C.* 1990. Pp. xiii, 156. (Eisenbrauns, Winona Lake IN. Price: $19.50. ISBN 0 931464 47 1)

The book presents an argument about the date of the transmission of the alphabet from the Phoenician coast to Greece on the supposition that one should take seriously Herodotus's claim that he had seen 'Cadmean letters' on cauldrons in Boeotia dating from before the Trojan War. In the process Bernal presents a far-reaching and wide-ranging critique of the long dominant view of Rhys Carpenter that the transmission took place in the eighth century BC. On the assumption that South Semitic forms from which the 'extra' letters of the Greek alphabet are derived are now attested in LBA Lebanon, Bernal regards even Naveh's more recent and influential view of an eleventh-century transmission as much too late. Following the dictum that the date of an alphabet is the date of its earliest letters, he argues for a mid second millennium date. This involves assuming that the Greek alphabet was not all borrowed at once: there were two major 'waves' with subsidiary 'ripples'. Because of the postulated early date of transmission, evidence is lacking in any one extant source and Bernal has to compile an eclectic 'alphabet of primary transmission'. In the process the argument from silence so greatly deplored by Carpenter is repeatedly invoked. There is no doubt that the author has fulfilled the claim expressed in the dedication to his maternal grandfather, Sir Alan Gardiner, that it is 'possible to combine Scholarship with Imagination'. A particularly regrettable feature, which turns a provocative book into an inflammatory one, is the dubbing of exponents of late dating 'anti-Semitic'.

W. JOHNSTONE

BIENKOWSKI, P. (ed.): *The Art of Jordan.* Foreword by Her Majesty Queen Noor al-Hussein of Jordan. 1991. Pp. xii, 178, 200 illus. (National Museums and Galleries on Merseyside, Liverpool. Price: £7.95. ISBN 0 906367 46 8)

This lavishly illustrated book was prepared for the exhibition 'Jordan: Treasures from an Ancient Land' held at Liverpool Museum in 1991. The introduction, 'Jordan: Crossroads of the Near East', is by the editor.

ARCHAEOLOGY AND EPIGRAPHY

F. Zayadine writes on sculpture, H. J. Franken provides a history of pottery-making, G. Philip describes art and technology, M. Piccirillo presents the mosaics of Jordan, W. Kawar explains traditional costume, and B. Mershen gives an account of folk jewellery. Of more specific interest will be A. R. Millard's contribution: 'Writing in Jordan: From Cuneiform to Arabic'. The presentation is superb: most of the photographs are in colour, and a map, a chronological table, bibliographies and an index are provided.

W. G. E. WATSON

BLOK, H. and STEINER, M.: *De onderste steen boven: Opgravingen in Jeruzalem.* 1991. Pp. 154. (Kok, Kampen. ISBN 90 242 3170 1)

This paperback book provides the Dutch reader with a good, clear, up-to-date, and authoritative summary of the archaeological discoveries that have been made in Jerusalem since the last century. The largest part of the work is a series of brief chapters discussing the discoveries chronologically from the Early Bronze Age to the end of the Byzantine era, while other chapters consist of an Introduction, a chronological summary of excavations in Jerusalem from the nineteenth century up to the present day, an account of the various ancient walls of Jerusalem, and a concluding section entitled 'Een bezoek aan Jeruzalem', which has the needs of the modern tourist in mind. The book also contains helpful line drawings and photographs (coloured and black and white), a bibliography and index, and each chapter is provided with scholarly end notes. The authors are experts in their field and disputed points are treated with due caution. All in all this is an attractive and useful volume which would merit translation into English.

J. DAY

BUNNENS, G.: *Tell Ahmar, 1988 Season.* (Abr-Nahrain Supplement Series Volume 2. Publications of the Melbourne University Expedition to Tell Ahmar, Volume 1). 1990. Pp. x, 151. (Department of Classical and Near Eastern Studies, University of Melbourne; distributed by Peeters, Leuven. ISBN 90 6831 322 3)

Tell Ahmar, also known as Til Barsip, is a site in northern Syria on the upper Euphrates river. It was excavated more than fifty years ago by a French team under the direction of F. Thureau-Dangin, but now is threatened by the proposed construction of a new dam. The present volume represents the preliminary report of the first season's work undertaken by members of Melbourne University. Two areas were excavated. One was on the acropolis, where it was possible to relate the results to those of the French excavations and where remains (probably domestic) from the Early Bronze Age were discovered. This work is fully reported by the editor with a detailed presentation of the pottery by A. Jamieson. The other area, a sounding on the 'Intermediate Terrace' between the acropolis and the lower city, is described more briefly by G. Wightman (little architecture, but the pottery is primarily third–fifth centuries AD). Other chapters record surface finds, present a detailed new publication of the city gate lions (A. Roobaert) and furnish a preliminary ethnographical description of the modern village. At this early stage, there is little of major significance to report.

H. G. M. WILLIAMSON

CRIBB, R.: *Nomads in Archaeology* (New Studies in Archaeology). 1991. Pp. xiv, 253. (Cambridge University Press. Price: £35.00. ISBN 0 521 32881 0)

This study will be of interest to biblical historians given the continued debate on the role of nomads in the origins and subsequent history of Israel. Cribb challenges the long-held assumption, deriving from the work of Childe,

28 ARCHAEOLOGY AND EPIGRAPHY

that nomads leave no trace. His observations of modern nomads lead him to believe that it is possible to recover the organizational features of nomadic campsites archaeologically, particularly such features as pottery, raised or level floors, mud or stone-lined hearths, stone storage platforms, alcoves, tent foundations, substantial walls and stone-built corrals. This wide-ranging methodological study, drawing upon published archaeological studies and personal fieldwork in Turkey and Iran, has important implications for the study of Israelite history.

Cribb views nomadism as an alternative specialization within a general agricultural–pastoral continuum and not as a stage on the way to sedentarization. The presence of nomadic and sedentary sections of the same tribe reflect a high degree of specialization and interdependence within a single political and territorial unit. However, the various permanent features of campsites are difficult to distinguish from sedentary sites. The implication here is that published archaeological data may contain evidence for the existence of nomads in close proximity to villages and towns which has not been recognized. His emphasis on the tribe as a political creation forming a territorial and migratory unit but lacking any notion of common agnatic descent is of particular interest in the context of the current debate about the nature of Israel. Moreover, he also challenges the migrationist theory which assumes that the breakdown of state power opens the way for invasion by nomads who replace the sedentary culture and population. The collapse of state power in Syria and Iran in recent times which has permitted large numbers to resume a preferred migratory life-style resulting in the destruction or abandonment of their villages may be analogous with Late Bronze Age Palestine. Cribb's study raises a series of important questions which are of interest to historians of Israel and ought to lead to a re-evaluation of published data and long-held assumptions about nomadic culture. K. W. WHITELAM

CUNCHILLOS, J.-L.: *La Trouvaille Épigraphique de L'Ougarit*. 2: *Bibliographie* (Ras Shamra-Ougarit V). 1990. Pp. 202*. (Éditions Recherche sur les Civilisations, Paris. Price: Fr 95.73. ISBN 2 86538 205 9; ISSN 0291 1655)

This is the second, bibliographical part of a comprehensive reference work on Ugaritic epigraphy prepared under the aegis of the French Archaeological Mission to Ras Shamra (see *B.L.* 1991, pp. 27–28). Like the first volume, it is primarily focused on the individual tablets (not on series of tablets forming whole compositions, though there are some global bibliographical entries for such series). The Ugaritic tablets are numbered according to *KTU* and bibliographical resources are listed for each, beginning with the *editio princeps*. As in the first volume, other sections are devoted to the tablets in Akkadian, Sumerian, Hurrian, etc., excavation numbers being the basis of order in the listing of these. Within each section the materials are ordered according to types (e.g. Akkadian — religious, literary, letters, legal, economic, scholastic, etc.; Ugaritic — religious, letters, legal, etc.). One pragmatic decision by the author which may be noted is the treatment of Gibson's *Canaanite Myths and Legends* (1978) as replacing Driver's (1956), so that the latter is ignored. It should also be noted that the bibliographies do not cover philological and historical studies in general, but only such works as are specifically based on the text in question. Nor does the author aim to replace the exhaustive *Ugarit-Bibliographie* of Dietrich, Loretz, and Sanmartin, which is purely chronological and lists (almost) everything. The great advantage of the present work is the fact that one can move directly from a text located in *KTU* (or in the publications containing texts in Akkadian, etc.) to a bibliographical guide both to the *editio princeps* and to secondary literature.

J. F. HEALEY

ARCHAEOLOGY AND EPIGRAPHY

DAHLBERG, B. T. and O'CONNELL, K. G. (eds): *Tell el-Hesi. The Site and the Expedition* (American Schools of Oriental Research Excavation Reports). 1989. Pp. xix, 214. (Eisenbrauns, Winona Lake IN. Price: $42.50. ISBN 0 931464 57 9)

This is one in a series of volumes representing the final publication of the first phase of excavations at Tell el-Hesi (four seasons, 1970–75). It is intended to serve as an introduction and background to the other more detailed reports, though it includes the full publication of several minor areas of the site as well, most notably the Persian period cemetery (M. D. Coogan). It is no secret that the members of the excavation staff have a particular interest in introducing new methods of working into Palestinian archaeology, and this may explain the sometimes self-conscious — even introverted — accounts of the progress of the excavation, the formative influences on its directors, and the development of the volunteer programme. Of particular interest to readers of the *Book List* will be the informative narrative by J. M. Matthers of the work of Petrie and Bliss at the site, including some previously unpublished material from the archives of the Palestine Exploration Fund. The environment of the site is described in detail by F. L. Koucky, and an especially valuable chapter (pp. 125–62) is contributed by L. E. Toombs in which he provides 'an overview of the stratigraphy and architecture associated with the archaeological periods represented at Tell el-Hesi'. Five strata have been completely excavated (Persian, Hellenistic, late Arabic, a Muslim cemetery, and recent military trenching), while partially excavated strata (on which work has continued since, of course) include the Iron, Late and Early Bronze, and Chalcolithic periods. Those looking for a summary of what was achieved during this opening phase of the work will find in this chapter a clear and authoritative description.

H. G. M. WILLIAMSON

DAVIES, G. I.: *Ancient Hebrew Inscriptions: corpus and concordance.* 1991. Pp. xxxiv, 535. (Cambridge University Press. Price: £75.00 ($110.00). ISBN 0 521 40248 4)

Dr Davies and his assistants (to whom he pays a gracious tribute) have put us all in their debt by producing this Corpus and Concordance of all the known classical Hebrew inscriptions, thus making the content of texts hitherto scattered over many different kinds of publication readily available to everyone. The Corpus's numbering of the inscriptions will surely become standard and at a stroke do away with the confusions which have plagued Hebrew epigraphy in the past. It does not claim to be a critical edition in the full sense. Photographs have been constantly consulted, but it has usually followed the majority view on doubtful readings and only introduced alternative readings or (on a few occasions) new readings where it has felt this to be absolutely necessary; and it has only filled lacunae where there exist parallel texts enabling this to be done without recourse to conjecture. Special care has been taken to distinguish in the case of doubtful letters between those where traces of their shape survive and those where appeal to the context has to be made. These careful and frugal editorial strategies are to be commended and add considerably to the value and authority of the collection. It does not simply gather material for us conveniently but does so in a way that we can trust. The same is true of the Concordance which eschews arrangement by root but does indicate by using a separate line for each instance of a word the immediate context in which it occurs.

The volume stops at around 200 BC, which will disappoint some, but a separate Cambridge project is in hand to cover Jewish inscriptions in all languages from the Graeco–Roman period and in due course, therefore, later Hebrew inscriptions will be available for consultation there. Dr Davies is also planning a successor volume which will list all instances of grammatical forms

30 ARCHAEOLOGY AND EPIGRAPHY

and thus put for the first time our non-biblical sources for the history of classical Hebrew into studiable order. A further note in the Introduction tells us that machine-readable copies of the text of the inscriptions will soon be available for purchase — this again must be a first! So there is more to come. Meanwhile Davies is to be warmly congratulated on this work of primary scholarship, which has made full use of the computer revolution, but as an aid to and not a substitute for the painstaking probing which our forefathers have taught us dare not be abandoned.

J. C. L. GIBSON

DEVER, W. G.: *Recent Archaeological Discoveries and Biblical Research.* The Samuel and Althea Stroum Lectures in Jewish Studies. 1990. Pp. x, 189. (University of Washington Press, Seattle and London. Price: $17.50. ISBN 0 295 96588 6)

This collection, designed to introduce the interested layperson to the complexities of the relationship between archaeology and biblical studies, was originally delivered as the Stroum Lectures in 1985. The lectures have not been revised for publication, although the endnotes have been updated to include work published in 1988.

Dever sketches the background to the demise of 'Biblical archaeology' (he modestly claims to have merely observed its passing and written its obituary) and the development of a multi-disciplinary Syro–Palestinian archaeology. Biblical archaeology is redefined as a dialogue between two disciplines in which biblical studies and Syro–Palestinian archaeology are equal partners, having similar concerns, but each with its own approach and individual contribution. The value of archaeology is that it provides the data for reconstructing the socio-economic environment out of which the Hebrew Bible emerged. His review of the debate on the settlement of Israel in Canaan in the light of new archaeological evidence dismisses the conquest and infiltration theories concluding that the evidence is most compatible with the peasants' revolt model. The endnotes refer to more recently published research but he does not discuss their implications for his current understanding of the problem. The final two essays deal with monumental art and architecture during the United Monarchy and Israelite religion. He maintains that the implications of the Kuntillet 'Ajrud material and Iron Age female figurines have been played down by biblical scholars because of the long-standing assumption that Israelite religion was unique. Dever attempts to redress the balance by emphasizing the degree of affinity and continuity between Israelite and Canaanite religion which has been minimized by Jewish and Christian scholars.

The essays provide masterly reviews and syntheses of archaeological excavations and surveys and their implications for understanding Israelite history and religion. There are a series of very useful charts, summarizing major sites and their significance, and illustrations. Although slightly dated, given the wealth of material published since 1985, this is a first-class introduction for laypersons, students, and scholars to a series of important methodological problems in the relationship between archaeology and biblical studies.

K. W. WHITELAM

DORSEY, D. A.: *The Roads and Highways of Ancient Israel* (The ASOR Library of Biblical and Near Eastern Archaeology). 1991. Pp. xviii, 300. (Johns Hopkins University Press, Baltimore. Price: £28.50. ISBN 0 8018 3898 3)

This attempt to provide a comprehensive treatment of Israel's Iron Age (1200–587 BCE) road system deals with the nature of Israel's roads, their physical character, and methods of transport, including evidence for the

ARCHAEOLOGY AND EPIGRAPHY

speed of travel in the ancient world. The work includes a survey of biblical and extra-biblical material with an appendix on road terminology in the Hebrew Bible. He comes to the somewhat surprising conclusion, on the basis of his literary study, that 'during the Iron Age the highways and byways of Israel were bustling with activity'.

The rest of the book is devoted to a reconstruction of a complex network of 245 roads and branches based on a valuable collection of published and unpublished archaeological survey results. The catalogue of over 1,000 sites, which were plotted on 1:50,000 maps, is to be published separately by ASOR. There are two major maps on the inside covers illustrating the entire reconstructed road system for the south and north of Israel with page size maps distributed throughout the book showing details of different regions. Dorsey acknowledges that he is forced to present a composite picture since the dating of many sites is imprecise and it is not possible to assign various roads precisely to the Iron I or Iron II periods. Dorsey is well aware of the limitations of much of the evidence, the subjective nature of the exercise, and that the conclusions must remain speculative given the paucity of evidence, particularly since there is no archaeological evidence of an open road datable to this period. However, the catalogue of archaeological sites and the literary evidence provide a valuable resource for the study of the settlement patterns, trade and economy of Iron Age Israel.

K. W. WHITELAM

GIBSON, S. (ed.): *Bulletin of the Anglo–Israel Archaeological Society*, Vol. 9 (1989–90). Vol. 10 (1990–91). Pp. 70, 115. (Anglo–Israel Archaeological Society, London. Price: £10.00 ($24.00) per volume. ISSN 0266 2442)

A joint review of these two volumes means that the two parts of G. J. Wightman's detailed discussion of 'Temple Fortresses in Jerusalem' can be noted together. After balanced scrutiny, he concludes the Seleucid Akra stood just south of the Dome of the Rock. He then investigates the site of the *baris* and the Antonia forts at the north-west corner of the Temple enclosure, offering sound arguments for preferring the minimal view of their areas, confining the forts to the rock podium between the Temple and the present Bab Sitti Marian street. Sketch plans, appropriately annotated, aid the reader. (The linguistic discussions are less expert.) In vol. 10, D. M. Jacobson's 'The Plan of Herod's Temple' complements Wightman's work, agreeing on the Akra site, arguing that the line of the north wall of Herod's Temple ran slightly north of the present line. He then shows how the buildings were laid out on a geometrical scheme, with the present Rock, trimmed since the first century, marking part of the site of the ancient shrine. This is a moderately presented counter to some recent speculations. In vol. 9 J. E. Taylor offers a re-examination of the conclusions drawn by the Franciscan excavators at Capernaum, refuting their suggestion that Jewish-Christians revered the site of Peter's house there from the second century. The supposedly Christian graffiti cannot be read as certainly as hoped, and ten allegedly in Aramaic can be read as Greek. In the same issue, P. Magrill identifies and discusses an Assyrian glazed vase from Lachish, S. Dar publishes five Early Bronze Age axe-heads from the Emeq Hefer region, while S. Gibson and D. Urman publish coins of Alexander Jannaeus in the Palestine Exploration Fund collection, which were found long ago in the Golan, in vol. 10. Both issues contain helpful book reviews, some quite lengthy, and summaries of lectures. Pride of place among the summaries is given to Denys Pringle's 'Crusader Jerusalem' (vol. 10, pp. 104–13). There are also reports from grant holders, and obituaries.

A. R. MILLARD

32 ARCHAEOLOGY AND EPIGRAPHY

GITIN, S. and DEVER, W. G. (eds): *Recent Excavations in Israel: Studies in Iron Age Archaeology* (The Annual of the American Schools of Oriental Research 49). 1989. Pp. xii, 152. (Eisenbrauns, Winona Lake IN. Price: $25.00. ISBN 0 89757 049 9)

This collection of papers, delivered at an ASOR Symposium in 1985, represents a sample of important archaeological work on the Iron Age. Some of the papers have been updated to include new information and published with numerous illustrations and charts. A number of the papers concentrate on the implications of new information from Tel Miqne-Ekron for our understanding of Philistia. T. Dothan stresses that cultural change during the transition period from Late Bronze–Iron I Age was not uniform or simultaneous but was characterized by regional diversity in which indigenous Canaanite, Egyptian, Philistine, and Israelite cultures overlapped. S. Gitin presents the results of work at the site since 1981 concentrating on striking discoveries from the seventh century BCE when Ekron was the largest olive oil production site known in the ancient Near East. M. Dothan uses archaeology to determine the geographical movements and settlement sites of early Sea People groups. A. Biran attempts to correlate archaeological evidence from Tel Dan with the biblical traditions of the Danite migration concluding that the collared-rim ware at the site was '. . . an innovation introduced by the tribe of Dan' whose migration must be dated to the beginning of the Iron Age. The results of neutron activation analysis on collared-rim ware from Tel Dan by Yellin and Gunneweg, illustrate that a majority of the repertoire came from seven different locations, thus indicating trade contacts with different areas. Y. Shiloh illustrates how the results of excavations in Jerusalem have enriched our knowledge of the Iron II period, while E. Stern finds evidence for a Greek settlement at Tel Dor dating to 440–400 BCE. An Edomite ostracon and sanctuary are interpreted by I. Beit-Arieh as evidence for an Edomite population in the eastern Negev prior to the end of the First Temple period. W. Dever closes the volume with a review of recent trends in archaeology and a call for a broader, truly inter-disciplinary archaeology. Scholars will disagree over the interpretation of much of the material, especially some of the biblical correlations, but it cannot be doubted that the volume contributes considerably to an understanding of the Iron Age.

K. W. WHITELAM

HEINTZ, J.-G. with the collaboration of D. BODI and L. MILLOT: *Bibliographie de Mari. Archéologie et Textes [1933–1988]* (Travaux du G.R.E.S.A., Université de Strasbourg). 1990. Pp. x, 128. (Harrassowitz, Wiesbaden. Price: DM 68.00. ISBN 3 447 03009 7)

This comprehensive bibliography of Mari studies, following the author's *Index documentaire des textes de Mari* (1975) (*B.L.* 1975, pp. 31–32), is to be welcomed and will prove useful both to Assyriologists and to Old Testament specialists. Full bibliographical information on the archaeology of the site, on the publication of the Mari texts and on monographs, articles and theses containing substantial material on Mari is provided. In the case of larger works the sections or pages dealing with Mari material are specified. Useful, particularly in the bibliography of the Mari texts, is the additional listing of published reviews of the individual text volumes. Of special Old Testament interest will be the supplementary note on the Mari 'prophetic' texts (pp. 125–28), which provides a concordance of the texts in question.

J. F. HEALEY

ARCHAEOLOGY AND EPIGRAPHY 33

HERZOG, Z., RAPP, G., Jr and NEGBI, O. (eds): *Excavations at Tel Michal, Israel* (Publications of the Institute of Archaeology, 8). 1989. Pp. xxiii, 462. (University of Minnesota, Minneapolis; The Sonia and Marco Nadler Institute of Archaeology, Tel Aviv University. Price: $59.95. ISBN 0 8166 1622 1)

Tel Michal, whose ancient name is unknown, lies on the coastal plain of Israel within the municipal boundaries of the modern Herzliya. It was excavated in four main seasons from 1977–80. This final report consists of some thirty-six chapters written by forty-three authors, together with numerous drawings, maps, plans, charts, and plates. Seventeen strata are distinguished, stretching from Middle Bronze IIB to early Arab, though there were a number of breaks in occupation. The Persian, Hellenistic and Roman periods are the best represented. As well as detailed descriptions of architectural remains, pottery, and numerous small finds (though unfortunately scarcely any inscribed material), attention is also paid to the regional geology, geography and history of the site. In view of the poor preservation of much of the site, which has been subjected to severe erosion, this decision to pursue the excavation as part of a wider regional archaeological project was sensible and has proved fruitful. This detailed and relatively prompt publication is to be welcomed.

H. G. M. WILLIAMSON

HOFTIJZER, J. and VAN DER KOOIJ, G.: *The Balaam Text from Deir 'Alla Re-evaluated. Proceedings of the International Symposium held at Leiden, 21–24 August 1989.* 1991. Pp. xi, 324. (Brill, Leiden. Price: fl. 150.00. ISBN 90 04 09317 6)

The volume presents eleven main papers, five responses, three short communications and an additional note 'based on remarks made during the symposium'. The main papers are by H. J. Franken ('Deir 'Alla re-visited'), M. M. Ibrahim and G. van der Kooij (archaeology of Deir 'Alla phase IX), A. Lemaire (historical and cultural significance of the inscriptions), B. A. Levine (general interpretation of the texts), P. K. McCarter (dialect of the texts), J. C. Greenfield (philological observations), J. Hoftijzer (the first combination), M. Weippert (the Balaam text and the Old Testament), H.-P. Müller (divinatory language and the bird-list), E. Puech (palaeography), and G. van der Kooij (book and script). The responses to papers or to pairs of papers are by J. A. Hackett, D. Pardee, G. I. Davies, and M. Dijkstra (twice). The short communications are by J.-M. Husser, J. Huehnergard and A. Wolters, and the additional note by F. Israel. The place of the Deir 'Alla dialect on the linguistic map clearly caused fluttering in the dovecots, but this and other uncertainties aside (and is it 'text' or 'texts'? — both are used freely), the potential of this difficult but rewarding text is very much in evidence throughout the various contributions. A most useful volume.

R. P. GORDON

HVIDBERG-HANSEN, F. O.: *Kana'anaeiske myter og legender. Oversaettelse med indledning og kommentar.* I–II (Bibel og Historie 13). 1990. Pp. x, 235; xvi, 247. (Aarhus Universitetsforlag. Price: Dkr 268.00. ISBN 87 7288 266 2; 87 7288 265 4)

The aim of this work is to meet a long felt need for a complete translation to a Scandinavian language of the largest and most important texts from Ras Shamra; the translations in F. F. Hvidberg's *Weeping and Laughter* (Danish ed. 1938) are till now the most complete. The first fifty pages of vol. I are introduction to the excavations, the texts, the language etc., and then follow translations with introduction to the texts in the following order, CTA 2, 3, 4, 5–6, 10–11, 24, 23, KTU 1.119, 1.114, CTA 17–19, 14–16. In vol. II very

34 ARCHAEOLOGY AND EPIGRAPHY

thoroughly and carefully made notes to the different sections and texts in vol. I
are found, This meritorious work will be indispensable to all Scandinavian
students of Old Testament and Near Eastern religion in years to come.

K. JEPPESEN

JAMES, P., in collaboration with THORPE, I. J., KOKKINOS, N., MORKOT,
R. and FRANKISH, J.: *Centuries of Darkness. A challenge to the conventional
chronology of Old World archaeology.* 1991. Pp. xxii, 434. (Jonathan Cape,
London. Price: £19.99. ISBN 0 224 02647 x)

In this book a group of young archaeologists have collaborated to
re-examine the foundations of ancient Mediterranean history. Separate
chapters consider Italy and the West, Greece (three chapters), the Hittites,
Cyprus, Palestine, Egypt (two chapters), and Mesopotamia; and there are
four useful appendices on specific problems. Their basic thesis can be put
quite simply: it is that the chronology for ancient Egypt accepted since
Flinders Petrie as the benchmark for dates in the remainder of the Mediterranean world leads to so many 'gaps' and other difficulties that it should be
discarded in favour of a chronology lower by two to three hundred years,
which was in fact unsuccessfully championed by some scholars in the late
nineteenth century. The relevance of this proposal for Old Testament studies
lies chiefly in its effects on the dating of archaeological remains from
Palestine, though if it were accepted correlations of biblical history with
Egyptian history would also be affected. The book is written in a lively and
readable style, and is also extensively documented with references to
scholarly literature. As one would expect, it is stronger in its discussion of
archaeology than in its treatment of written sources. An adequate assessment
of the different chapters can only be given by specialists in the various fields:
initial reactions have been negative as far as the alternative chronology is
concerned, even if some issues are acknowledged to remain open (see
especially the *Cambridge Archaeological Journal*, 1/2 (October 1991),
pp. 227–53). The most recent scientific information (multiple radiocarbon
dates, dendrochronology) appears to support the generally accepted dates or
even higher ones, and the literary evidence from Egypt and Mesopotamia
does not permit the compression of history required by the theory advocated
in this book. As far as the history of Palestine is concerned (see pp. 162–203),
the equation of Shishak (1 Kings 14) with Ramesses III rather than Sheshonq I
is surely perverse, and the interpretations of the archaeological evidence
proposed create many more problems than they solve. Nevertheless the book
may perform a useful service by arousing interest in chronological problems
and by showing that it is not only in biblical studies that many uncertainties
remain.

G. I. DAVIES

JAMIESON-DRAKE, D. W.: *Scribes and Schools in Monarchic Judah. A
Socio-Archeological Approach* (JSOT Supplement Series 109; Social World
of Biblical Antiquity Series 9). 1991. Pp. 240. (Almond Press, Sheffield.
Price: £30.00 ($48.50). ISBN 1 85075 275 3; ISSN 0265 1408; 0309 0787)

Arguing that the case for schools in Judah has been made on inadequate
grounds, principally by R. J. Williams and A. Lemaire, the author defines
schools as places outside the home where fees were paid for instruction in
scribal skills, mainly for administrative purposes. 'Scribalism' went hand-in-
hand with growing urbanization, social stratification, and increased craft
specialization. The work aims to investigate the existence of schools from
excavated remains independent of the biblical texts. The analysis is based on
recent archaeological and anthropological theories developed to produce
sociological information from the classification and distribution of the

ARCHAEOLOGY AND EPIGRAPHY 35

excavated objects. The deductions are that 'all of the seven sites in the eighth–seventh centuries containing direct evidence of writing' were 'to some degree administratively dependent on Jerusalem', and that was the centre for 'formalized scribal training', perhaps exclusively (pp. 147 f). Within the author's strict definitions this may be true, but they are a strait-jacket which cannot contain the material. Detailed charts and lists derived from excavators' reports summarize the finds on which Jamieson-Drake draws, and are basic to the study (pp. 160–216), followed by 'Bibliography of Sites' and 'Selected Bibliography' (pp. 217–37). Unhappily, these are inaccurate and incomplete, the references stop in 1984, and several works published earlier than that cited in the text are not listed, while other highly relevant ones are ignored. The omission of Y. Aharoni's *Arad Inscriptions* (Hebrew 1975, English 1981) is inexplicable: it presents 91 ostraca, plus graffiti and seals, but here only nineteen ostraca are credited to Arad (Table 13). At least two dozen of these ostraca are letters, which may be local transcripts of oral messages, or epistles written elsewhere and carried to Arad, a factor not considered. The variety, quantity, and distribution of other relics of ancient Hebrew writing in Judah and their significance is ignored totally. The supposition that the greater number of ostraca from the seventh century results from a decrease in the use of papyrus (p. 124) exemplifies the inadequate base of this study; the recent finds of hundreds of bullae once sealing papyri in that century contradict that idea. Official administrative instruction may have been given in Jerusalem alone, but there was clearly a wide use and knowledge of writing throughout Judah from at least 700 BC, and the contrary conclusion here is simply at variance with the facts.

A. R. MILLARD

KEEL, O., SHUVAL, M. and UEHLINGER, C.: *Studien zu den Stempelsiegeln aus Palästina/Israel* (OBO 100). 1990. Pp. xiii, 455 and XXII plates. (Universitätsverlag, Freiburg (CH); Vandenhoeck & Ruprecht, Göttingen. Price: SwFr 120.00. ISBN 3 7278 0692 3; 3 525 53732 8)

O. Keel's enterprising investigations of ancient iconography continue to focus on seal designs, often interpreted in the light of other monuments and texts. This volume deals with Late Bronze Age and Iron Age seals (for Vol. II see *B.L.* 1990, p. 122). C. Uehlinger argues for the existence of a temple of Ramesses III at Gaza on the evidence of scarabs, ostraca from Tel Sera' and Egyptian texts, while O. Keel discusses the bow as a symbol of rule in hunting and warfare in Egypt and Israel, as various scarabs depict. These two essays are reprinted from *ZDPV* 104 (1988) and 93 (1977) respectively, with additions, and O. Keel's 'La glyptique de Tell Keisan' is reprinted from the 1980 excavation report. The major original contribution is M. Shuval's 'Catalogue of Early Iron Stamp Seals from Israel', the translation of a Tel Aviv M.A. dissertation (pp. 67–161). Shuval has collected 82 pieces from controlled excavations, grouped them by design, and analysed the elements occurring, concluding that there are temporal and spatial distribution patterns, with Egyptian influence dominant in the Coastal Plain, local and northern influences in Jezreel and the Central Hills. O. Keel also wrote additional notes to his essay on the bow (pp. 263–79), commented on Shuval's Catalogue, eliciting replies from Shuval on points of interpretation, then added various comparisons and remarks on his Tell Keisan study, notably identifying a figure stabbing with a spear with Seth-Baal. C. Uehlinger shows convincingly that marks understood as the letters *gd* 'Gad' on three scaraboid seals are poorly incised *ankh* symbols. Finally, Keel offers a long survey of Early Iron Age Glyptic from Palestine, asking what evidence it gives for religious beliefs and concluding little can be learnt to shed light on early Israel's. The multitude of careful drawings alone makes this a valuable compilation.

A. R. MILLARD

36 ARCHAEOLOGY AND EPIGRAPHY

McNutt, P. M.: *The Forging of Israel. Iron Technology, Symbolism, and Tradition in Ancient Society* (Journal for the Study of the Old Testament Supplement Series 108; The Social World of Biblical Antiquity Series 8). 1990. Pp. 307. (Almond Press, Sheffield. Price: £30.00 ($50.00); sub. price: £22.50 ($37.50). ISBN 1 85075 263 x)

McNutt's wide-ranging study of iron technology and its symbolism adds further weight to the now commonplace denial that iron played a crucial role in the settlement of the Palestinian hill country during the Late Bronze–Iron Age transition or that the Philistine threat was a result of a monopoly on iron working. She demonstrates by means of a long, sometimes unstructured, review of previous studies and archaeological finds that iron technology was adopted in Palestine very gradually over several centuries. It was not until the tenth century BCE, the period usually assigned to the formation of an Israelite state, that the new technology was finally accepted and adopted, although it is not clear how this affected social, political, and economic processes. An extensive treatment of African traditions is used to explore the importance of iron as a cultural symbol on a variety of levels. It is used in the Hebrew Bible to convey important meanings about Israel's social and religious identity, often expressing notions of relationship, particularly between Israel and its god. Its symbolic significance in terms of transformation is used of the two major transitions in Israel's history, the exodus from Egypt and the Babylonian exile which are symbolized in terms of a furnace or of the metalworking process: Yahweh is represented as the Divine Smith purifying and transforming the people in order to bring them into a new relationship with the Divine. One of the primary threads of this study is the attempt to draw attention to the importance of understanding and exploring the symbolic intentions of biblical texts as conveying significant information about social and religious values rather than as representations of historical reality. K. W. Whitelam

Meyers, E. M., Meyers, C. L. and Strange, J. F.: *Meiron Excavation Project* Vol. v. *Excavations at the Ancient Synagogue of Gush Halav* (Excavation Reports of the American Schools of Oriental Research). 1990. Pp. xx, 292. (Eisenbrauns, Winona Lake IN. Price: $40.00. ISBN 0 931464 59 5)

As an off-shoot of the Meiron Excavation Project Eric Meyers directed in 1977 and 1978 two short seasons on the ruins of the synagogue in the lower town of ancient Gush Halav, the Gischala of Greek sources, domicile of Josephus' notorious rival, John of Gischala, during the First War against Rome (*Vita* 70–76; *Bellum* ii, 590–92). Because the site was located in a flourishing olive grove, the archaeologists had to confine themselves to the synagogue itself and to a few metres beyond its outer walls. Consequently little was discovered about the relationship between the synagogue and the immediate settlement which it served, or about the relationship between that settlement and upper Gush Halav, situated in the modern village of El-Jish up the hill. However, the synagogue itself proved to be, in Meyers words, 'a gem'. Four phases of development were distinguished covering a period of some three hundred years (*c.* 250 CE–*c.* 550 CE). The building is of a 'unique' basilica type and incorporates 'spatial elements that find few, if any, parallels elsewhere' (p. 246). The synagogue was orientated on Jerusalem, and, through all its architectural modifications, the bema remained a central feature, suggesting liturgical continuity, with a steady emphasis on the reading and expounding of Torah. With each new site excavated it becomes ever clearer that the Galilee, even Jewish Galilee, did not constitute a homogeneous region. Gush Halav in Upper Galilee was, as Meyers has argued, probably much more semitic in character than hellenized towns like Sepphoris in Lower Galilee. The elegant little synagogue at Gush Halav, so

ARCHAEOLOGY AND EPIGRAPHY

professionally reported in this excellent monograph (which contains some superb architectural reconstructions), is a welcome addition to the inventory of Galilean synagogues. It gives an interesting, if teasing, glimpse of Judaism as it was practised in the Galilee in the period when the Yerushalmi Talmud was in gestation.

P. S. ALEXANDER

MOOREY, P. R.: *A Century of Biblical Archaeology*. 1991. Pp. xvii, 189. (Lutterworth, Cambridge. Price: £9.95. ISBN 0 7188 2825 9)

This is a good read by any standard. It begins with the period 1800–1890, giving a judicious account of the great decipherments and the first steps towards a scientific methodology. (It is particularly good to see the role of Edward Hincks in the decipherment of cuneiform emphasized). The author's survey of Biblical Archaeology in the period 1890–1990 manages to combine a concise survey of what has been achieved with a clear presentation of the methodological issues which emerged. Despite his protestations of lack of expertise, he also gives a very adequate account of the Biblical side of the topic. Inevitably Albright's colossal figure is a central focus. He and other scholars of the older generation are treated critically but judged fairly in terms of the best excavation methods available to them. Their achievement is thus seen in a clear light, as is the progress of the whole discipline, despite some ups and downs. The author rightly reminds us of how far we have moved since the earlier part of the last century, or even the earlier part of this century, when the nature of Middle Eastern *tells* was still not quite understood. It is easy to forget how important has been the relatively recent insight that changes in pottery style might provide a clue to the dating of the successive stages of occupation of an archaeological site. Moorey looks favourably on the more modern approaches to the subject emphasizing the study of Palestinian archaeology in the wider context of developing landscapes and societies rather than individual political events. He is clearly optimistic that Biblical Archaeology can climb out of the 'proving the Bible' true' bog into which it fell.

J. F. HEALEY

PETTINATO, G.: *Ebla. A New Look at History*. Translated by C. Faith Richardson. 1991. Pp. x, 290. (Johns Hopkins University Press, Baltimore and London. Price: £26.50. ISBN 0 8018 4150 x)

This is a translation of the author's *Nuovi orizzonti della storia* (see *B.L.* 1988, p. 126). As an introduction to Ebla studies it has the advantage over some earlier publications of having been written in a calmer atmosphere than that which prevailed in the early days of Ebla and on factual matters it gives a clear and, on the whole, reliable account. It is particularly strong on Ebla's commercial activities and its international links. To the earlier *B.L.* review by Watson a few things may be added. First the English translations of technical terms are sometimes rather strange — 'Old Babylonian' and 'Old Assyrian' appear as 'Paleo-Babylonian' and 'Paleo-Assyrian'. The subtitle too seems off-beat. 'A New Look at *Syrian* History' might be thought more appropriate, though the grand claim for significance is pursued throughout the book. Ebla, according to the author, is 'the discovery of the twentieth century', the pivot of the Fertile Crescent. Its importance is not to be doubted and exaggeration is, perhaps, understandable in the popular history-writing genre. To which genre Pettinato's book is intended to belong is difficult to define, since it combines the most elementary statements about the background (explaining, for example, what cuneiform writing is) with long lists of place-names in Assyriological transliteration. The treaty between Ebla and Ashur (despite E. Sollberger, *Studi Eblaiti* 3 (1980) 129 ff., who read Abarsal instead of

38 ARCHAEOLOGY AND EPIGRAPHY

Ashur) is given in full in transliteration and translation and it plays a prominent role in the historical reconstruction. The sections on Eblaite language and religion are very short and one would have to look elsewhere for information on these. There is, appropriately, only passing reference to the Old Testament. There are useful bibliographies. The style is sometimes anecdotal and autobiographical, but the book is well written and informative, constituting a good introduction to the subject.

J. F. HEALEY

READE, J.: *Mesopotamia*. 1991. Pp. 72. (British Museum Publications, London. Price: £5.95. ISBN 0 7141 2078 2)

A clearly written and well illustrated survey from prehistoric hunting through agriculture, irrigation, and technological developments to the establishment of civilization, marked by urbanization and state organization and writing *c.* 3000 BC, in Mesopotamia. The title is not obvious but covers ancient Iraq and E. Syria. The influence of Sumerians, Akkadians and early Babylonians on the West (e.g. Ebla and Mari) is shown as are the importance of trade, temple (thus the priestly control of much land), and the environment (the flood in the Early Dynastic period). This will serve as a useful introduction to the geographical, historical, cultural, and religious background down to the Patriarchal period. The story ends in the early second millennium so that necessarily little relates directly to the Old Testament.

D. J. WISEMAN

SASS, B.: *Studia Alphabetica. On the Origin and Early History of the Northwest Semitic, South Semitic and Greek Alphabets* (Orbis Biblicus et Orientalis 102). 1991. Pp. 124, 16 plates. (Universitätsverlag Freiburg (CH); Vandenhoeck & Ruprecht, Göttingen. Price: SwFr 39.00. ISBN 3 7278 0729 6 (Universitätsverlag); 3 525 53734 4 (Vandenhoeck & Ruprecht))

Sass, lecturer in archaeology at Haifa, himself credited with the discovery of two proto-Sinaitic inscriptions, has written, as the title suggests, not a monograph with a single, coherent, argument, but a series of studies. These are of quite unequal length.

The first, which has already appeared in Hebrew in abbreviated form in *Eretz Israel* 20, 1989, re-examines the theory that the alphabet was evolved by Egyptian scribes in the Middle Kingdom in their effort to transliterate foreign names. This idea was borrowed by the Semites, who derived their alphabet by acrophony from a selection of hieroglyphs now given Semitic names.

The second, and major, article (pp. 28–93) concerns the evolution of the South Semitic alphabet. Sass provides a valuable corpus of inscriptions with 52 photographs and a table to give a conspectus of the letter forms. He argues that some ten of the 29 letters are derived from north-west Semitic. The date of the borrowing and development he argues, on the historical grounds of the conditions favourable to the emergence of the kingdom of Sheba, cannot be before the twelfth century, perhaps a century or two later (contra Cross's date of fourteenth–thirteenth centuries).

The third article is little more than note (though it is complemented by a pull-out table of letter forms) on Naveh's theory of the eleventh century borrowing by the Greeks of the Phoenician alphabet. Sass argues that this theory virtually boils down to the dot in the *'ayin/omicron* not attested in Phoenician after the eleventh century, but occurring in early Greek texts. Historical conditions for contacts between Greece and Phoenicia point to one or two centuries later. Sass prefers the ninth century to avoid Naveh's 'tercentennial epigraphic void', though a slightly higher date would be justified palaeographically. More precision on the matter, he suggests, will depend on studies of the history of the alphabet on the Greek side.

W. JOHNSTONE

ARCHAEOLOGY AND EPIGRAPHY

SMELIK, K. A. D.: *Writings from Ancient Israel. A Handbook of Historical and Religious Documents.* Translated by G. I. Davies. 1991. Pp. ix, 191. (T. & T. Clark, Edinburgh. Price: £12.50. ISBN 0 567 29202 9)

Can there be epigraphy without tears? I doubt it, but if there can be, this lively and informative little book by Klaas Smelik, ably translated by G. I. Davies, is it. After a brief introduction on the origin of the alphabet and the place of writing in ancient Israel, it takes us through the quite sizeable deposit of inscribed objects now available in Old Hebrew and its related dialects of Moabite and Ammonite. Chapters are devoted to the Gezer Calendar, the Mesha stele, the Samaria ostraca, the Siloam tunnel inscription and other texts from Jerusalem, the Deir Alla and Ammonite finds from Jordan, the Yavneh-Yam letter, the Arad ostraca, and the Lachish letters. The archaeological background of the texts is described, a translation is given, and the significance of the texts for biblical history, civilization, and religion helpfully discussed. Two final chapters deal with seals and weights, and with a number of smaller texts like those from Khirbet Beit Lei and Kuntillet Ajrud. This nicely produced volume will give students without Hebrew and an interested general public an invaluable insight into the bearing of the inscriptions on Old Testament concerns, and will surely be a spur for students with Hebrew to begin studying them in the original. The excellent select bibliography is clearly designed with the latter in mind, and a plaintive note in the Preface regrets that it was not possible, no doubt for financial reasons, to print the text in the original languages.

J. C. L. GIBSON

WOOD, B. G.: *The Sociology of Pottery in Ancient Palestine. The Ceramic Industry and the Diffusion of Ceramic Style in the Bronze and Iron Ages* (Journal for the Study of the Old Testament Supplement Series 103; JSOT/ ASOR Monographs 4). 1990. Pp. 148. (Sheffield Academic Press. Price: £25.00 ($42.50); sub. price: £18.75 ($32.50). ISBN 1 85075 269 9; ISSN 0267 5684; ISSN 0309 0787)

This concise study seeks to switch attention from the study of pottery itself, which forms such a fundamental part of archaeology, to an understanding of the nature of pottery production in ancient Palestine. In the course of this, Wood raises a series of questions which have implications for the study of Palestinian trade and economy. He presents a wide range of archaeological and particularly ethnographic material, coupled with a very useful bibliography, which is of great value to historians of Palestine. The first part concentrates on the nature of the ceramic industry including the methods and organization of production. He proposes that the village workshop mode of production would have predominated during periods of a decentralized economy, such as EBIV-MBI, although the evidence discussed relates to LBIIA at Hazor and Iron I at Lachish. However, during periods of urbanization, a fairly standardized range of good quality pottery was mass produced in urban centres. In the second part of the study, Wood proposes a model for the commercial sale of ceramic wares in order to answer the question of why it is that similar ceramic styles are found throughout Palestine and that these styles change over time: pottery-making was an urban craft specialism with markets in urban centres and their satellite villages, while itinerant merchants diffused the wares even further by transporting them to adjacent urban centres and beyond. This he believes would answer Franken's concern that there might have been a significant time lag in development between coastal urban centres and a site such as Deir ʿAlla. Thus he confirms the fundamental assumption of Palestinian archaeology that the study of changes in ceramic morphology in the context of stratified deposits, along with comparative analyses of material from other sites, remains a reliable chronological tool.

40 ARCHAEOLOGY AND EPIGRAPHY

Yet in arriving at this conclusion, he raises many questions about archaeo-logical assumptions based upon pottery analysis while shedding light on aspects of Palestinian economy and trade.

K. W. WHITELAM

3. HISTORY AND GEOGRAPHY

ANBAR, M.: *Les tribus amurrites de Mari* (Orbis Biblicus et Orientalis 108). 1991. Pp. 248. (Universitätsverlag, Freiburg (CH); Vandenhoeck & Ruprecht, Göttingen. Price: SwFr 66.00. ISBN 3 7278 0750 4 (Universitätsverlag); ISBN 3 525 53741 7 (Vandenhoeck & Ruprecht)).

Sufficient is known from the enormous archives of Mari (over 20,000 tablets) to enable special studies to be prepared, although publication of the texts continues. The author built on the seminal work of J.-R. Kupper, *Les nomades en Mésopotamie* (1957) in his thesis published in Hebrew in 1985. His re-written study takes account of the recent surge in editions and discussions of Mari texts, up to 1990. After a summary of the chronology and history of Mari, useful in themselves, ch. III describes organisation of the four major tribes, and ch. IV their location in various districts from the Tigris to Aleppo. The tribes are Hanûm, Bini-Yamina (the preferred reading of the name, but not connected with Benjamin), Bini-Sim'āl, and Sutûm. The second and third may have been divisions of the first. Rule by kings, sheikhs and elders is the topic of ch. V, and the economy of the tribes of ch. VI. Intricacies of relationships between rulers of urban states and the mobile tribesmen are examined in ch. VII and the origins of the tribes in ch. VIII – they moved from the Jebel Bishri area in the twentieth century BC. Anbar concludes there was little tension at the social level, problems of authority and control arose at the political level. The tribesmen were ready to abandon nomadic life for a semi-sedentary situation, raising crops and following pastures. Apart from the book's value as a study of a type of society at a certain period, and some comparisons are made with more recent tribes in the Near East, many small points of comparison with the Old Testament arise, e.g. villages divided between tribes (p. 100), tribes invading a settled area, settling and often separating (p. 214). The work abounds with quotations and references to the Mari texts, and occasionally to the Bible, stressing the labour of the author in sifting and sorting a mass of sources to present their evidence about these famous tribes in an intelligible and enlightening way.

A. R. MILLARD

VON ARX, U.: *Studien zur Geschichte des alttestamentlichen Zwölfer-symbolismus*. Bd 1: *Fragen im Horizont der Amphiktyoniehypothese von Martin Noth* (Europäische Hochschulschriften, Reihe XXIII, Bd. 397). 1990. Pp. 583. (Lang, Frankfurt (Main)–Bern–New York–Paris. Price: SwFr 42.00. ISBN 3 261 04250 8; ISSN 0721 3409)

The volume under review is a modified version, both contracted and expanded, of a doctoral thesis accepted by the 'Christkatholisch' Faculty of the University of Bern in 1984. The first main chapter (pp. 23–52) argues that the conception of an Israel in twelve tribes developed in Canaan. The second (pp. 55–84) reviews Noth's amphictyony thesis, and modifications proposed by Smend and Seebass. The third looks briefly at the spectrum of twelve-formations in Graeco–Roman antiquity (pp. 85–94). The much more detailed survey in the fourth (pp. 95–197) of groupings of twelve in the environs of Israel insists that since this information comes from the Bible itself, mostly in fact from genealogies in Genesis, it offers no sound testimony to extra-Israelite conceptions. And the fifth chapter offers an excursus (pp. 199–246) on 'Nasi' in Jewish tradition. The supporting end-notes, set in the came case

HISTORY AND GEOGRAPHY

as the main text, occupy even more space (pp. 247–497). The following bibliography contains some 1,000 items, and yet has not a few gaps. Unhappily the indexes, generously spaced over only five pages, are much too select for easy access to so detailed a treatment.

The author, Professor since 1986 of New Testament and Homiletics in his Bern Faculty, is candid that his massive project developed from asking the New Testament question: What all is actually implied by the number of Jesus' closer circle of disciples? He hopes to be able to publish his planned third volume, on examples of twelve in Jewish tradition between the fourth century BCE and third CE. Yet the complexities of the issues relating to the planned second volume — genealogical and geographical-territorial tribal listings, tribal sayings, and the definition of the meaning of 'tribe' — have led von Arx to a crisis of confidence whether he can bring into focus the divergent views about the traditions of the Hexateuch and their redaction. All reviewers will have much sympathy with him; but many will blame him for including the word 'all' in his initial question. There is much of value within these first results of a massive personal quest; yet von Arx should not have published so much without coming to closer terms with the issues presently defeating him. Were he to persevere, for example, with studies of the meaning of the Hebrew words conventionally translated as 'tribe', he might find that they refer more often than is commonly thought to representative insignia and less often to territorial entities. He might also find that many relevant texts were not far distant in date from the fourth century BCE.

A. G. AULD

ASALI, K. J. (ed.): *Jerusalem in History*. 1989. Pp. 295. (Scorpion Publishing, Essex. Price: £13.95. ISBN 0 905906 70 5)

Himself a Jerusalemite, the former Director of the Jordan University Library has done debate a service in commissioning and editing nine essays on the history of Jerusalem. Joined by scholars from seven other countries, he has sought to counter a flow of writings on Jerusalem more favourable to Israeli perspectives on the present and future of the city. Inevitably his own claim of balance and objectivity will not go uncontested. It is the first two very different essays which overlap most clearly with the interests of the *Book List*. H. J. Franken offers a fresh if difficult discussion of written, archaeological, and religious evidence for 'Jerusalem in the Bronze Age, 3000–1000 BC'. The limitations of the available data lead him to claim less in his concluding short historical sketch than is often done. This is particularly true of his reassessment of the archaeological evidence as he works on the materials of the Kenyon excavations. The Middle Bronze Age town of the eighteenth century may not have lasted long; for no traces of habitation can be traced to the period from seventeenth to fifteenth centuries. G. E. Mendenhall, by contrast, tells a story, period by period, of 'Jerusalem from 1000–63 BC' which surprises this reader in the conservative literalness of its handling of many biblical texts. The remaining chapters treat 'Jerusalem under Rome and Byzantium, 63 BC–637 AD' (J. Wilkinson); 'Jerusalem in the Early Islamic Period, 7th–11th Centuries AD' (A. A. Duri); 'Crusader Jerusalem, 1099–1187 AD' (M. A. Hiyari); 'Jerusalem under the Ayyubids and Mamluks, 1197–1516 AD' (D. P. Little); 'Jerusalem under the Ottomans, 1516–1831 AD' (Asali); 'Jerusalem in the 19th Century, 1831–1917' (A. Schölch); and 'The Transformation of Jerusalem, 1917–1987 AD' (M. C. Hudson) carries the story to the outbreak of the *intifada*.

A. G. AULD

42 HISTORY AND GEOGRAPHY

COOTE, R. B.: *Early Israel: a New Horizon*. 1990. Pp. ix, 197. (Fortress, Minneapolis. Price: $11.95. ISBN 0 8006 2450 5)

This is more than a synthesis of recent work on Israelite origins and early history; it sets this work within the framework of a new perspective that makes an original contribution to our historical understanding. The author points to three chapters in particular, those which focus on Israel in the thirteenth century, on the arrival of the Sea Peoples, and on the settlement of the highlands, for his own contribution to the ongoing discussion. Here there is a strong emphasis on the political dimension of tribalism, the Israel of the Merneptah Stele being a tribal group in northern Palestine brought under the control of Egypt to form a buffer between Egyptian controlled Palestine and the Hittites. Israel's chiefs, such as Moses, were part of the Egyptian imperial system of control. The arrival of the Sea Peoples in the late thirteenth and early twelfth centuries, and the decline of the Egyptian New Kingdom, left Israel and the Philistines as the two proxy powers of Egypt in Palestine, locked in a struggle for control which was essentially a conflict between lowland Philistines and highland Israelites.

Israel thus originated before the end of Egyptian control in Palestine, but the latter event was one of the factors which led to the very marked extension of highland settlements, so facilitating the survival of Israel. Other factors involved included the removal of the Hittite presence, and so of the constraint on Israelite tribal expansion formed by the Hittites and Egyptians. Coote makes very effective use of Finkelstein's recent results, though some of Finkelstein's conclusions, including his general understanding of Israel's origins and his specific interpretations of the evidence from some particular sites, are not adopted.

Coote thus describes the origin and development of Israel in thoroughly political terms, explicitly rejecting any religious, ethnic, cultural, or ethical foundation for its appearance. The idealism of Mendenhall and Gottwald is allowed little effective role, the admission that 'the new tribal settlements seemed more inviting to many farming families and groups than life under Egyptian or Philistine rule, not least because they provided the option of indigenous rule, or nominal self-rule, in contrast to foreign rule' (pp. 170f.), being no more than an incidental concession in a treatment which concentrates on 'normal political relationships' in Palestine.

This is a well written, well argued, and persuasive study which offers a very credible and wholly realistic treatment of a complex topic. It offers a coherent and consistent picture, with excellent analysis of life in tribal society, and a thorough but clear integration of archaeological, geographical, and literary evidence. At the same time, it avoids much of the technical discussion to be found in other presentations (though bibliographies are provided for each chapter), and so is fully accessible to a wide readership.

A. D. H. MAYES

DERFLER, S. L.: *The Hasmonean Revolt: Rebellion or Revolution* (Ancient Near Eastern Texts and Studies, Vol. 5). 1989. Pp. vi, 115. (The Edwin Mellen Press, Lewiston/Lampeter/Queenston. Price: $49.95. ISBN 0 88946 258 5)

The reason why D. wrote this book is unclear to me. Most of the ground it covers is well known, and the author is clearly not abreast of scholarship in a number of areas. For example, he does not seem to be aware of Bringmann's seminal work and his assumptions about the Hasidim show no knowledge of the debate in the past fifteen years. The one original question he does seem to want to tackle is whether the Maccabean revolt was a 'revolution' or a 'rebellion'. Perhaps there is something of value here if properly examined,

HISTORY AND GEOGRAPHY 43

but D.s brief treatment does not give any new insights into the revolt. On the contrary, he propagates simplistic socioeconomic views by making assumptions about 'class conflict' and the like without any evidence. For a little more than 100 pages, the price is excessive.

L. L. GRABBE

DUS, J.: *Israelitische Vorfahren–Vasallen palästinischer Stadtstaaten?*. *Revisionsbedürftigkeit der Landnahmehypothese von Albrecht Alt* (Europäische Hochschulschriften Series XXIII Bd. 404). 1991. Pp. 118. (Lang, Frankfurt (Main). Price: DM 16.00. ISBN 3 631 42974 6; ISSN 0721 3409)

This brief monograph from a Czechoslovakian scholar offers a revision of Alt's theory of a peaceful infiltration by 'Israel' into Canaan, which seeks to improve that particular model of the way in which Israel came into being. Dus argues that the nomadic, non-Canaanite ancestors of Israel were already living in a symbiotic, vassal relationship with various Canaanite city states at least as early as the fifteenth century BCE. The kind of relationship which he has in mind is that which he argues must have existed between kings of Mari and Amorite nomads in the eighteenth and nineteenth centuries BCE, and which is also reflected in Genesis 20:15, 34:10, 47:5–6. Israel came into being when several groups of these nomadic vassals united in successful revolt against their Canaanite overlords, switching their covenant-allegiance, as it were, from these sovereigns to Yahweh.

This is an interesting variation on some well-known themes. It remains to be seen how the new theory will stand up once it is fleshed out rather more in the author's projected history of Israel, with all the archaeological evidence, both old and new, fully integrated with it.

I. W. PROVAN

HELTZER, M. and LIPINSKI, E. (eds): *Society and Economy in the Eastern Mediterranean (c. 1500–1000 B.C.) Proceedings of the International Symposium held at the University of Haifa from the 28th of April to the 2nd of May 1985* (Orientalia Lovaniensia Analecta 23). 1988. Pp. xiv, 398. (Peeters, Leuven. ISBN 90 6831 135 2)

The symposium from which this volume derives brought together specialists in Mycenaean, Levantine, and Hittite studies, including both historians and archaeologists. The intention was to identify common features and interrelationships within the different civilizations of the Eastern Mediterranean, as highly centralized palace states flourished and then suddenly disintegrated, to be replaced by new social and economic patterns of organization. The Mycenaean crater from Tel Dan forms an apt frontispiece, and there are over thirty other figures. A number of important survey articles are included, as well as a report of the closing discussion, and Old Testament scholars will have particular interest in a series of articles on the 'Sea Peoples' (by I. Singer, A. Mazar, A. Raban, and M. Dothan), in two articles on settlements in the highlands of Palestine (by D. Eitam and A. Zertal) and in M. Weinfeld's comparative study entitled 'The promise to the patriarchs: an analysis of foundation stories'.

G. I. DAVIES

VON RAD, G.: *Holy War in Ancient Israel*. Translated and edited by Marva J. Dawn. Introduction by Ben C. Ollenburger. Bibliography by Judith E. Sanderson. 1991. Pp. vii, 166. (Eerdmans, Grand Rapids MI; Gracewing, Leominster. Price: $14.95; £8.95. ISBN 0 8028 0528 0; 0 85244 208 4)

Gerhard von Rad's short study of *Der Heilige Krieg*, which first appeared in 1951, has been variously described as a classic and a work which has proved itself to be seminal, influential, and definitive. In view of such acclamations,

44 HISTORY AND GEOGRAPHY

which are in no way exaggerations, it is surprising that it has taken half a century to prepare and publish an English translation of such an important work. However, the appearance of this translation is not too late to be welcomed, and not least because it has the added bonuses of an introduction and a descriptive bibliography relating to 'War, Peace and Justice in the Hebrew Bible'. Ben Ollenburger's Introduction begins by setting von Rad's study against two significant backgrounds, firstly, that of previous study and secondly, that of von Rad's own work. The Introduction is concluded with a brief review of subsequent treatments of the subject. Judith Sanderson's bibliography, which extends to some thirty pages, is also a valuable addition.

It is only to be hoped that the English translation will be as widely read and used as was the German original.

G. H. JONES

REVIV, J.: *The Elders in Ancient Israel. A Study of a Biblical Institution.* Translated from the Hebrew by Lucy Plitmann. 1989. Pp. 222. (Magnes, Jerusalem. Price: $22.00. ISBN 965 223 701 1)

The aim of this study is to describe the function of the elders by reference to the nature of Israelite society and to extra-biblical references in the ancient near eastern context, and by using social and cultural anthropology. After a discussion of the relationship of 'elders' and 'heads', the presentation follows a historical progression, tracing the function of the elders from pre-settlement times through the pre-monarchic and monarchic periods, with full discussion of the relationship of the elders to other leadership institutions and of the influence of the state on their role in society. Although it is clear that the political, military, legal, and general leadership powers of the elders increased with the development of urbanism, it is maintained that there was a strong continuity in the significance of the institution, their various functions in Deuteronomy being dependent on ancient tradition. The discussion of the biblical material perhaps assumes too quickly the basic historicity of the biblical scheme of Israelite origins; but this study is generally useful, particularly in its incorporation of non-biblical material, first that deriving from Alalah, Ugarit, and El-Amarna for the situation in Syria–Palestine, and, secondly, that deriving especially from Mari for Mesopotamia. The authority of the elders in Israel, where they never formed part of the state administration, is perceived as greater than elsewhere in the ancient near east, but throughout this area they represented a foundational leadership institution deeply rooted in the basic and original structures of society.

A. D. H. MAYES

4. TEXT AND VERSIONS

CATHCART, K. J. and GORDON, R. P.: *The Targum of the Minor Prophets. Translated with a Critical Introduction, Apparatus and Notes* (The Aramaic Bible 14). 1989. Pp. xvi, 259. (T. & T. Clark, Edinburgh. Price: £39.95. ISBN 0 567 09471 5)

This edition of the Targum of the twelve Minor Prophets represents an excellent addition to *The Aramaic Bible* series. It follows the conventional format of English translation of the Targum with succinct textual and exegetical notes at the foot of each page. The Introduction deals briefly with such matters as translational characteristics, theology, life and setting, text and versions, language, rabbinical citations and date.

P. W. COXON

TEXT AND VERSIONS 45

CLARKE, E. G. (ed.): *Newsletter for Targumic and Cognate Studies*, Vol. 18.1 (1991). 1991. Pp. 8. (Department of Near Eastern Studies, University of Toronto. Price: $5.00. ISSN 0704 59005)

About seventy-five items, mainly in article form, are noted in this issue. The editorial work has been hampered by a strike in the main library of the University of Toronto; it is hoped to make up any deficiencies in the next fascicle.

R. P. GORDON

COX, C. E. (ed.): *VII Congress of the International Organization for Septuagint and Cognate Studies. Leuven 1989* (Society of Biblical Literature Septuagint and Cognate Studies Series 31). 1991. Pp. xxxi, 459. (Scholars Press, Atlanta, GA. Price: $44.95 (members price: $29.95); paperback price: $29.95 (members price: $14.95). ISBN 1 55540 647 5; 1 55540 648 3)

The twenty-four papers and one abstract made more widely available in this volume represent all but two of the papers presented at Leuven in 1989, and demonstrate the range of interests customarily displayed at IOSCS Congresses. L. Greenspoon discusses the eclectic and unsatisfactory use of the Septuagint in modern English versions of the Bible. A. Aejmelaeus writes on translation technique and the intention of the translator, and A. van der Kooij on the ending of the book of 1 Esdras. J. W. Wevers offers some post-partem reflections on the Göttingen Pentateuch. There is an abstract of an already published paper by P. W. Flint on the Septuagint version of Isa.23:1–14 and the Massoretic Text. S. Sipila writes on the Septuagint version of Josh.3–4, and R. Sollamo on the pleonastic use of the pronoun in connection with the relative pronoun in the Greek Pentateuch. J. Lust discusses Messianism and the Greek version of Jeremiah; while J. Bajard and R.-F. Poswick of the Maredsous Centre 'Informatique et Bible' review statistical aspects of the connections between the Septuagint and the Massoretic Text. E. Tov and G. Marquis offer in turn a progress report on and the transcript of a demonstration of the CATSS (Computer Assisted Tools for Septuagint Study) project. T. Muraoka discusses Hebrew hapax legomena and Septuagint lexicography, and A. Voitila the translation of the Yiqtol in the Greek story of Joseph (Gen. 37, 39–50). M. Harl reviews LXX lexical choices through the eyes of early Greek recensions, revisions, and commentaries; and R. G. Jenkins uses colophons of the Syrohexapla to probe the textual history of the recensions of Origen. V. Spottorno discusses the Lucianic text of Kings in the New Testament; J. Trebolle, the text-critical use of the Septuagint in the Book of Kings; and N. Fernández Marcos, the Antiochian text in I–II Chronicles. P. Lefebvre writes on Solomon and Bacchus, editor Cox on the exegesis of the Greek text of Job 29–31, J. Cook on hellenistic influence in the LXX book of Proverbs, and J. R. Busto Saiz on the meaning of Wisdom 2:9a. R. Martin offers a syntax criticism of Baruch; S. P. Cowe discusses the parent text and the translation technique of the Armenian version of the Epistle of Jeremiah; and J. Annandale-Potgieter writes on the high priests in 1 Maccabees and the writing of Josephus. In a substantial Introduction (pp. ix–xxvii), Claude Cox has summarized each paper and in many cases indicated its place in recent discussion.

A. G. AULD

DRAZIN, I.: *Targum Onkelos to Exodus. An English Translation of the Text with Analysis and Commentary.* 1990. Pp. xiii, 383. (KTAV, Hoboken NJ; Center for Judaic Studies, University of Denver; Society for Targumic Studies. Price: $59.50. ISBN 0 88125 342 1)

Drazin has already published a commentary volume on Targum Onkelos to Deuteronomy (1982) and has further volumes on Pentateuchal books in

46 TEXT AND VERSIONS

preparation. The Aramaic text and English translation are presented on facing pages which also include extensive notes. Some account is taken of modern Targumic scholarship, but the commentator's energies are directed mainly to discussion of the Targum in relation to the other Targums, other ancient versions, and rabbinic literature. The introduction reflects the strongly statistical approach favoured by Drazin for the analysis of the translation character of the Targum. He notes in his second sentence that over 2,385 deviations from the MT are 'noted, explained, and tabulated'. Drazin is very concerned to show that Onkelos follows only the *peshat* line of interpretation, and he illustrates in some detail the ways in which a number of scholars have mistakenly identified *derash* in this Targum. Some other very specific conclusions are reached, for example that in Exodus Onkelos draws its interpretations quite consistently from the Mekilta of Rabbi Ishmael, that Onkelos was composed after the fourth century CE, and that this Targum does not represent exclusively the views of R. Akiba or of any particular school. A quite definite profile of Onkelos in Exodus thus emerges, and the basis for some fresh discussion.

R. P. GORDON

NORTON, G. J. and PISANO, S. (eds): *Tradition of the Text. Studies offered to Dominique Barthélemy in Celebration of his 70th Birthday*. With a preface by Carlo Maria Card. Martini (Orbis Biblicus et Orientalis 109). 1991. Pp. xi, 310, plates. (Universitätsverlag, Freiburg (CH); Vandenhoeck & Ruprecht, Göttingen. Price: SwFr 84.00. ISBN 3 7278 0761 x (Universitätsverlag); ISBN 3 525 53742 5 (Vandenhoeck & Ruprecht))

This collection, coming some seventy numbers later in the series OBO than the volume in honour of Barthélemy's 60th birthday, contains eighteen articles, for the most part dealing with the early transmission of the biblical text. Particular passages covered are: Gen. 9:6, Hebrew and Greek (J. Lust), Deut. 29:19–20 LXX (M. Harl), Is. 3:7 (R. D. Weis), Jer. 52 (P.-M. Bogaert), Neh. 8:8 (A. van der Kooij). An *editio princeps* of 4QJerᶜ is provided by E. Tov, and other contributions cover: *Tiqqune Sopherim* and the Targum tradition (L. Diez Merino), LXX or LXXII translators (G. Dorival), Ephrem's Commentary on the Sermon on the Mount (C. McCarthy), 'Textual criticism and entropy' (E. A. Nida), problems concerning any re-edition of hexaplaric materials (G. J. Norton), *Okhlah we-Okhlah* (B. Ognibeni), the definite article in LXX Psalms (A. Pietersma), 'Stability and fluidity in text and canon' (J. A. Sanders), the relationship between 1 Esdras and Ezra-Nehemiah (A. Schenker), 'The interim and final Hebrew OT Text Project and the translator' (J. de Waard), Lectionary texts of LXX Exodus (J. W. Wevers), 'Egypt' in LXX Hosea (S. Pisano), and a calendrical reference to a celebration of Easter on a Wednesday in the thirteenth century (S. Szyszman).

S. P. BROCK

(Peshitta): *The Old Testament in Syriac According to the Peshitta Version*, edited on behalf of the International Organization for the Study of the Old Testament by the Peshitta Institute, Leiden. Part I, fasc. 2; Part II, fasc. 1b: *Leviticus, Numbers, Deuteronomy, Joshua*, prepared by D. J. Lane, A. P. Hayman, W. M. van Vliet, J. H. Hospers, H. J. W. Drijvers, and J. E. Erbes. 1991. Pp. xxix, 79; xxiv, 111; xxiv, 99; xix, 65. (Brill, Leiden. Price: fl. 240.00; $133.33. ISBN 90 04 09091 6)

This volume completes both Part I and Part II of the invaluable Leiden edition of the Syriac Old Testament; for Part I, fasc. 1 (Gen.-Exod.), see *B.L.* 1978, p. 44; and for Part II, fasc. 1a (Job), *B.L.* 1984, p. 47; fasc. 2 (Jud.-Sam.), *B.L.* 1980, p. 46; fasc. 3 (Pss), *B.L.* 1981, pp. 46–47; fasc. 4 (Kings), *B.L.* 1977, p. 38; and fasc. 5 (Prov.-Wis.-Qoh.-Cant.), *B.L.* 1981, p. 47. The

TEXT AND VERSIONS

editorial principles and layout of the editions and introductions follow the general pattern established in the more recent volumes of the edition (there is some small variation of practice in matters of detail between differents editors). The fact that here, for the first time, scholars are now provided — mostly in the apparatus — with all the evidence available for reaching back to the earliest text form of the Peshitta of these books, highlights the significance of this long-awaited volume (some of the editors completed their basic work a considerable time ago). A companion monograph on the Peshitta of Joshua, by Erbes, is to appear in *Studia Semitica Upsaliensia.*

S. P. BROCK

VAN DER PLOEG, J. P. M.: *The Book of Judith* (Moran 'Etho Series, 3). 1991. Pp. 53, 38. (St Ephrem Ecumenical Research Institute [SEERI], Kottayam, Kerala. Available through E. Kornhardt, Academic Bookseller, 42 Hill View Road, Oxford OX2 OBZ)

This is an edition and translation of an intriguing new form of the Syriac translation of Judith, preserved in an Indian manuscript of 1734. There is a short introduction and some brief notes; the text itself is reproduced from the manuscript. As the editor points out, a proper assessment of the text must await the Leiden edition of the Peshitta; the mixture of Peshitta and LXX elements reminds one of the work of Jacob and Edessa. For ease of reference the editor provides his translation with the verse numberings (often very different) of both the Göttingen edition of the LXX and of the Mosul edition of the Peshitta (whose verse numbers, and text, have evidently been followed in the hand-copied Apocrypha provided in the UBS reprint (1979) of Lee's edition of the Peshitta).

S. P. BROCK

SALVESEN, A.: *Symmachus in the Pentateuch* (Journal of Semitic Studies Monograph 15). 1991. Pp. xviii, 329. (University of Manchester, Manchester. Price: £30.00. ISBN 0 951612425; ISSN 0022 4480)

The monograph is a slightly revised and updated version of the author's 1988 Oxford D.Phil. dissertation, written under the supervision of Sebastian Brock. It attempts to solve the ancient mystery of the identity and religious affiliation of Symmachus by means of a systematic study of the fragments on the Pentateuch. The models are the work of Busto Saiz on the Psalms and González Luis on the Major Prophets, but the emphasis is on exegesis rather than translation-technique. Part I (the bulk of the book) examines all the extant material, verse by verse throughout the Pentateuch, and compares it with what is available in the Septuagint, Theodotion (i.e. the Kaige Recension), Aquila, the Vulgate, the Targumim, the Peshitta, and the Samaritan Pentateuch. This method of identifying exegetical positions is reinforced by references to a wide range of other sources, both Jewish and Christian. The section ends with an evaluation of the main features of Symmachus' theology and exegetical techniques. Part II looks more briefly at the syntactical and lexical aspects of the Version and its influence on Jerome. The book ends with an attempt to unravel the confusing patristic evidence about Symmachus in the light of the preceding analyses. The conclusions reached are that Symmachus was not an Ebionite (against Eusebius and e.g. Schoeps) but a Jew, possibly of Samaritan origin (thus in line with Epiphanius and e.g. Geiger, Barthélemy), perhaps even to be identified with 'Sumchos', the disciple of Rabbi Meir; and that the version was probably made c. 200 CE at Caesarea in Palestine. Whether or not one feels convinced by the final detective-work, the presentation of the 'clues', together with such a wealth of comparative material, is immensely valuable, not only for the study of Symmachus' version

48　　　　　　　　TEXT AND VERSIONS

itself, but for the history of early exegesis of the Pentateuch. The complex textual material is lucidly presented, and is a tour-de-force of 'camera-ready' techniques.

J. M. Dines

Vetus Latina. Die Reste der altlateinischen Bibel, nach Petrus Sabatier neu gesammelt und herausgegeben von der Erzabtei Beuron. 12: *Esaias*. Herausgebeben von R. Gryson. 5. Lieferung: Is. 10, 20–14, 13. 1990. Pp. 321–400. (Herder, Freiburg im Breisgau. Price: DM 81.50; sub. price: DM 72.00. ISBN 3 451 00444 5)

This richly detailed edition continues on its way. The density of the patristic quotations displayed (cf. *B.L.* 1989, p. 50), becomes even more striking: thus for Isa 11:1–2, as against a few lines of actual text, multiplied by five to display the LXX and four Latin traditions, something like fourteen pages of citations are provided. Will thought be given to the eventual production of a simplified edition which might include only the biblical texts themselves, in their varous forms, and could thus be condensed into a volume or two for the entire Bible as a convenient instrument for the average textual critic?

J. Barr

Vetus Latina. Die Reste der altlateinischen Bibel, nach Petrus Sabatier neu gesammelt und herausgegeben von der Erzabtei Beuron. 12: *Essais*. Herausgegeben von R. Gryson. 6. Lieferung: Is. 14, 13–22, 5; 7. Lieferung: Is. 22, 5–26, 20. 1991. Pp. 401–480; 481–560. (Herder, Freiburg im Breisgau. Price: DM 81.50; sub. price: DM 72.00, each fascicle. ISBN 3 451 00445 3; 3 451 00475 5)

Two further fascicles mark the steady progress of this majestic edition, and will be universally welcome.

J. Barr

5.　EXEGESIS AND MODERN TRANSLATIONS

Beaucamp, É.: *Livre de la Consolation d'Israël. Is XL–LV* (Lire la Bible). 1991. Pp. 255. (Cerf, Paris. Price: Fr 95.00. ISBN 2 204 04370 2; ISSN 0588 2257)

This book is intended for a non-specialist public, and will undoubtedly help Christian laypeople to a deeper understanding of this part of the Bible, and provide devotional nourishment. The author's analysis of the text, however, is unusual; and it is unfortunate that he has not been able to submit it to the scholarly world with full argumentation. After the prologue (40:1–11), the prophecy falls into two discourses. 40:12–49:13 and 49:14–52:12. The first is divided into three sections by the doxologies at 42:10–12, 44:23, and 49:13. The Servant Songs are attributed to the same prophet, but have been inserted in their present positions by a disciple or editor. The Servant's experience in the first two Songs is identical with that of Israel; but in the last two Songs he seems to be an individual, perhaps the prophet himself or an eschatological figure. The satires against idolatry (40:19–20, 41:6–7, 44:9–20, and 46:5–7) are also regarded as extraneous, and represent a later perspective than that of Second Isaiah. Chapters 54 and 55 are treated as an appendix, the last four verses serving as an epilogue.

A. Gelston

EXEGESIS AND MODERN TRANSLATIONS 49

BRATCHER, R. G. and REYBURN, W. D.: *A Translator's Handbook on the Book of Psalms* (Helps for Translators Series). 1991. Pp. xi, 219. (United Bible Societies, New York. Price: $20.00. ISBN 0 8267 0118 3)

This massive work, intended primarily for translators of the Psalms, will be of great value also to other students of the Psalms, so extensive and varied is the information which it contains. The core of the work is the treatment of translational problems. The entire text of the Psalms in TEV (which was the original basis of the commentary) and RSV (which was added when TEV was found to be unsatisfactory) is printed in very short sections. Unfortunately, NRSV and REB appeared too late to be used throughout. A number of other modern translations are referred to in the running commentary which accompanies the text. The discussion of translational problems often inevitably involves exegetical as well as philological treatment. Occasional notes on textual problems are added where necessary. There is a brief introduction to the Psalms including a summary account of literary types, and also a commendably judicious treatment of Hebrew poetry. Guidance for further reading is provided; and a glossary explains technical terms. It is impossible in a short notice to take up points of detail which call for discussion. Suffice it to say that this is a first class work of reference.

G. W. ANDERSON

BRÉSARD, L. and CROUZEL, H., with the collaboration of M. BORRET: *ORIGÈNE: Commentaire sur le Cantique des Cantiques – Texte de la Version Latine de Rufin, Introduction, Traduction et Notes* (Sources Chrétiennes 375). 1991. Pp. 470. (Cerf, Paris. Price: Fr 256.00. ISBN 2 204 04397 4; ISSN 0750 1978)

This is the first of two volumes presenting the extant portion of Origen's commentary on the Song of Songs, preserved only (apart from some catena fragments) in Rufinus's Latin version. The critical text is prefaced by an Introduction and accompanied by a French translation and notes. This is the nineteenth work of Origen to appear (in whole or in part) in *Sources Chrétiennes*; his homilies on the Song have been republished in a revised edition (*SC* 37*bis*, 1966). The translation, some of the notes, and parts of the Introduction are by Dom Brésard of Cîteaux, the rest of the Introduction by H. Crouzel, probably the leading living Origen scholar. Origen's approach and method are carefully described; he saw the 'literal sense' as an *epithalamion* by King Solomon, but was mainly interested in the allegorical interpretation in which the male partner is Christ, the female both the Church and the individual Christian soul. Origen's method is compared with that of Jewish exegesis, and its influence on subsequent Christian exegesis and mystical theology is traced. The whole production is of the high standard one expects of this splendid series.

R. P. R. MURRAY

CASSIODORUS: *Explanation of the Psalms*. Volume I *Psalms 1–50*. Volume II *Psalms 51–100*. Volume III *Psalms 101–150*. Translated and annotated by P. G. Walsh (Ancient Christian Writers; the Works of the Fathers in Translation 51; 52; 53). 1990; 1991; 1992. Pp. vi, 618; 528; vi, 543. (Paulist Press, New York, Mahwah NJ. Price: $36.95; $34.85; $34.95. ISBN 0 8091 0441 5; 0 8091 0444 X; 0 8091 0445 8)

These volumes present in translation the Psalms commentary by the sixth-century rhetorician Cassiodorus who, half-way through his life, retired from high political office under Theoderic to devote himself to Christian studies. His commentary is dependent on Hilary, Jerome and especially Augustine. Cassiodorus's Latin text is normally a form of the *Vetus Latina*; any knowledge he shows of what is in the Hebrew or in Origen comes usually

50 EXEGESIS AND MODERN TRANSLATIONS

from Jerome. Besides the theological perspectives of his sources, whom he follows in relating everything possible to Christ and the Church, Cassiodorus constantly reveals his own interest in rhetoric; he clearly aimed to promote the study of the Psalter both for spiritual profit and as a text for rhetorical education, and this twofold purpose made his commentary much used by western monks for centuries. This concern with rhetoric needed a classical scholar of a quality today increasingly rare, but still happily to be found in Professor P. G. Walsh. The excellent translation is supported by a useful Introduction and appendices on textual variants and etymologies mentioned by Cassiodorus, and on rhetorical technicalities; also notes throughout, though these are rather bare. For example, 'Diapsalm' (I, p. 33) would be slightly less mysterious if there were a note explaining that *diapsalma* is *selah*. Throughout the commentary, the psalms are read as written by a prophet who, in as many cases as possible, spoke either in the person of Christ or about him; but occasionally, as on Ps. 104 (105), the viewpoint comes nearer to an Antiochene appreciation that the original context is of intrinsic value. The third volume, like the others, is enlivened by little excursuses: on *Alleluia* (which fascinates Cassiodorus), on alphabetical psalms, and on the nature and number of the *Cantica graduum*: the mysterious significance of $15 = 7+8$ comes up again, apropos of the number 150, in the conclusion of the whole work. Students of the history of exegesis and of Latin rhetoric alike will find this presentation of Cassiodorus most valuable.   R. P. R. MURRAY

FRETHEIM, T. E.: *Exodus* (Interpretation. A Bible Commentary for Teaching and Preaching). 1991. Pp. vii, 321. (John Knox Press, Louisville KY. Price: $21.95. ISBN 0 8042 3102 8)

A thorough exposition of the 'final form' of the book, especially its narrative sections, with suitable cross-reference to the New Testament and allusion to modern (American) life, this should provide its primarily envisaged audience, the preacher and bible-study leader, with a wealth of material for stimulus and reflection. The occasional colloquialism (e.g. 'nary', 'zap', 'upping the ante' [so that's how it's spelt?!]) no doubt reflects the intended user. Other interpreters should not however ignore it: it is alive to redactional questions (though the obtruding of editorial material is typically represented as 'retardation' of the narrative of the final form); while it has neither footnotes nor critical apparatus (it is based on NRSV), it does directly engage on occasion with other scholars (e.g. Childs, Durham, liberation theologians) on controversial issues and supplies five pages of bibliographical material. A basic thesis is that Exodus should be interpreted not so much in terms of the 'mighty acts of God' (how times have changed! — though the author may not have disengaged himself quite enough from historicist questions in discussing e.g. the morality of the divine slaughter of the Egyptians and their animals) as of creation: 'God's redemptive work should . . . not be seen in interventionist terms but as an intensification of the ongoing activity of the Creator God' (p. 25); parallels are drawn with Genesis 1–9 (even to Exod. 32 as 'Fall'); the atrocities of the Pharoah have cosmic/environmental significance (hence the plagues affecting nature); the exposition has a distinctly 'green' tinge.

W. JOHNSTONE

GAEBELEIN, F. E. (general editor): *The Expositor's Bible Commentary with the New International Version of the Holy Bible in Twelve Volumes*. Volume 5: *Psalms–Song of Songs*. 1991. Pp. xvi, 1244. (Zondervan, Grand Rapids MI. Price: $34.95. ISBN 0 310 36470 1)

Of the six Old Testament volumes in this substantial conservative exegetical set, that on Isaiah–Ezekiel was reviewed in *B. L.* 1988, p. 57. Three

EXEGESIS AND MODERN TRANSLATIONS 51

others have been published but not noted; only that on Deuteronomy–Samuel now remains. In the present volume the bulk of the space naturally goes to Psalms, by W. A. VanGemeren of Reformed Theological Seminary. His worthwhile detailed treatment works within a traditional framework (e.g. in its approach to the headings which refer to incidents in David's life) in an open-minded way and in dialogue with a wide range of scholarship. It is interspersed with a number of 'appendices' on different divine titles, 'Zion theology' etc., and incorporates very thorough bibliographical references. I was not persuaded by its inclination to find chiasms in scores of Psalms. The treatment of Proverbs by A. P. Ross of Trinity Episcopal School for Ministry includes a topical index to the sayings though does not consider the possible significance of their order in the book; again there are thorough bibliographical references. Ecclesiastes is covered by J. S. Wright (1905–85), one of the handful of British contributors to the series; his work has been usefully updated by J. H. Walton of Moody Bible Institute. In his brief treatment of the Song of Songs D. F. Kinlaw of Asbury College argues briskly for the literal interpretation of the Song but sees the allegorical interpretation as intuitively grasping that sexual relationships do have a heavenly background and significance.

J. GOLDINGAY

GLASSNER, G.: *Vision eines auf Verheissung gegründeten Jerusalem. Textanalytische Studien zu Jesaja 54* (Österreichische Biblische Studien 11). 1991. Pp. ix, 278. (Öst. Kath. Bibelwerk, Klosterneuburg. Price: DM 39.00; SwFr 34.00. ISBN 3 85396 082 0)

This dissertation, inspired initially by a study of Galatians 4:21–31, is a detailed study of Isaiah 54. The Hebrew text is set out in transliteration, broken into 'units of expression', of which each verse consists of from two to seven. This is followed by a concise but thorough review of the evidence of text and versions where the text itself is uncertain. Next comes a section on the relation of this chapter to the rest of Second Isaiah and on its form-critical analysis. Then follows a translation and initial interpretation in the light of the analysis into 'units of expression'. The longest section is devoted to a triple analysis of the chapter. First there is an analysis of the chapter into five sections (verses 1–3, 4–6, 7–10, 11–14a, 14b–17). Then there is a detailed analysis of each section in turn. Finally there is an analysis of the form of the whole chapter in the light of the detailed analysis of the sections. A short section returns to the role of the chapter within its immediate context in Second Isaiah and explores a correspondence with a contracting passage in Jeremiah 4:5–31. This dissertation will be indispensable to future students of Isaiah 54.

A. GELSTON

GOLKA, F. W.: *Jona* (Calwer Bibelkommentare). 1991. Pp. 108. (Calwer, Stuttgart. Price: DM 34.00. ISBN 3 7668 3115 1)

This is an expanded version, in German, of the author's commentary in the series *International Theological Commentary*, already reviewed (see *B.L.* 1989, p. 57).

R. B. SALTERS

GÖRG, M.: *Josua* (Die Neue Echter Bibel Altes Testament). 1991. Pp. 115. (Echter, Würzburg. Price: DM 28.00. ISBN 3 429 01398 4)

The twenty-sixth volume of this series of popular commentaries on the books of the Old Testament is devoted to Joshua. A brief introduction deals with the nature and contents of the Book, the variety of types of material within it, and the complexities of its growth. In chapters 1–12, three principal

52   EXEGESIS AND MODERN TRANSLATIONS

stages of development are distinguished — pre-Deuteronomistic material, Deuteronomistic redaction, and post-Deuteronomistic commentary — although it is noted that its history is more complex; the earliest material may go back to a 'spät- oder nachjahwistischen Stufe (J^E)' (p. 6), while the latest may have affinities with the Priestly tradition. It is suggested that the nature of the material in the first half of the book is such that it cannot really help with the task of understanding the complex processes whereby indigenous and external elements came to make common cause against the urban centres. The possibility is noted that at least at the J^E level there may have been some contemporary relevance in stories of God's interventions, in the face of the Assyrian threat, and that 'die dtr Darstellungsweise assyrische Kriegs-phraseologie rezipiert' (p. 7). Chapters 13–19 are regarded as a large insertion reflecting the P-tradition, which underwent Deuteronomistic redaction and Priestly adaptation. Chapters 20–22 belong to the post-Deuteronomistic phase, chapter 23 is Deuteronomistic, while chapter 24 is a knitting together of material from all the book's main literary phases. It seems that perhaps the Hexateuch is still alive and well in some circles!

The text of the book according to the *Einheitsübersetzung* is given on each page, along with a running commentary. There are also a number of textual footnotes and marginal cross-references.

A. H. W. Curtis

Hamilton, V. P.: *The Book of Genesis, Chapters 1–17* (NICOT). 1990. Pp. xviii, 522. (Eerdmans, Grand Rapids MI. Price: $27.95. ISBN 0 8028 2308 4)

Evangelical scholars, pastors, and students are being well served these days, being the three groups at which both the New International and the Word Biblical series are aimed. In both series the word evangelical is broadly interpreted to mean a commitment to the inspiration and authority of Scripture and not at all to a particular line of approved exegesis. Recently I reviewed favourably Gordon Wenham's first Genesis volume in the Word Biblical series (*B.L.* 1989, p. 63), and I am equally impressed by Professor Hamilton's first Genesis volume in the New International series. There is a quite specific break with Mosaic authorship and a recognition that it is not essential to read Genesis as a 'seamless garment' for its evangelical truth to be grasped. There is still a concern with unity, however, and Hamilton points with some satisfaction to the 'final form' emphasis in many other scholars who have no conservative axes to grind and are every bit as suspicious as he is of old style source criticism. I am sure he is right to draw attention to this meeting of minds, and I hope that it presages a time when the term evangelical will no longer be regarded by one party as a kind of *nihil obstat* and by the other as the equivalent of a government health warning. The commentary is judicious in its use of cognate Ancient Near Eastern material, satisfyingly rich in its detailed exegesis, and if it is openly directed towards the needs of a particular faith community, it reminds that community of its duty to respond to and not manipulate the words of Scripture. A rather unique feature is the attention devoted to the interpretation of Genesis in the New Testament. Hamilton naturally regards this as authoritative for the Christian, but it is not allowed a privileged position in his own exegesis of the text of Genesis in terms of its message for its first hearers.

J. C. L. Gibson

Maarsingh, B.: *Ezechiel*. Deel III (De Prediking van het Oude Testament). 1991. Pp. 310. (Callenbach, Nijkerk. Price: fl. 87.50; sub. price: fl. 79.50. ISBN 90 266 0284 7)

Parts I and II of this commentary were reviewed in the Book Lists for 1986 (pp. 55–56) and 1989 (p. 58). Part III completes the work, covering

EXEGESIS AND MODERN TRANSLATIONS 53

chapters 33–48. There are various excursuses on the picture of the shepherd in Egypt and Mesopotamia, the expectation of David in the Old Testament, and Old Testament notions of resurrection, for example. The visions of the restored city and temple are illustrated with diagrams. The text is expounded with particular reference to text-critical and philological matters, and to the message of Ezekiel from a Christian perspective.

J. W. Rogerson

MEINHOLD, A.: *Die Sprüche.* Teil 1: *Sprüche Kapitel 1–15.* Teil 2: *Sprüche Kapitel 16–31* (Zürcher Bibelkommentare). 1991. Pp. 262; viii, 263–542. (Theologischer Verlag, Zürich. Price: DM 34.00 [each vol.]. ISBN 3 290 10132 0)

This is a full commentary in two volumes whose function is not to wrestle with the textual and lexicographical problems of Proverbs. The author does not lose sweat on this activity, though he pays some attention to the Hebrew text and the Septuagint in brief footnotes to his translation. The commentary is well-organized and knowledgeable and will be a useful guide to students who are unfamiliar with this territory and are seeking a more detailed knowledge of its contours.

Proverbs is divided into three principal collections (1–9; 10:1–22:16; 25–29) and four small collections (22:17–24:22; 24:23–24; 30:1–14; 30:15–33). 31:1–9 is described as *Lehre* and so is associated with 1–9; the piece on the woman of parts (31:10–31) is entitled *Gedicht*. 22:17–24:22 is identified as material which is dependent on an Egyptian model (Amenemope), but which has been modified, and so it too has links with 1–9.

The Introduction (pp. 15–41) contains a review of international wisdom literature (pp. 26–37) and has contributions on *Gattungen*, authorship, theology, the final redaction, and canonicity. Solomonic authorship is not to be taken literally, but is an indication of earliness and may be glossed as an affirmation that the contents of the book have an intellectual quality which befits the wisest of kings (p. 21). The final redaction (pp. 39–40) should be set in the Greek period, prior to Ben Sira and the Septuagint of Proverbs whose structure is mostly that of the Hebrew. Meinhold's discussion of Greek loan words is slight and his tentative identification of *spyh* (31:27 not 30:27, p. 40) as a word-play on Greek *sophia* should be discounted. I do not follow his statement that 30:5f. presupposes the existence of the three parts of the Hebrew Bible.

W. McKane

The Metsudah Chumash/Rashi. A New Linear Translation by Rabbi A. Davis, with Rashi Translation by Rabbi A. Kleinkaufmann. I. *Bereishis.* 1991. Pp. ix, 575. (KTAV, Hoboken NJ. Price: $27.50. ISBN 0 88125 389 8)

Inlike many mediaeval Jewish Bible commentators, Rashi has been translated and explained in English editions. The edition of Rosenbaum and Silbermann (London, 1929–34) and the linear translation of Abraham ben Isaiah and Benjamin Sharfman (New York, 1949–50) have already helped many generations of those less familiar with this kind of rabbinic commentary, even if they are currently looking somewhat dated. It now appears that even the most traditional circles among Jewish communities in English-speaking countries feel such a need and are anxious to meet it within their own terms of religious reference. The current version has therefore been produced for synagogal use in such circles, with a transliteration reflecting (not always consistently) Ashkenazi Hebrew pronunciation, divisions according to the sabbath lectionary, and the inclusion of the prophetic readings. Critical

54 EXEGESIS AND MODERN TRANSLATIONS

scholarship is avoided but the traditional translations and the brief but helpful notes may nevertheless be found useful in wider circles than those of the intended readership.

S. C REIF

MILGROM, J.: *Leviticus 1–16.* A new translation with introduction and commentary (Anchor Bible 3). 1991. Pp. xix, 1163. (Doubleday, New York. Price: $42.00. ISBN 0 385 11434 6)

This is the most significant commentary on Leviticus ever to have been written in English. For the last twenty years Milgrom has published a stream of monographs and articles on the cultic law. Now in this commentary and in another on Numbers (JPS, 1990) he has gathered up his insights in a masterful synthesis. A third volume on Leviticus 16–27 is promised to complete his work. Though he builds on his earlier studies in this volume, there is much here that is completely fresh.

The introduction begins by outlining his methodology. Milgrom is primarily committed to the exegesis of the final form of the text, though he does think he can discern four main layers in the text, P^1, P^2, H^1, and H^2. Leviticus 1–16 is largely P^1, but it is supplemented by P^2 and H. H^1 and H^2 constitute the bulk of Lev 17–27. P^1 reflects the worship of the tabernacle at Shiloh and the temple in Jerusalem in the early monarchy. P's revision was complete by the mid-eighth century, when H originated. H reached its final form in the exile. A short section entitled Priestly Theology highlights Israel's rejection of the demonic: human sin not demonic activity is the chief danger to Israel and is the rationale of the sacrificial system. Milgrom also draws attention to the public nature of the priestly cult and the avoidance of anthropomorphism in Leviticus.

Most of the book, nearly 1000 pages, is commentary, which despite its length avoids undue verbosity. The author's enthusiasm and clear style are enhanced by diagrams, a few pictures, and ample quotation of Near Eastern ritual texts and later Jewish exegetes. Each section of text is first translated, then under 'Notes' commented on phrase by phrase. Finally under 'Comment' longer reflective discussion is found. In these comments Milgrom offers his own illuminating syntheses of the issues raised by Leviticus. For example Comments on the Diet laws in chapter 11 prompt a discussion of Leviticus's central ideas on holiness and ethics as well as a full treatment of all the biblical dietary laws and the interpretations they have prompted.

This commentary is thus essential reading for anyone concerned with the history of Israelite religion or Old Testament theology. Not all of Milgrom's critical or exegetical views will command assent, but his commentary is a wise, learned and lucid guide to a difficult Old Testament book.

G. J. WENHAM

NAKAZAWA, K.: *Yobuki: Shinyaku to Ryakuchu* (Job: a new translation with comments). 1991. Pp. 204. (Shinkyo Shuppansha, Tokyo. Price: ¥2200)

This is a Japanese translation, with brief comments, of the Book of Job. The author had previously published a translation of the book excluding chapters 28 and 32–37 in *Yobuki no Mochifu* (The Motif of the Book of Job) in 1978. The author marks in bold fonts the 'key words' and 'key sentences' which he thinks indicate the 'motif' of each chapter or paragraph. As an appendix, the author gives a brief history of the interpretation of the Book of Job in Japan and explains why he has translated some passages differently from the ordinary way.

D. T. TSUMURA

EXEGESIS AND MODERN TRANSLATIONS 55

PÉTER-CONTESSE, R. and ELLINGTON, J.: *A Translator's Handbook on Leviticus* (Helps for Translators Series). 1990. Pp. ix, 458. (United Bible Societies, New York. Price: $9.50. ISBN 0 8267 0102 7)

This book is designed for missionaries, who, not knowing Biblical Hebrew, are engaged in translating Leviticus into tribal languages. It therefore aims to do two things: first, to clarify how English translations understand Leviticus, and second, to suggest ways of expressing its ideas in a receptor language that may lack precise equivalents for the English (or Hebrew) terms.

In pursuing the first aim of clarifying the meaning of the English versions, the book sets out side by side the RSV and TEV and explains their differences citing many other versions where relevant. In this respect it is little different from a good popular verse-by-verse commentary. But, being primarily interested in translation, it says relatively little about the historical setting or theology of Leviticus. It is exegetically up-to-date, but it does not try to offer new views. For those engaged in Bible translation its discussion of potential problems would be invaluable, but the typical reader of the *Book List* would be better served by an ordinary commentary.

G. J. WENHAM

PROVAN, I. W.: *Lamentations* (New Century Bible). 1991. Pp. xviii, 142. (Marshall Pickering, London; Eerdmans, Grand Rapids MI. Price: £8.95; $14.95. ISBN 0 551 02323 6; 0 8028 0547 7)

Before the commentary proper there is an introduction dealing with the name of the book and its place in the canon, its literary character, its authorship and date of composition, the theology of the book, and the text and interpretation. There is a good bibliography, and author and scripture indexes. This is a worthy member of the series, refreshingly written, and timely.

Provan exercises great caution as to authorship, background and date, and argues strongly that there is too little evidence for conclusions to be reached with any confidence. If hyperbole is employed in the poems, as it seems to be, it is wrong, exegetically, to deduce from such language any precise historical background; yet that is the kind of exegesis which is found in many commentaries. We may not even conclude that Jeremiah is not the author, for we know very little about Jeremiah's life and background; and we may not deduce that vivid imagery points to an eye witness description: it may have something to do with the author's imagination and creativity. Further studies in Lamentations will have to take this work into account.

R. B. SALTERS

RICE, G.: *Nations Under God. A Commentary on the Book of I Kings* (International Theological Commentary). 1990. Pp. xv, 198. (Eerdmans, Grand Rapids MI; Handsel, Edinburgh. Price: $10.95. ISBN 0 8028 0492 6; 1 871828 06 6)

Faithful to the first declared aim of the International Theological Commentary, Gene Rice identifies the main theological themes of 1 Kings as follows: the covenant people are struggling with the problem of political existence; their past is recounted in the light of the first two commandments; in relating their history to morality the book contains warnings against a divided heart, calls for obedience, and summons to repentance. As he moves on to the second task, which is to emphasize the relevance of the book to the life of the Church, the author tries to identify the equivalent of Canaanite religion in our own society, to prod us to value our own efforts, and to look for God's presence in areas of public life and service.

56   EXEGESIS AND MODERN TRANSLATIONS

Those seeking the minimum of exegesis to give a basis for preaching in a style which is then named 'exegetical preaching' will be interested in this kind of commentary.

G. H. JONES

RICHTER. W.: *Biblia Hebraica transcripta das ist das ganze Alte Testament transkribiert, mit Satzeinteilungen versehen und durch die Version tiberisch-masoretischer Autoritäten bereichert, auf der sie gründet.* 1. *Genesis*; 2. *Exodus, Leviticus*; 3. *Numeri, Deuteronomium* (Arbeiten zu Text und Sprache im Alten Testament 33.1, 2, 3). 1991. Pp. viii, 485; 629; 701. (EOS Verlag, St. Ottilien. Price: DM 58.00; DM 68.00; DM 78.00. ISBN 3 88096 533 1; ISBN 3 88096 582 X; ISBN 3 88096 583 8)

I find myself completely puzzled by these volumes. They contain the text of BHS transcribed into a form suitable for computer analysis, with the pointed and accented Hebrew text on the right hand pages and the transcription facing it. There is a very short Introduction in the first volume. Even allowing for German vocalization, there are curious features. For example, segholates are represented in their short form, so that what might conventionally be transcribed as $way^e h\hat{\imath}$-$\underline{b}\bar{o}qer$ becomes $wa=yihy\ buqr$. The verses are divided into numbered short lines, and syntactical relations noted by marginal codes. It is claimed that the work contains complete morphological data and that the details about the clauses allow precise citation. When the whole text has been published it will be made available on disk or tape, with user programs. Apart from serving the needs of proof reading, the present editions of the BH^t appear to be valueless. Only computer analysis of the Hebrew text using this data base can reveal its usefulness. But perhaps I have missed the point.

C. S. RODD

SAYDON, P. P.: *Bibbia Saydon. It-Testament il-Qadim,* II: *Il-Kotba tal-Gherf u il-Kotba tal-Profeti.* Edited by Carmel Attard. 1990. (Museum, Malta)

It was in the Twenties that the linguist Saydon planned the translation of the entire Bible into Maltese. His efforts coincided with the attempts to establish Maltese as a literary language. Being a specialist in semitic languages Saydon preferred the semitic to romance elements present in spoken Maltese. The result of his endeavours which lasted thirty years (1929–59) was a highly literary and technically precise translation into Maltese of both Old and New Testament. In spite of being an enormous achievement Saydon's Maltese bible possessed an inherent Achilles heel. Following promulgation on 4 December 1963, of the *Constitution on the Sacred Liturgy* (Sacrosanctum Concilium) by the Vatican Council II, the Catholic Church in Malta needed a translation of the Bible in the common vernacular for both the Liturgical purposes and for private reading. Professor Saydon was currently revising his opus, but was unwilling to submit his translation to a radical adaptation to contemporary Maltese. This impasse led, in December 1966, to the decision by the Malta Bible Society (founded in 1958 by the same Professor Saydon together with other collaborators) to embark on a new translation which was finally published in one volume in 1984.

The present volume, therefore, is posthumous and we owe its publication to a local Institution to which Saydon entrusted his copyright. This volume is the final one of the series. The first volume published in 1977, included the entire New Testament, while the second, published in 1982, consisted of the Old Testament historical books; the present volume contains Old Testament wisdom and prophetic literature. The updating of Saydon's notes was done by the general editor Rev. Carmel Attard, who also wrote a useful introduction to the traditional complexes as well as to the single books. The appendices

EXEGESIS AND MODERN TRANSLATIONS 57

include a short discussion on Hebrew prosody (pp. 1541–44), a glossary of terms (now obsolete) employed by the translator (pp. 1547–51), a number of beautifully printed maps, and a design of the ideal Temple as conceived by the Prophet Ezechiel. Also noteworthy are the black and white reproductions of a number of paintings by Giuseppe Cali (1846–1930), that are treasured in several parish churches in Malta. Lovers of the Maltese language and of the Bible have several reasons to be grateful to the publishing house, MUSEUM, for this monumental series under the general title *BIBBJA SAYDON*.

A. ABELA

STINE, P. C. (ed.): *Bible Translation and the Spread of the Church. The Last 200 Years* (Studies in Christian Mission 2). 1990. Pp. xii, 154. (Brill, Leiden. Price: fl. 75.00; $38.46. ISBN 90 04 09331 1 1; ISSN 0924 9389)

The nine contributions to this book were delivered at a conference convened by the United Bible Societies at the Centre of Theological Inquiry at Princeton in 1988. L. Sameh, writing on 'Gospel and Culture', claims that translating the Bible indigenizes Christianity in different locations and thus strengthens it. In 'The Translation Principle in Christian History' A. Walls contrasts the approach of Patrick, who expected the Scriptures to be read in Latin, with that of Wulfila, who translated the Bible into Gothic, thus exemplifying the view that Bible translation corresponds to the incarnation. D. C. Arichae ('Theology and Translation') contrasts formally equivalent with audience-centred translation and maintains that translation for a specific readership involves exegesis. S. Batalden ('The Politics of Modern Russian Biblical Translation') discusses the effect of political authority on translation. The role of translation in developing indigenous theologies is considered by S. Escobar (a Latin American View) and K. Koyma (an Asian view). L. J. Luzbetak ('Contextual Translation: The Role of Cultural Anthropology') examines the nature of translation as cross-cultural communication. D. L. Whiteman investigates 'Bible Translation and Social and Cultural Development'. In a concluding paper ('Future Bible Translation and the Future of the Church'), U. Fick argues that the diversity and unity of the Bible can be a safeguard against disunity in the Church and mankind. G. W. ANDERSON

STONE, M. E.: *Fourth Ezra: A Commentary on the Book of Fourth Ezra* (Hermeneia). 1990. Pp. xxii, 496. (Fortress, Minneapolis; SCM, London. Price: £35.50. ISBN 0 8006 6026 9)

During the past twenty years Michael Stone has published a series of preliminary studies on various aspects of 4 Ezra. He here brings this work to a conclusion with the publication of a fine commentary that is fully worthy of the remarkable apocalypse to which it is devoted. In broad terms Stone's interpretation follows the 'psychological' approach developed by Gunkel, but he also builds on and refines the observations of scholars who have been critical of weaknesses in Gunkel's approach. Stone maintains that 4 Ezra is a literary unity incorporating certain preexistent materials, and that it was written by an author of considerable skill and subtlety. In contrast to some previous commentators he argues that there is a definite development within the argument of the first three versions. He believes that the religious experiences attributed to Ezra in the book, although often described in a conventional manner, reflect the actual religious experiences of the author. And in relation to the fourth vision, whose pivotal position in the development of the book he rightly emphasises, he suggests that the experiences that Ezra undergoes as he witnesses the transformation of the mourning woman into a city (10:25–27) 'is analogous to the major sort of reorientation of

58 EXEGESIS AND MODERN TRANSLATIONS

personality that is usually associated with religious conversion'. It is this 'conversion' that provides the key to the change in Ezra's attitude in the second part of the apocalypse.

Stone's commentary is based on the RSV, but he has not hesitated to depart from the RSV where, in his judgement, the textual evidence warranted this; the translation is accompanied by textual notes. The exegetical comment is usually divided into three sections: Form and Structure, Function and Content, and Commentary; and although this arrangement sometimes leads to a degree of repetition, the exegetical comment contains many acute and interesting observations both on the meaning of the book as a whole and on the interpretation of disputed points. The volume also contains a fifty-page Introduction, a bibliography, and full indexes.

M. A. KNIBB

STUDIUM BIBLICUM FRANCISCANUM: *Yoshuaki. Genbun Kotei ni yoru Kogoyaku* (The Book of Joshua: Translation into Modern Japanese from the Oriental Languages). 1991. Pp. 180, *3. (Chuo Shuppansha, Tokyo. Price: ¥2400)

Studium Biblicum Franciscanum has issued Japanese translations of the Old Testament and Apocrypha, and this volume on Joshua is the twentieth one. Only Kings, Chronicles, Isaiah, Jeremiah, and Ezekiel are yet to be translated among the thirty-nine Old Testament books. The book also has an Introduction and Comments. Studium Biblicum Franciscanum is to be congratulated on this significant contribution to Biblical scholarship in Japan.

D. T. TSUMURA

TOWNSEND, J. J.: *Midrash Tanhuma. Translated into English with Introduction, Indices, and Brief Notes* (S. Buber Recension). Vol. I: *Genesis*. 1989. Pp. xvii, 334. (KTAV, Hoboken NJ. Price: $39.50. ISBN 0 88125 087 2)

Townsend offers a straightforward rendering of the so-called Buber recension of Midrash Tanhuma, with little attempt at emendation and with only brief notes. He has, perhaps, followed Buber a little too closely. Buber, though an indefatigable editor of midrashic texts, did not produce good editions. Some of his work is extremely poor and drew strong criticism even in his own day. (Note, for example, the strictures of Schechter and others on his *Midrash Zuta*.) Townsend might have done better to have followed the example of Hans Bietenhard, who based his German translation of Midrash Tanhuma (*Midrasch Tanhuma B*, Judaica et Christiana 5, Bern and Frankfurt, 1980–82) directly on a manuscript, Vat. Ebr. 34. Townsend could have chosen Buber's base-text, Bodleian 154, which contains a different recension from the Vatican ms, and recorded important variants in the footnotes. Certainly, it is regrettable that he has carried over into the English Buber's annoying system of brackets, braces, and parentheses. He adds material on his own account within angle brackets, and the result is visually rather messy and a little confusing. The Introduction is short and confines itself largely to explaining the conventions behind the translation (which include a conscious attempt to avoid sexist language!). In passing Townsend proposes a date for the Buber Tanhuma no earlier than the ninth century, on the grounds that it quotes a chapter from the *She'iltot* of R. Ahai (eighth century). At least a footnote reference to Felix Böhl's discussion of the relationship of the Tanhuma to the *She'iltot* in *Aufbau und literarische Formen des aggadischen Teils im Jelamdenu-Midrasch* (Wiesbaden 1977) would have been helpful. Böhl shows that the problem is more complex than is often supposed. Townsend suggests southern Italy as the provenance of the Buber Tanhuma, but again does not elaborate on an important issue. Though some of Townsend's editorial decisions are disappointing, there is no doubt that he

EXEGESIS AND MODERN TRANSLATIONS 59

has performed his central task of translating the text conscientiously and well. Midrash Tanḥuma is the last of the classic midrashim to be rendered into English. It is good to see this great treasure-house of Rabbinic bible-exegesis made available to a wider public.

P. S. ALEXANDER

Tre bibelböcker i översättning av bibelkommissionen: Första Moseboken, Ordspåksboken, Jeremia. 1991. Pp. 368, incl. 2 maps. (Atlantis. Printed by Schmidts Boktryckeri, Helsingborg. ISBN 91 7486 971 X)

This, the most substantial specimen hitherto of the new Swedish translation of the Old Testament, was published just 450 years after the appearance of Gustav Vasa's Bible, the first translation of the whole Bible into Swedish. It contains three books of considerable length (Genesis, Proverbs, and Jeremiah) which differ markedly in literary character and in their length and diversity exemplify the approach which the translators have adopted to their task. The vocabulary and style of the new translation present a striking contrast to the 'professor's Swedish' of the 1917 translation. This is particularly evident in Proverbs where the terse style of the new translation is more appropriate than the rather ponderous verbosity of its predecessor. The vocabulary used in Proverbs, however, is slightly nearer to the 1917 translation (old fashioned even then), on the ground that the vocabulary of contemporary usage is less appropriate in a proverb. Elsewhere vocabulary and style are modern and no attempt has been made to use high-flown language for literary effect or to produce the atmosphere of antiquity by antiquated vocabulary or idiom. On the other hand, differences of style in the original are reflected in corresponding differences in translation, notably in the somewhat dry, matter-of-fact style used in the prose passages in Jeremiah in contrast to the poetry. Where necessary, the translation is accompanied by concise explanatory notes and at the end of the volume there are some 20 pages of text-critical notes. Brief but illuminating essays, relating to both content and style, are prefixed to the books. These are the work of distinguished writers who have taken part in the work of translation: Karl–Gustav Hildebrand (Genesis), Gunn-Britt Sundström (Proverbs), and Gunnar Harding (Jeremiah). This volume is in every way an outstanding achievement. It is appropriate that Atlantis should have included it in it series of world classics. The format is altogether admirable.

G. W. ANDERSON

WEINFELD, M.: *Deuteronomy 1–11*. A new translation with introduction and commentary (Anchor Bible 5). 1991. Pp. xv, 458. (Doubleday, New York. Price: $34.00. ISBN 0 385 17593 0)

Professor Weinfeld's views on the origin, significance and background of the book of Deuteronomy were widely publicized in his detailed study of 1972 entitled *Deuteronomy and the Deuteronomic School* (*B.L.*, 1973, p. 46). He has subsequently published a substantial number of detailed studies of individual topics relating to the book and now offers this excellently set out and detailed commentary on the text. It follows the established format for the series and reaffirms positions that Weinfeld has already argued for earlier. Much of the background of the book is claimed to have a North Israelite origin, it displays a dependence on the form of ancient Near Eastern vassal-treaties, both Hittite and Assyrian, and the book is closely related to Josiah's reform, which it antedates and for which it came to provide the central focus. The book itself probably originated among scribes working in the seventh century BCE so that Josiah's reform must have begun with a task of temple renovation before the lawbook was discovered.

60   EXEGESIS AND MODERN TRANSLATIONS

Weinfeld argues for an original shortform of the Decalogue, which antedates both Exodus 20 and Deuteronomy 5, and the school of nationalist pious devotees of Yahweh, who were the authors of Deuteronomy, had a strong link with wisdom. Accordingly the book is supportive of the cultus in principle, but strongly separated from it in intellectual outlook, which is more rational and formalistic than the cult would enjoin.

All of these positions have been advocated and discussed for some years, and have increasingly become the subject of critical re-examination and revision. Weinfeld takes note of such criticisms, as for instance those which favour the late date for the Decalogue, but rejects them. Similarly the case for recognizing that Deuteronomy was more the product of Josiah's reform than its cause, is dismissed too readily. Over a number of issues one cannot help feeling that Weinfeld, in a desire to be open to too many viewpoints and to defend too many fondly held hypotheses, has arrived at an unconvincing synthesis. This is not to fail to recognize the comprehensiveness and value of this clearly set out, and well-written, commentary, but to question seriously whether many of its critical assumptions will last as long as such a full-blooded presentation properly merits.

R. E. Clements

ZAKOVITCH, Y.: *Ruth* (Mikra le-Yisrael). 1990. Pp. viii, 124. (Am Oved, Tel Aviv, Magnes, Jerusalem. ISBN 965 13 0646 7)

In their brief introduction to this new series of commentaries for the Hebrew reading public, the editors (M. Greenberg and S. Ahitub) set what many would regard as an impossibly comprehensive agenda. They require up-to-date scholarly treatment alongside attention to traditional Jewish exegesis as reflected in the ancient versions and the later commentators, extra- and inner-Biblical comparisons, sound textual and linguistic analysis, explanation of *realia* in the light of archaeological research and the like, and discussion of scholarly issues while not ignoring the Bible's cultural heritage. Even in the case of so short a book as Ruth, Zakovitch has naturally had to be selective, and he concentrates on a sensitive appreciation of the narrative's artistry, its links and echoes with other Biblical material, and frequent reference to earlier Jewish exegesis. Other matters are not neglected, of course, though a weakness is the very restricted treatment of modern scholarly work (the bibliography is less than two pages, there are no footnotes and secondary literature is rarely referred to). The commentary's format is straightforward: after a forty-page introduction, each paragraph of the Massoretic Text is reproduced, followed by a general analysis and then phrase-by-phrase commentary.

H. G. M. Williamson

6. LITERARY CRITICISM AND INTRODUCTION

ACKROYD, P. R.: *The Chronicler in His Age* (Journal for the Study of the Old Testament Supplement Series 101). 1991. Pp. 397. (JSOT Press, Sheffield. Price: £40.00 ($60.00). ISBN 1 85075 2540; ISSN 0309 0787)

In his brief Preface, Peter Ackroyd notes that this second collection of his essays (on *Studies in the Religious Tradition of the Old Testament* see *B.L.* 1988, p. 99) 'concentrates attention on the post-exilic period', a lively concern of his for well over thirty years, and 'gathers conveniently around "the Chronicler"', a title used for the figure or figures lying behind both the books of Chronicles and the books of Ezra and Nehemiah'. The title of the volume is adapted from that of the first and longest piece, 'The Age of the Chronicler' (pp. 8–86); and the collection as a whole is marked by careful sifting of evidence. Although only chapter 8 had not been set in print before, many

LITERARY CRITICISM AND INTRODUCTION   61

others reprint lectures which had been printed only in private or very local collections abroad. The many readers of the author's *Exile and Restoration* and of his commentary on Chronicles, Ezra, and Nehemiah will now be able to chart his ongoing engagement with these issues which he nicely describes, borrowing words of Ronald Eyre, as a rearrangement of his uncertainties (pp. 156 f).

A. G. AULD

BAK, D. H.: *Klagende Gott — klagende Menschen. Studien zur Klage im Jeremiabuch* (BZAW 193). 1990. Pp. xiii, 273. (De Gruyter, Berlin, New York. Price: DM 104.00. ISBN 3 11 012341 X)

Yet another monograph on the laments in the book of Jeremiah, but in many ways a superior piece of work in an already over-subscribed subgenre of writing on Jeremiah. Dong Hyun Bak looks not only at the laments in Jer. 11–20, but also considers the other lament elements in the book of Jeremiah (e.g. 30:5–7, 12–15; 31:15, 18–20; 48:31–39). This wide-ranging scrutiny allows him to treat the whole lament phenomenon in Jeremiah, as well as paying particular attention to the lament poems in chs 11–20 (the so-called 'confessions'). The treatment of the secondary literature (in the footnotes) strikes me as being very comprehensive and therefore this monograph is to be welcomed for its survey of the literature and for its well-balanced treatment of a considerable amount of scholarly writing. The research behind the monograph was undertaken in Berlin under the supervision of Peter Welten (Richard Hentschke also is acknowledged as an influence in co-refereering the work). Bak is Korean, so there is a Korean dimension to this theological analysis of a very important aspect of the book of Jeremiah (the influence of Minyung theology is evident throughout the book). In fact, the book is a nice blend of conventional Western scholarship and contemporary Korean piety — a shape of things to come in biblical scholarship. The biblical texts have been raked over a thousand times before and have therefore very little to yield by way of new insights, unless their analysis is accompanied by new approaches, new theories or new cultural insights. Bak's monograph belongs to this third category and, while learning little new about the book of Jeremiah, I enjoyed this trawl of an ancient text in the company of a modern voice.

R. P. CARROLL

BARTON, J.: *What is the Bible?* 1991. Pp. vi, 169. (Triangle, SPCK, London. Price: £4.99. ISBN 0 281 04528 3)

This short popular book treats in very readable form various topics commonly rising in people's minds about the Bible — both Old and New Testaments. Topics include modern pluralist views and relevance/irrelevance of the Bible as a historical document. Questions of biblical morality are addressed: particularly notable is Barton's well-balanced treatment of liberation theology and appeals to the Bible to justify political systems. Similarly contemporary is his treatment of sexist material in the Bible with regard to modern feminist movements — particularly the apparent maleness of God. He concludes with advice to 'would-be Bible readers' on reading the Bible: assessment of popular paraphrases (like Alan Dale's), modern translations, and books designed to help beginners. Indices are replaced by lists of books in Protestant and Catholic Bibles, of Old Testament books by genre and of books in both Testaments in probable chronological order. An excellent handbook for newcomers to biblical study.

J. G. SNAITH

62 LITERARY CRITICISM AND INTRODUCTION

BECKER, U.: *Richerzeit und Königtum. Redaktionsgeschichtliche Studien zum Richterbuch* (BZAW 192). 1990. Pp. ix, 326. (De Gruyter, Berlin, New York. Price: DM 118.00. ISBN 3 11 012440 8)

This substantial Bonn dissertation offers a helpful review of a largely German-language contribution to study of the development of the book of Judges. To be fair, the relevant studies of Auld, Boling, Mayes, Soggin, and many others are regularly acknowledged and frequently discussed; yet sometimes these appear to be refugees from another world, tolerated but not knowing quite how to behave. Other would-be visitors, like those Anglo-American scholars whose literary work 'is based on wholly different philosophical and literary premisses', would hardly be issued a visa by Becker. To the claim of B. G. Webb (see *B.L.* 1988, p. 95) that 'synchronic analysis . . . will help to facilitate finer discrimination' he responds by regretting that Webb has in fact completely screened out 'literarkritische' considerations. Following an introductory chapter, eleven chapters short and long discuss in turn all sections of the book except for the Samson series 1:1–2:5; 2:6–9; 2:10–19; 2:20–3:6; 3:7–11; 3:12–30; 4–5; 6–9; 10:6–12:6; 10:1–5/12:7–15; and 17–21. A thirteenth chapter briefly reviews the resulting picture of the formation of the book of Judges, and offers some remarks on 'Judges' Period and Monarchy'.

The Deuteronomistic Historian had available to him traditions of the murder of Eglon, the basic stock of the Song of Deborah, some Gideon and Abimelech stories, the anti-royal Jotham fable, the fragmentary list of minor judges, and a short account of the rise of Jephthah (and possibly part of the Samson tradition) — but no connected version of any of these, as argued by W. Richter. He himself (DtrH) provided his collection with a programmatic introduction (2:11–18*), an exemplary story (3:7–11); supplemented his source materials where necessary (6:1–6*; 9:42–45*; and 10:17f*); and also composed a developed narrative (4) on the basis of Deborah's song. Becker attributes two groups of texts to 'late Deuteronomistic' supplementers: remarks about the disobedience of the people in chapter 2, the added Ephod note in 8:24–27, and moralizing about the kingdom of Abimelech are attributed to the 'nomistic' DtrN; then the list of unconquered cities (1:21, 27ff), the related angel-speech (2:1–5), and the Micah narrative (17f*) branding the northern cult as heretical belong at least to the vicinity of DtrN. Finally, an author indebted to Pentateuchal P and from the vicinity of the redactor of the Pentateuch contributed the outer portions, 1:1–18, 22–26 and 19–21; and added the pro-monarchial refrain from his new concluding chapters to 17:6 and 18:1, so completing the production of the now independent book of Judges.

Against Veijola he argues that it was the original DtrH and not the later DtrN who included Jotham's fable and formulated Gideon's saying; and though in 1 Sam. 8, when he is facing the institution itself, the same writer's criticism of monarchy is milder, Becker is sure that Dtr's own views come to clearer expression as he describes the earlier period. The DtrN supplements share and sharpen DtrH's attitude to kingship. But the final edition of the book involves a radical reshaping of the whole Dtr understanding: the period of the Judges becomes a failure to be rescued only by the monarchy.

A. G. AULD

BEN ZVI, E.: *A Historical–Critical Study of the Book of Zephaniah* (Beihefte zur Zeitschrift für die alttestamentliche Wissenschaft 198). 1991. Pp. xii, 390. (De Gruyter, Berlin. Price: DM 148.00. ISBN 3 11 012837 3; ISSN 0934 2575)

Two-thirds of this book, which originated as a doctoral dissertation, consists of a detailed verse by verse study of Zephaniah, concentrating on

LITERARY CRITICISM AND INTRODUCTION 63

textual, linguistic, and lexical matters. Particular attention is paid to the use of the words and expressions found in Zephaniah in other biblical material. This is followed by the Commentary, which is an analysis of the Book, its units, and the traditions embedded in it. The conclusion reached is that it is a post-monarchical composition, in all probability not the work of a single author, embodying traditional material, and itself expanded by later additions. Some of the author's more general comments, e.g. on the oracles against the nations or the nature of the community responsible for the composition of the Book, are more debatable. Unfortunately the style is turgid, and the proof-reading inaccurate. Hebrew quotations extending over two lines are generally wrongly divided, and a Murabba'at reading is given in two different forms on p. 240. Ben Zvi has collected a great deal of material which will be indispensable to the serious student of Zephaniah, but his work must be used with caution.

A. GELSTON

BODI, D.: *The Book of Ezekiel and the Poem of Erra* (Orbis Biblicus et Orientalis 104). 1991. Pp. 324. (Universitätsverlag, Freiburg (CH); Vandenhoeck & Ruprecht, Göttingen. Price: SwFr 78.00. ISBN 3 7278 0731 8 (Universitätsverlag); 3 525 53736 0 (Vandenhoeck & Ruprecht))

This book represents a revised and expanded version of a PhD dissertation completed at Union Theological Seminary, New York, in 1987, under the supervision of George Landes.

Bodi attempts to demonstrate the likelihood that in the formulation of certain themes and motifs in the book of Ezekiel, its author or redactor knew and used the somewhat earlier Akkadian composition called the Poem of Erra. He analyses twelve features shared by both works. His main concern is with four features which appear uniquely in the book of Ezekiel (that is, nowhere else in the Old Testament), but also in the Poem of Erra. These are Hebrew *š'ṭ* in its various forms (e.g. Ezek. 16:57) and Akkadian *šēṭu/leqû šēṭūtu* ('to show contempt'); Hebrew *ḥašmal* (e.g. Ezek. 1:4) and Akkadian *elmēšu* ('amber'); the motif of the seven executioners in Ezek. 9 and the Divine Seven (*Sebetti*) in the Poem of Erra; and details of the motif of preservation from the flood (c.f. Ezek. 22:24). It is argued that the source of these four features of Ezekiel is most probably the Poem of Erra. Bodi considers a further eight features (including both vocabulary and theological motifs) which Ezekiel shares with other Old Testament traditions and also with the Poem of Erra. It is argued that the source of these is probably antecedent Old Testament prophetic traditions, but that the Poem of Erra might have influenced the formulation and presentation of some aspects of these motifs within Ezekiel.

Bodi places this work within the context of a detailed review of research undertaken on the Babylonian influence on the Book of Ezekiel during the nineteenth and twentieth centuries. The concluding section of the book explores the poetic strategy which Bodi describes as 'literary emulation', a creative synthesis of traditional material which Bodi sees as exemplified by the cases he has presented in detail.

This is a valuable study. Bodi is sensitive to problems of method, and to the limitations of the comparative study of Ancient Near Eastern literature; but, this said, he perhaps tries to prove too much in tracing as much as he does to the direct or indirect influence of the relatively short Poem of Erra. Our sources, both biblical and non-biblical, are so selective that a degree of agnosticism is appropriate. The book has a clear layout, though at points it still reads very much like a dissertation. It has an index of biblical, Akkadian, and other texts discussed, but lacks other indexes.

P. M. JOYCE

64 LITERARY CRITICISM AND INTRODUCTION

DE BOER, P. A.: *Selected Studies in Old Testament Exegesis*. Edited by C. Van Duin (Oudtestamentische Studiën xxvii). 1991. Pp. ix, 246. (Brill, Leiden. Price: fl. 120; $61.54. ISBN 90 04 09342 7; ISSN 069 7226)

This collection of twenty-four articles by the late Professor de Boer, originally planned as a congratulatory volume, has sadly become a memorial volume. Three of the articles are in French, two in German, and the remainder in English. Of those which now appear in English, seven have been specially translated from the original Dutch. The volume represents the whole of Professor de Boer's career, the earliest piece dating from 1938. The articles cover a wide range of topics but with a strong emphasis on the exegesis of biblical passages (from Genesis, Exodus, Deuteronomy, Samuel, Job, Psalms, and Ecclesiastes). Two are on wider topics (Israelite kingship and Egypt in the Old Testament). Two are wholly related to the author's Syriac studies. A photograph of Professor de Boer forms the frontispiece. The volume is prefaced by an appreciation of de Boer's work and influence as scholar and teacher by the editor, and concludes with a list of his published works (127 items), a plate of the Ṣo'ar inscription illustrating one of the articles, and an index of biblical references. The whole is a fitting tribute to an important and well-loved scholar who was a personal friend of many members of this Society, and will be a permanent memorial of his work.

R. N. WHYBRAY

BOZAK, B. A.: *Life "Anew"*. *A Literary–Theological Study of Jer. 30–31* (Analecta Biblica, 122). 1991. Pp. xviii, 196. (Editrice Pontificio Istituto Biblico, Roma. ISBN 88 7653 1223 X)

This is a slightly revised version of Barbara Bozak's doctoral dissertation (directed by Charles Conroy) defended at the Gregorian University in May 1988. Written without the benefit of having had access to Holladay 2 (published in 1989) or McKane 2 (yet to be published) on Jeremiah, this is an excellent in-depth analysis of Jeremiah 30–31 (the so-called 'Book of Consolation'). It develops the work of Böhmer and Bracke on those two chapters, but is a superior work because of its treatment of 30–31 as an integrated literary unit. Bozak undertakes a close reading of the text (à la New Criticism), but goes beyond such a close reading in her poetic analysis of the text to an integrative reading of the chapters as constituting and communicating a single message. There is a great wealth of detailed exegetical and linguistic analysis in this book which will make it very valuable for any close reader of the text. Apart from the extremely valuable structural analysis of the poems constituting 30–31 and the prose conclusion, there is a very useful treatment of the unifying elements which make 30–31 more than just a mere anthology of poems and a good presentation of the seven motifs forming the themes of 30–31. Bozak isolates three themes in 30–31: the transformation of reality; the gratuitousness of Yhwh's salvific deed; and the representation of future events as being passed on, yet different from, the known (past and present) — i.e. notions of continuity and discontinuity between past and future. The concluding chapter on the feminine address and imagery in 30–31 (pp. 155–72) touches on one of the most striking features of the text, using Jungian archetypes discourse to make some important points. Altogether I found this a very thoughtful and thought-provoking piece of work and a most useful contribution to contemporary Jeremiah studies.

R. P. CARROLL

LITERARY CRITICISM AND INTRODUCTION 65

Brekelmans, C. and Lust, J. (eds): *Pentateuchal and Deuteronomistic Studies: Papers read at the XIIIth IOSOT Congress, Leuven 1989* (Bibliotheca Ephemeridum Theologicarum Lovaniensium xciv). 1990. Pp. 307. (University Press, Leuven; distributed by Peeters, Leuven. Price: BFr 1,500. ISBN 90 6186 423 2; 90 6831 306 1)

An interesting volume consisting of twenty-two articles of varying length. On the Pentateuch side, E. van Wolde uses the serpent of Genesis 2–3 to illustrate a reader-oriented semiotic approach to texts (pp. 11–21). J. Vermeylen offers a reading of Genesis 27 in terms of successive redactional layers (pp. 23—40). P. Kevers finds the 'sons of Jacob' in Genesis 34 to be an original part of the story, which derives from a pre-Israelite Jacob clan living in Canaan (pp. 41–46). J. Krasovec finds unifying themes in Exodus 7–11 (pp. 47–66); while M. Vervenne takes Exodus 13:17–14:31 as a test case for the contention that Pentateuchal P is both document and redactional layer (pp. 67–90). N. Lohfink asks whether there is a Deuteronomistic redaction of the Book of the Covenant, answering in the negative (pp. 91–113). A. Schenker outlines the difference between the *hattat and 'asham* offering in the light of Leviticus 5:1–6 and 5:17–19 (pp. 115–23). C. Schäfer-Lichtenberger discusses divine and human authority in Deuteronomy (pp. 125–42); and L. Laberge looks at the state of the text in Deuteronomy 31:1–30 and 32:44–47 (pp. 143–60). Finally, H. Lubsczyk discusses the origin and influence of Deuteronomy (pp. 161–77).

On the side of Deuteronomistic studies, E. Cortese, in dialogue with the 'Smend school', argues in favour of an initial Josianic redaction of the Deuteronomistic History (pp. 179–90). M. Nobile discusses the significance of the four Passover accounts in Genesis–Kings for an understanding of the final form of this corpus (pp. 191–96). Z. Kallai explains the explanatory note in Joshua 17:14–18 (pp. 197–205). D. Edelman argues that a sensitive literary reading of the current form of the story of Saul makes implausible the view that it is made up from pre-existing blocks of material (pp. 207–20). V. Peterca examines 1 Samuel 15:24–31 (pp. 221–25); and E. Eynikel argues that 1 Kings 13 comprises, not two separate old legends, but one story which has been edited (pp. 227–37). K. Smelik considers the literary function of 1 Kings 17:8–24 (pp. 239–43); and A. Lemaire argues for a first redaction of the Elisha cycle around 800 BCE at the court of King Joash (pp. 245–54). C. Conroy makes some proposals about method in exegesis, suggesting that chronological priority should be given to 'final-form' study (pp. 255–68). M. J. Paul explores the implications of a distinction between covenant restoration and covenant renewal for our reading of 2 Kings 22–23 (pp. 269–76); and R. J. Coggins uses various translations of 2 Kings 23:29 which seek harmony with history as we know it from other sources to illustrate the danger of translators 'improving' their text (pp. 277–81). Finally, B. Becking argues for the historical reliability of 2 Kings 25:27–30 and discusses the theological significance of the passage (pp. 283–93).

I. W. Provan

Carr, D. M.: *From D to Q: A Study of Early Jewish Interpretations of Solomon's Dream at Gibeon* (The Society of Biblical Literature Monograph Series 44). 1991. Pp. xii, 257. (Scholars Press, Atlanta GA. Price: $29.95 (pbk). ISBN 1 55540 528 2; 1 55540 529 0)

This revision of a Claremont dissertation offers an interesting scrutiny of the influence of the narrative of Solomon's vision at Gibeon on, and the transformation of that story in, biblical tradition. After a short Introduction (pp. 1–5), substantial chapters discuss 'The Redaction History of 1 Kgs 3:2–15' (pp. 7–30) and 'The Pre-Deuteronomistic Vorlage to the Gibeon Story' (pp. 31–56); and their implications are teased out in a discussion of 'Interpretation in Redaction' (pp. 57–87). The retellings of the story by the

66 LITERARY CRITICISM AND INTRODUCTION

Chronicler and by Josephus are treated as 'Interpretations in Histories of Israel' (pp. 89–132). Then 'Interpretations in Instructions' (pp. 133–72) reviews the influence of motifs within the story on Qohelet 1:12–2:26, on a number of passages in the Wisdom of Solomon, and on Q ('the last Second Temple Jewish interpretation of the Gibeon story'). The 'Summary and Concluding Reflections' (pp. 173–202) both review the argument and present some contemporary analogies from the work of Phyllis Trible and Carter Heyward. An Appendix (pp. 203–14) argues for the proposed reconstruction of Q from Luke 12:22–31 and Matthew 6:25–33.

Many details of this treatment may prove contentious. This reader, for example, would not argue that Chr. was, like Josephus, a re-reading of 1 Kgs 3, but rather that both biblical stories developed a shared earlier narrative in the light of their different aims, much as Carr claims Luke and Matthew reworked Q. Yet, though this different starting point would lead him to many readjustments of the argument, he fully agrees with Carr's view that the early Jewish interpretations reviewed here 'exemplify an interpretative flexibility which corresponds in exciting ways with the contemporary methodological pluralism in Biblical scholarship'.

A. G. AULD

DANIELS, D. R: *Hosea and Salvation History. The Early Traditions of Israel in the Prophecy of Hosea* (Beihefte zur Zeitschrift für die alttestamentliche Wissenschaft 191). 1990. Pp. vii, 148. (De Gruyter, Berlin. Price: DM 78.00. ISBN 3 11 012143 3; ISSN 0934 2575)

This closely argued work is a revision of the author's doctoral dissertation accepted by the University of Hamburg in 1987. The main part of the book consists of an exegetical study of those passages in Hosea which make explicit reference to Israel's historical traditions. Translation and textual notes are followed by sections sub-titled Form, Comment, and Results. Fundamental to the author's argument is his particular view of the growth and development of the book of Hosea. Chapter 3 as a whole originated with Hosea himself; chapters 1–2 are the work of the prophet's disciples, a collection existing prior to the complexes of 4–11 and 12–14 whose compiler is, he believes, Hosea himself. The author argues that for Hosea Israel's history as a whole can be described as 'salvation history', for this depends not on Israel's conduct, but on the continuity of Yahweh's will for his people. Even the coming disaster is to be seen as a work of salvation in that it negates the effects of Israel's conduct which militated against God's saving purposes. For Hosea the historical traditions demonstrate not Israel's special status but the extant and nature of her sin. Although his eschatology is not to be seen as 'a typological interpretation of Israel's salvation traditions', yet his expectations for the future are clearly formulated in the light of his understanding of Israel's history. One conclusion which emerges is that theologically motivated presentations of the formative period of Israel's history existed at a date significantly earlier than the late seventh century BC.

G. I. EMMERSON

DELL, K. J.: *The Book of Job as Sceptical Literature* (Beihefte zur Zeitschrift für die alttestamentliche Wissenschaft 197). 1991. Pp. x, 259. (De Gruyter, Berlin. Price: DM 104.00. ISBN 3 11 012554 4; ISSN 0934 2575)

This revised Oxford thesis argues the importance of characterizing *Job* as sceptical literature. Not only the challenging speeches, but also aspects of form and structure express sceptical intent. Examination of small units reveals a deliberate 'misusing' of form for achieving parody, while the juxtaposition of contradictory sections in the overall structure is all part of the ironical thrust. However, it is allowed that the effects of paradox intended by the great poet were weakened or confused by additions made by later editors,

LITERARY CRITICISM AND INTRODUCTION 67

especially the Elihu speeches and Ch. 28. Questions are raised about the classification of *Job* as a wisdom book, and it is suggested that its origin may be sought in an intellectual tradition akin to the Greek sceptics.

This is a readable and informative study which shows sober judgment. A survey of how *Job* was received in Jewish and Christian circles down to the Middle Ages is a valuable feature.

J. H. EATON

DENNIS, T.: *Lo and Behold! The Power of Old Testament Storytelling*. 1991. Pp. 164. (SPCK, London. Price: £8.99. ISBN 0 281 04491 0)

This book by the Vice-Principal and Tutor in Biblical Studies at Salisbury & Wells Theological College is aimed at a readership outside the academic world, but also hopes to bridge the gap between academic and devotional studies by seeking to enrich faith (so the author's preface). In a series of focused studies of different stories in the Hebrew Bible Trevor Dennis attempts the impossible and probably succeeds as much as any reader of the Bible might be deemed to have succeeded in such an ambitious aim. The biblical stories analysed are: Genesis 1–3, Genesis 22–23, Genesis 32–33, Exodus 16/Numbers 11, Joshua 6/1 Samuel 4, 1 Kings 19:1–18/2 Kings 5, and the book of Jonah. Each analysis consists of a careful reading of the text (in some cases the analysis is essentially an intertextual one), with simple theological observations and a certain tendency to make the stories yield pointers to Christian truth. Dennis's readings of these well-known stories (the two creation stories of Genesis, the attempted murder of Isaac and Abraham's purchase of an overpriced burial plot for Sarah, Jacob's wrestling with the angel and his reconciliation with Esau, the stories about manna and quails in the desert, the destruction of Jericho and the capture of the ark, Elijah on Horeb and Elisha and Naaman, and the story of Jonah) are intelligent, sensible readings of the text, though I suspect the text is less amenable to his theological comments. I doubt if any reader of the book of Jonah will find with Dennis that 'It will leave us at the foot of the Cross' (p. 133; cf. p. 155). Such judgements apart, this is an excellent wee volume which may be recommended thoroughly to any literate person wishing to gain an entry into the wonderland of biblical stories.

R. P. CARROLL

DOORLY, W. J.: *Prophet of Love. Understanding the Book of Hosea*. 1991. Pp. 138. (Paulist, New York. Price: $8.95. ISBN 0 8091 3241 9)

The author sees the book of Hosea as 'a mural to which several inspired artists contributed'. These artists are four in number; the eighth century prophet, a collector of his oracles after the fall of the northern kingdom, a redactor from the time of Josiah, and finally an exilic redactor. The approach is broadly that of Gale Yee in *Composition and Tradition in the Book of Hosea, A Redactional Critical Investigation* (reviewed in *B.L.* 1988, p. 98f.). Hosea's concern with unfaithfulness to Yahweh demonstrated in foreign political alliances has been reinterpreted by the Josianic redactor in terms of cultic evils. Ideas of repentance and restoration, indeed any elements of compassion and future hope, belong to the last redactor who alone merits the designation 'prophet of love'. The book is interestingly written and is stimulating as a hypothesis. The final bibliography wisely indicates other possible approaches to Hosea. References to the Hebrew plural of *beth 'ab* are incorrectly recorded (p. 16), and on p. 63 in the review copy the last two letters of the lines are missing.

G. I. EMMERSON

68 LITERARY CRITICISM AND INTRODUCTION

DUKE, R. K.: *The Persuasive Appeal of the Chronicler. A Rhetorical Analysis* (Journal for the Study of the Old Testament Supplement Series 88; Bible and Literature Series 25). 1990. Pp. 192. (Almond Press, Sheffield. Price: £25.00 ($43.75); sub. price: £18.75 ($32.75). ISBN 1 85075 228 1; ISSN 0260 4493; ISSN 0309 0787)

The application of literary criticism to biblical texts continues apace. Here Aristotle's categories of rhetoric are called upon to illustrate the techniques used in 1 and 2 Chronicles to engage the sympathies of the reader. After an introductory chapter offering a sketch of Chronicles research in terms of its literary rather than its historical claims, and outlining the relevance of Aristotelian rhetorical analysis to the study of the biblical text, we are introduced to the 'enthymeme', an inferential argument setting out a conviction and why that conviction should be accepted. Duke then devotes chapters to *logos*, *ethos*, and *pathos*, showing how rational, ethical, and emotional modes of persuasion form part of the Chronicler's technique. A series of appendices classify the different types of rhetorical devices used. The danger of studies of this kind is their tendency to find new ways of telling us what we already know, but Duke certainly enables us to see some aspects of the Chronicler's work from a different angle. R. J. COGGINS

EDELMAN, D. V.: *King Saul in the Historiography of Judah* (Journal for the Study of the Old Testament Supplement Series 121). 1991. Pp. 347. (Sheffield Academic Press. Price: £40.00 ($70.00); sub. price: £30.00 ($52.50). ISBN 1 85075 321 0)

This clearly presented reading of the story of Saul in 1 Sam. 8–2 Sam. 1 represents the source-evaluative opening chapter of a historian's study of King Saul grown to such proportions and perceived as sufficiently autonomous to merit separate publication. An Introduction and Overview of structuring devices in the narrative precede twenty-five chapters handling each biblical chapter in turn and a short statement of Conclusions. Edelman the historian, well aware that audience and narrator are far removed from Saul, sets herself the proper task of seeking to intuit how the audience of the original narrator would have read the artistically composed material she is studying. Yet she may have damaged her project by enquiring too little historically before accepting the whole Hebrew text of these chapters, give or take a few emendations, as an integral part of a seventh century Judahite Deuteronomistic History. Though for the sake of argument we might grant that assumption in face of a wide North American consensus, it would be dangerous to suppose Judges 19–21 echoed in a pre-exilic text of Samuel or to accept the originality of the longer (Hebrew) text of 1 Sam. 17–18. How to read the traditional Hebrew text of Samuel is a proper prior study for historians of Saul. But its literary context and absolute date are more contentious than Edelman is ready to admit. A. G. AULD

ELLIS, E. E.: *The Old Testament in Early Christianity. Canon and Interpretation in the Light of Modern Research* (Wissenschaftliche Untersuchungen zum Neuen Testament 54). 1991. Pp. xiii, 188. (Mohr, Tubingen. Price: DM 78.00. ISBN 3 16 145660 2)

A learned monograph which surveys scholarly opinion on the New Testament's 'canon' of the Old Testament and the ways in which the early church interpreted that canon. Conclusions are quite close to those of R. Beckwith, *The Old Testament Canon of the New Testament Church*, but more weight is allowed to evidence that documents outside our present Bible were recognized as possessing at least some measure of authority. There is a

LITERARY CRITICISM AND INTRODUCTION 69

good survey of exegetical methods, and a useful section on 'Perspectives and Presuppositions', which sketches the point of view from which New Testament authors read the older Scriptures. The presuppositions include ideas about eschatology, typology, corporate personality, and the 'hiddenness' of the word of God in Scripture. This is a useful book, not highly original but comprehensive in its coverage of important material.

J. BARTON

ELLUL, J.: *Reason for Being. A Meditation on Ecclesiastes.* Translated by J. M. Hanks. 1990. Pp. viii, 306. (Eerdmans, Grand Rapids MI. Price: $18.95. ISBN 0 8028 0405 5)

'Another book on Ecclesiastes?' is how the author begins, and one suspects that he feels a little guilty about adding to the already extensive list of publications in recent times. But this is a book which Ellul had to write. Qoheleth is a favourite book for him, and he has meditated on it for more than fifty years! As the title suggests, it is not a commentary. Indeed, the author confesses that, although he had read many works on Ecclesiastes, he chose to read nothing at the outset of his work. After he had finished writing he began to read everything he could find on Ecclesiastes. This explains the various footnotes which were inserted later in order to comment on the scholarly literature then encountered.

Ellul discusses what he sees to be the three themes of the book, *viz.* vanity, wisdom and God, and in doing so examines specific passages — often looking closely at the meaning of the original Hebrew — considering theological, philosophical, and literary aspects of the text and arguing for the book's place in scripture. He acknowledges contradictions in the book but will not allow that these may be the result of oversight or editorial activity. 'They guide us when we must recognise the true character of human existence and not just its reality: human existence is essentially self-contradictory.' This is, in places, a refreshing piece of work which will appeal more to the theologian than the exegete but it will serve to encourage renewed effort to understand a very difficult book.

R. B. SALTERS

EVANS, C. A.: *To See and Not Perceive. Isaiah 6.9–10 in Early Jewish and Christian Interpretation* (Journal for the Study of Old Testament Supplement Series 64). 1989. Pp. 261. (Sheffield Academic Press. Price: £30.00 ($52.50); sub. price: £22.50 ($40.00). ISBN 1 85075 172 2)

Evans introduces this work as a complete revision of his dissertation. Like Carr's (above, p. 65) this too is a Claremont essay in comparative midrash. The substantial opening chapter, entitled 'Isaiah 6.9–10 in the Context of Isaiah', offers a grammatical analysis of these two fascinating verses, then discusses them within the context of the Prophet Isaiah (which means for Evans, depending here heavily on Hasel and Jensen, the context of the first thirty-nine chapters of the Book of Isaiah) and of the Book of Isaiah (i.e. Isaiah 40–66), and mentions at the end the obduracy texts elsewhere in the Hebrew Bible. Subsequent chapters review the interpretation and use of these verses in Qumran, Septuagint, Targum, and Peshitta; in Paul, Mark, Matthew, Luke-Acts, and John; and in the Rabbis and the Fathers. The range of materials assembled will make this volume a very helpful teaching resource, although some teachers will find aggravating the loose statement of a number of linguistic and translational issues.

A. G. AULD

70   LITERARY CRITICISM AND INTRODUCTION

FARMER, K. A.: *Who Knows What is Good? A Commentary on the Books of Proverbs and Ecclesiastes* (International Theological Commentary). 1991. Pp. xii, 220. (Eerdmans, Grand Rapids MI; Handsel, Edinburgh. Price: $15.95. ISBN 0 8028 0161 7; 1 871828 08 2)

The *International Theological Commentary* series aim is: the Old Testament alive in the Church; and it is addressed to ministers and Christian educators. It does not claim to deal with critical problems but 'offers a theological interpretation of the Hebrew text'. The author begins with an introduction which describes the shape of the book of Proverbs: the longer poetic units, instructions, the personifications, the sayings of the wise, the words of Agur, and the poetic conclusion. There follows a brief commentary which is clearly written and helpfully set out. This is followed by a stimulating appendix 'Theology and Piety in Proverbs' in which the author argues that behind the apparent secularity of Proverbs lies a theology which is vibrant. The commentary on Ecclesiastes is similarly brief and is preceded by observations which encourage the reader to be cautious in interpreting the book. There follows a short chapter on the role of Ecclesiastes in the Canon, and an appendix which discusses the place of Ecclesiastes in the development of biblical ideas about life after death. There is a good bibliography and an index of scriptural references.   R. B. SALTERS

FOKKELMAN, J. P.: *Narrative Art and Poetry in the Books of Samuel. A full interpretation based on stylistic and structural analyses.* III *Throne and City (II Sam. 2–8 & 21–24)* (Studia Semitica Neerlandica). 1990. Pp. vi, 441. (Van Gorcum, Assen/Maastricht. Price: fl. 85.00. ISBN 90 232 2546 5)

Fokkelman's ambitious and impressive project, to offer a 'full interpretation' of the books of Samuel via a close reading of twelve levels of the text, from the sounds of the individual phrase to the compositional structure of the largest units, is by now well known. This volume fills the gap between volume 2, *The Crossing Fates*, on 1 Sam. 13–31 and 2 Sam. 1 (see *B.L.* 1987, pp. 62f), and volume 1, *King David*, on 2 Sam. 9–20 and 1 Kings 1–2 (see *B.L.* 1982, p. 60). As we have come to expect, the commentary is uncompromising and rebarbative to the casual reader. At every turn, at the very moment the reader is being seduced by the brilliance of the *apercus* the question keeps forming itself in the mind: To what end is this inordinate observation of detail, this endless accumulation of knowledge, this 'fulness'? Who can use this book, and to what end? And as we read on, increasingly the 'scientific' polish to the work wears thin, and we find ourselves constantly confronting Fokkelman's own individual, idiosyncratic judgements. Here, for example, is a case of 'breakneck speed' (p. 26), and here is a case of verbal economy (p. 27); here is Fokkelman's 'word of non-cynical appreciation' of David as God's elect (p. 36), and here is Fokkelman's opinion that 'terrible perfection' like the slaughter by the pool at Gibeon could not be 'so precise and so synchronous in reality' (p. 45). Despite the technicality of the work, let the reader understand: this is not science, it is art.   D. J. A. CLINES

FOX, M. V.: *The Redaction of the Books of Esther. On Reading Composite Texts* (Society of Biblical Literature Monograph Series 40). 1991. Pp. x, 195. (Scholars Press, Atlanta GA. Price: $29.95; paperback price: $18.95. ISBN 1 55540 444 8 (cloth); 1 55540 4448 (paper))

A review of this length cannot do justice even to the theme of this wide-ranging book, let alone to its detailed and meticulous argumentation. Its focus is upon two extant texts of Esther (the 'books' of the title), the

LITERARY CRITICISM AND INTRODUCTION 71

Masoretic text and the Greek alpha-text (AT), which combined a pre-Septuagintal translation with some of the Septuagint's own special material. Fox's primary concern is not the reconstruction of the sources but a analytic description of the redactional processes that can be uncovered now that we know the relationship between these texts. In two further chapters, Fox compares the shape and thrust of the various redactions with one another, and offers some interesting reflections on the lessons that can be gleaned for hypothetical source and redaction study from tracing the process of redaction in texts still extant. In a final excellent chapter, which inevitably leaves certain issues out of account, he considers the nature of redaction generally as an artistic process and as an object of reading.   D. J. A. CLINES

GABEL, J. B. and WHEELER, C. B.: *The Bible as literature. An introduction*. 2nd edition. 1990. Pp. viii, 286. (Oxford University Press, New York and Oxford. Price: £11.95. ISBN 0 19 505933 6)

The first edition of this excellent Introduction was reviewed in *B.L.* 1988, p. 76. Apart from some minor corrections, some bibliographical additions, and an interesting appendix on writing in biblical times, the second edition is unchanged. This means, unfortunately, that there is still no section on the Psalms.   J. C. L. GIBSON

GARSIEL, M.: *Biblical Names. A Literary Study of Midrashic Derivations and Puns*. 1991. Pp. 296. (Bar-Ilan University Press. Price: $30.00. ISBN 965 226 115 7)

Readers of Phyllis Hackett's translation will certainly endorse the appreciative review in *Book List* 1989, p. 75 of the prior Hebrew edition of Garsiel's enjoyable and erudite study. It is often stated and well known that Biblical names are rich in significance — but just how rich has now been ably documented.   A. G. AULD

GARSIEL, M.: *The First Book of Samuel: A Literary Study of Comparative Structures, Analogies, and Parallels*. 1990. Pp. 169. (Revivim, Jerusalem; distributed by Rubin Mass Ltd, PO Box 990, Jerusalem 91009. Price: $21.75)

This is an unaltered reprint of the 1985 English translation of Garsiel's work on First Samuel which was welcomed in *B.L.* 1986, p. 70. The outside cover still suggests publication by Revivim as before; however, on the page facing the beginning of the Preface, the work is said to be published by Rubin Mass, PO Box 990, Jerusalem, and they claim the 1990 copyright. Distribution in North America is by Eisenbrauns.   A. G. AULD

GITAY. Y.: *Isaiah and his Audience. The Structure and Meaning of Isaiah 1–12* (Studia Semitica Neerlandica, 30). 1991. Pp. ix, 283. (Van Gorcum, Assen/Maastricht. Price: fl. 49.50. ISBN 90 232 2493 0)

Professor Gitay's study presents a detailed exegesis of Isaiah 1–12 based primarily on principles of a rhetorical analysis. The presence of thirteen carefully structured units, when viewed from the perspective of their rhetorical impact, is taken to point to their Isaianic origin as speeches, with a heavy political import. The background is provided by the events of the Syro–Ephraimite war, and they are taken to have been recorded virtually as delivered. The advent of Assyria as an agent of oppression against Judah and Israel is interpreted as divine punishment, which must then in turn be

72 LITERARY CRITICISM AND INTRODUCTION

succeeded by a time of punishment for the oppressor. In contrast to the unfaithful Ahaz, who sought to establish an alliance with Assyria in order to protect his throne from the attempt by the Syro–Ephraimite alliance to dethrone him, Isaiah proclaimed, in portrait form, a promise of the coming of the ideal Davidic king.

The central thrust of Gitay's interpretation is clear and follows what is a reasonably well-established approach to the material. What is new is the emphasis upon rhetorical structures, with the strong contention that evidence for these undermines any need to deny Isaianic authorship to the material, or to look for secondary additions and reinterpretations. Overall rhetorical analysis is presented as rendering literary and redaction criticism obsolete.

R. E. CLEMENTS

GRESSMANN, H.: *Narrative and Novella in Samuel. Studies by Hugo Gressmann and Other Scholars 1906–1923* (JSOT Supplement Series 116; Historic Texts and Interpreters in Biblical Scholarship 9). 1991. Pp. 183. (Almond Press, Sheffield. Price: £19.50 ($32.50). ISBN 1 85075 281 8; ISSN 0263 1199; 0309 0787)

This volume brings together in translation, partly with a view to illustrating some continuities which exist between older and more recent readings of the books of Samuel as literature, four pieces of work by scholars of the early part of this century — Hugo Gressmann's *Die älteste Geschichtsschreibung und Prophetie Israels* (1921; selected editions only); Wilhelm Caspari's 'Literarische Art und historischer Wert von 2 Sam. 15–20' (1909); Bernhard Luther's 'Die Novelle von Juda und Tamar und andere israelitische Novellen' (1906); and Alfons Schulz's *Erzählungskunst in den Samuelbüchern* (1923). All four scholars have in common that they share a fine sense of the passages with which they deal as narrative art. Luther's seminal piece centres upon an appreciation of Genesis 38 as *Novelle* (a highly crafted, literary short story), though much of the article is devoted to material in the David literature of similar type. Caspari, developing Luther's ideas, gives more extended consideration to one such section within Samuel. The pieces extracted from Gressmann's book take a broader view of all the material in 2 Samuel 10–20 and 1 Kings 1–2; while Schulz ranges still more widely across both books of Samuel. Throughout the volume there is much of interest to the modern exegete. The continuities between this material and some modern reading of Samuel are clear, though it is also clear that the scholars concerned are in the main both more interested in the history behind the text, and more convinced of the value of reading Samuel in self-contained sections, than many of similar persuasion today. It is of particular interest, as the editor himself points out in the Preface, to read the essays in the light of Rost's *Die Überlieferung von der Thronnachfolge Davids*, which was to follow in 1926.

I. W. PROVAN

GUINAN, M. D.: *The Pentateuch* (Message of Biblical Spirituality 1). 1990. Pp. 138. (Liturgical Press, Collegeville, Minnesota. Price: $8.95. ISBN 0 8146 5567 X)

A series of fifteen brief outline commentaries, intended to cover the whole Bible, is here inaugurated. The series title denotes that the intended readership will be found among Christians, and particularly Roman Catholics; it does not indicate a revival of the older tradition of 'spiritual commentary'. Here one's attention is caught from time to time by perceptive comments, but for the most part this is standard introductory material, aimed at showing believers that biblical scholarship need not corrode their faith.

R. J. COGGINS

LITERARY CRITICISM AND INTRODUCTION 73

HAILE, G. and AMARE, M.: *Beauty of the Creation* (Journal of Semitic Studies Monograph 16). 1991. Pp. x, 87. (Journal of Semitic Studies, Manchester. Price: £25.00. ISBN 0 951612433)

Dr Getatchew Haile here presents the text and an annotated translation of the Amharic and the Geez versions of the Ethopian work known as *sənä fəträt* ('Beauty of the Creation'), which belongs within the hexaemeric literature. For readers of the *Book List* the volume is likely to be of most interest in the context of the history of the exegesis of Gen. 1–3, and it complements Roger Cowley's major study, *Ethiopian Biblical Interpretation* (1988). But the Amharic text shows a number of archaic features, on which Dr Getatchew Haile comments in his notes, and the text is also of interest as a specimen of Old Amharic.

M. A. KNIBB

HASEL, G. F.: *Understanding the Book of Amos. Basic Issues in Current Interpretations.* 1991. Pp. 171. (Baker Book House, Grand Rapids MI. Price: $10.95. ISBN 0 8010 4353 0)

It may ill behove this reviewer to complain about yet another introduction to the issues faced by critical readers of Amos. For he himself has contributed such a volume; and recent numbers of the *Book List* have attested the ongoing publication of studies large and small of this prophetic book, some of which ably add to the list of 'issues'. Hasel's conservative leanings are not concealed, though irenically expressed. He writes clearly, introduces the familiar questions, and makes available quite a large and up-to-date 'select' bibliography of over 800 items — yet the jacket oversells the volume in its claim that it 'survey[s] some 800 separate contributions', for the discussion fails to suggest awareness of many of these items. Indeed, although he records many of the critical issues, Hasel barely contributes to the *understanding* of them. His readers are left assured, for example, that the narrative in Amos 7:10–17 belongs where it is and should not be relocated; but they are not encouraged to savour discussion of whether its intimate relatedness to its context is also a guarantee of its 'authenticity'.

A. G. AULD

HERRMANN, S.: *Jeremia. Der Prophet und das Buch* (Erträge der Forschung, Band 271). 1990. Pp. xiii, 233. (Wissenschaftliche Buchgesellschaft, Darmstadt. Price: DM 45.00. ISBN 3 534 09047 0; ISSN 0174 0695)

Currently writing the Biblischer Kommentar volume(s) on Jeremiah, Siegfried Herrmann here gives us a masterly account of the current state of the play in Jeremiah studies. In five chapters Herrmann discusses the historical background and effectiveness of the book of Jeremiah, the contents and composition of the book (usefully schematized on pp. 41–52), critical analyses of Jeremiah, the textual tradition of the book (briefly), and the theological concepts in Jeremiah. The longest and (therefore) central section of his discussion is the one dealing with the critical analyses of the book (pp. 53–181). Starting with Duhm he examines all the major analyses of Jeremiah (Mowinckel, Rudolph, Hyatt, Cazelles, Rowley, Herrmann, Thiel, Robinson, Bright, Holladay, Weippert, Nicholson, Carroll, Lundbom, Holladay), including various specific approaches to and interpretations of the book, and briefly surveys the commentaries of Holladay, Carroll, McKane, and Herrmann (pp. 167–78). The brief concluding chapter on the theological concepts in the book of Jeremiah looks at the work of Raitt, Seitz, and Unterman before discussing five aspects of Jeremiah: the Hosea/Deuteronomic Gedankenkeis (God, people, land; false gods; the inner state of the nation); the sins of the nation and of individuals and the poems of lament; the overcoming of sin; repentance, forgiveness, the new covenant

74   LITERARY CRITICISM AND INTRODUCTION

and the gracious God; prophetic self-consciousness and false prophecy; the prophet of the nations and Israel's universal mission. Readers familiar with Herrmann's work over the past decades will find the treatment of the book of Jeremiah here follows Herrmann's well-known approaches to Jeremiah with no surprises in store. Nearly twenty pages of bibliography complete a very useful survey volume.

R. P. CARROLL

HILL, A. E. and WALTON, J. H.: *A Survey of the Old Testament.* 1991. Pp. xviii, 461. (Zondervan. Grand Rapids MI. Price: $22.95. ISBN 0 310 51600 5)

An 'innovative textbook' this, according to the publishers. This refers to the fact that, unlike many other such works, it does not spend much time on summarizing the contents of the Biblical books, but concentrates on their composition, their background, their purpose and message, and their major themes. It also offers questions for further study and discussion. In other respects, the book is all too similar to many another such conservative evangelical work. Although it does not pretend that critical views do not exist (indeed its lists some in its bibliographies) it defends such causes as the Mosaic authorship of Genesis, the literary unity of Isaiah, the historicity of Jonah, and the sixth century composition of Daniel.

B. P. ROBINSON

HONIGWACHS, Y.: *The Unity of Torah. A Commentary on the Organization and Purpose of the Five Books.* Volume 1. 1991. Pp. 350. (Feldheim, Jerusalem and New York. ISBN 0 87306 802 5)

Though convinced that the 'Torah . . . can be understood only within the context of its own world-view' (p. 10), Rabbi Honigwachs is sufficiently analytical, perceptive, and self-critical to challenge the impartial reader with at least some aspects of his theory. Since the Torah is not a haphazard collection of history and the law but an 'intricately planned and neatly executed construction' (p. 85), he explains it by reference to five principles found in the Ten Commandments that relate to divine and human existence, exclusive rights in divinity and marriage, the abuse of God's name and human property, cooperation with God and assistance to people, and self-effacement. He identifies sets of these principles in the Pentateuch as a whole, in each of its five books, in smaller groups of texts sub-divided by Masorah, introductory word and subject, and in legal terminology. The broadness of the definitions and the acknowledged difficulty in consistently applying the principles do, however, call into question the scientific validity of the thesis.

S. C. REIF

JAGERSMA, H.: *Numeri.* Deel III (De Prediking van het Oude Testament). 1990. Pp. 204. (Callenbach, Nijkerk. Price: fl. 71.50. sub. price: fl. 64.50. ISBN 90 266 0231 6)

Parts I and II were reviewed in the *Book List* for 1984 (p. 54) and 1989 (p. 55). Part III completes the commentary, dealing with chs. 25–36. The material is divided into three sections, 25–27 which may contain older material but which is of exilic date, 28–31 whose first two chapters date from shortly after the exile with the remainder being later, and 32–36. The main

LITERARY CRITICISM AND INTRODUCTION 75

theme of these chapters is the land, and the need for responsible living in the land in the presence of God. An index of names, subjects, and Hebrew words and terms for all three parts concludes the commentary.

J. W. ROGERSON

KARRER, M.: *Der Gesalbte. Die Grundlagen des Christustitels* (FRLANT 151). 1991. Pp. 482. (Vandenhoeck & Ruprecht, Göttingen. Price: DM 138.00. ISBN 3 525 53833 2)

The widely accepted explanation for the origin and development of the term 'Christ' is that in the first century AD the Jewish future hope centred on the figure of an eschatological Anointed One, that the first Christians saw this figure realized in Jesus and hence applied the term 'anointed' to him, but that when Christianity moved into the Graeco–Roman world, which knew nothing corresponding to the Jewish belief, the title lost its original significance and became little more than a proper name. Karrer finds this view inadequate and attempts to provide an alternative.

He begins with a survey of actual or conceptual instances of anointing in Judaism and concludes that royal anointing never had the significance in Israel that many have attributed to it and in any case ended at least no later than Zerubbabel, to be supplanted by the anointing of the high-priest, which in turn ceased after Onias III. Memories of these anointings as ideals were all that remained in New Testament times and the latter was more prominent than the former. By contrast, the living experience of anointing was in the cult, through the anointing of the apparatus of worship, in particular the Holy of Holies: the Holy of Holies became the criterion for the understanding of anointing, which marked the locus of God's presence and activity. The various eschatological figures of Judaism, and there were a number of them, were viewed as 'anointed' because they were close to God and he worked through them. The appellation 'anointed' for Jesus did not derive directly from any one of these, though they had a part to play: rather, his follows saw him as a unique being who, so to speak, replaced the Holy of Holies as the centre of the divine presence and work. Because the pagan world was familiar with cultic anointings which, *mutatis mutandis*, had a similar significance to those in Judaism, the concept of Jesus as 'the anointed' was able to be at home there also.

A brief summary cannot accommodate all the nuances and qualifications of Karrer's discussion: his work is very detailed, to the extent that it is not always easy to follow the thread of the argument. He is right to emphasize the wide variety of 'messianic' expectations which formed the background of Jesus' ministry and his contention that the title 'Christ' could have had real theological significance in the Graeco–Roman sphere deserves serious consideration. But doubt remains about his central thesis of the source of the anointing concept in later Judaism: he does not produce convincing evidence for his statement that 'in all probability, the Holy of Holies is to be considered as "the Anointed"' and one wonders if there really is any.

J. R. PORTER

KINZIG, W.: *Erbin Kirche. Die Auslegung von Psalm 5, 1 in den Psalmenhomilien des Asterius und in der Alten Kirche.* 1990. Abhandlungen der Heidelberger Akademie der Wissenschaften. (Carl Winter (Universitätsverlag), Heidelberg. Price: DM 65.00; DM 35.00 (pbk), ISBN 3 533 04321 5; 3 533 04320 7)

This monograph is a by-product of the writer's studies on the Asterius to whose authorship a number of 'pseudo-Chrysostomic' homilies on the Psalms were restored by M. Richard, who, however (by deductions from citations in catenae), supposed that he was an Asterius known as 'the Sophist' and as an Arian. Dr Kinzig has argued elsewhere that this one is not yet identifiable; but

76 LITERARY CRITICISM AND INTRODUCTION

the language shows links with Hesychius and especially Chrysostom, which suggest a date around 400. Leontius of Constantinople (mid-sixth century) must have known these homilies. Though surely Syrian or Palestinian, the exegetical method is in many respects individual. The present study focuses on an interpretation of the heading of Ps 5 in the LXX, *eis to telos, huper tēs klēronomousēs, psalmos tō Daueid*, which Asterius uses several times in the extant homilies. His understanding of it might be rendered: 'At the end [*of the life of Christ*], on behalf of the inheriting heiress-dowered bride [*no longer Israel but the Church*], a song by David' [*to Christ as testator, endower and spouse*]. The exposition is so full of the technical language of inheritance law as to be almost a main source for this in its period; this may throw light on Asterius's professional training. The anti-Jewish interpretation of *klēronomousēs* (emphatically continuous present) has links with earlier works of both east and west, but these are probably due to common roots in Christian paschal liturgy. However, the reading of *nᵉḥilot* as *naḥalot* ('inheritances') which must underlie the LXX is also attested in the *Midrash on Psalms* with reference to the Land and the Temple, and Asterius might perhaps have known of this interpretation.

This is a fascinating example of the structures that could be built on the presuppositions that the LXX and its Psalm titles were inspired and, if obscure, must mysteriously refer to points of early Christian belief. The monograph is lucidly argued and fully documented.　　　R. P. R. MURRAY

KRATZ, R. G.: *Kyros im Deuterojesaja-Buch. Redaktionsgeschichtliche Untersuchungen zu Entstehung und Theologie von Jes 40–55* (Forschungen zum Alten Testament 1). 1991. Pp. x, 254. (Mohr, Tübingen. Price: DM 148.00. ISBN 3 16 145757 9; ISSN 0940 4155)

The sub-title gives a clearer indication of the aim and contents of this study, which attempts to account for the tension between the overall unity of Isaiah 40–55 and its lack of any self-evident structure. The writer seeks a solution in the detection of several layers of material in these chapters. The Cyrus oracles and their context are analysed in detail, and provide a clue to the demarcation of the stages in the evolution of Second Isaiah. The *Grundschrift* consists of disputation speeches and oracles of salvation addressed to Jacob-Israel, and of oracles of judgement against the nations and their gods. The hope of Israel's liberation is founded on the world-rule of the Creator. This *Grundschrift* has been expanded by the addition of further supplementary layers of material, which offer either interpretations or developments of it. One of these displays a consistent heightening of the role of Cyrus as conqueror in the plan of world history. The Servant Songs, which are reflected in this layer, are thought to have been added to the *Grundschrift* at the same time. Further layers contain the passages about the manufacture of idols and additional material about the Servant. The argument is close, and must await detailed evaluation by other scholars, but no commentator on Second Isaiah can afford to neglect this book.　　　A. GELSTON

LOADER, J. A.: *A Tale of Two Cities. Sodom and Gomorrah in the Old Testament, early Jewish and early Christian Traditions* (Contributions to Biblical Exegesis and Theology 1). 1991. Pp. 150. (Kok, Kampen. Price: fl. 42.50. ISBN 90 242 5333 0)

This short book covers an extensive terrain, from the earliest origins of the biblical Sodom story to the classical patristic and rabbinic sources. The main focus is on the narrative of Genesis 18–19: the author argues that this text constitutes a unified narrative by a single author of the ?seventh century BCE, exploiting (but not merely compiling) earlier materials. Some of

LITERARY CRITICISM AND INTRODUCTION 77

these (or similar) materials are used in other, earlier parts of the Hebrew Bible. Different emphases are found in different places. The two chapters on post-biblical sources, both 'Jewish' and Christian, argue that these writings tend to exploit certain basic themes while displaying a great variety of interpretations. The disappointingly vague conclusions are perhaps the inevitable consequence of a rather unsympathetic approach. The eight-page bibliography is weighted towards older work in English and German, and is particularly short on references in the patristic and rabbinic areas.

N. R. M. DE LANGE

LOHFINK, N.: *Studien zum Deuteronomium und zur deuteronomistischen Literatur* II (Stuttgarter Biblische Aufsatzbände: Altes Testament 12). 1991. Pp. 303. (Katholisches Bibelwerk, Stuttgart. Price: DM 49.00. ISBN 3 460 06121 9)

The second volume of Lohfink's collected studies in this series includes thirteen publications from 1976 to 1990. A greater proportion of the articles here than in the first volume is devoted to deuteronomistic texts outside Deuteronomy, particularly from Kings (e.g. 'Zur neueren Diskussion über 2 Kön 22–23'; 'Die Kultreform Joschijas von Juda') and the book of Jeremiah ('Der junge Jeremia als Propagandist und Poet'; 'Die Gotteswortverschachtelung in Jer 30–31'), and the relationship of deuteronomic to earlier texts, rather than to oral tradition ('Hos xi 5 als Bezugspunkt von Dtn xvii 16'; 'Zur deuteronomischen Zentralisationsformel'), is examined. Yet the focus here is still Deuteronomy. While all the articles have been previously published and are still generally accessible (in two cases, however, it is the German original MS version of articles subsequently published in English which is here presented), and while none of the articles has been updated, the value of having them together is very considerable. There is an impressive originality, comprehensiveness, and consistency in Lohfink's direct engagement with the text of Deuteronomy, which gives these studies an abiding reference value. Themes reappear in different contexts, but in such a way that their impact is enriched rather than dulled.

The first article, 'Das Deuteronomium' (the German version of Lohfink's contribution, 'Deuteronomy', to the *IDB* Supplement), appropriately introduces the volume, and is continued by several articles which effectively explore in more detail many of its summary statements and ideas. All of these are impressive and important, but perhaps one of the most significant is 'Gott im Buch Deuteronomium', for this not only works within the frame of a historical and literary understanding of the structure, origin, and development of Deuteronomy, but in doing so clearly demonstrates how it is that it is this book which is really the centre of the Old Testament. It is here that, in response to the faith and culture crisis of the late pre-exilic period that traditional Israelite belief was selectively systematized; the problem which that systematization created for Israelite faith in the exilic and post-exilic periods then led to subsequent editing of that book in sometimes close association with the thinking which found its deposit in Second Isaiah and the priestly writing.

The volume is supplied with various indexes, and also with a seven page introduction providing information on reactions to the original articles and an indication of the author's present views.

A. D. H. MAYES

LONGACRE, R. E.: *Joseph: a Story of Divine Providence. A Text Theoretical and Textlinguistic Analysis of Genesis 37 and 39–48.* 1989. Pp. xiv, 322. (Eisenbrauns, Winona Lake IN. Price: $27.50. ISBN 0 931464 42 0)

The Joseph story is here subjected to detailed analysis so as to bring out its distinctive linguistic characteristics. In the main body of the book the

78 LITERARY CRITICISM AND INTRODUCTION

functioning of the different verbal forms is analysed, and the development of the story is illustrated by discourse analysis: the way in which particular characters play their roles reflected in the use of particular speech-forms. One of the most interesting chapters is that on socio-linguistics, showing how linguistic usage reflects the social status of the speaker and addressee. The whole is rounded off by an elaborate display-table (pp. 101) setting out the constitutent structure of the whole story, prefaced by a warning that the table is incomprehensible to those who have not followed the preceding detailed analysis. A brief appendix refers to tagmemics, a term not used in the body of the book, but the source of much of its methodology. An interesting study, though one is too often aware of the hidden agenda of the determination to exclude source-division as having any role in analysing the Joseph story: the explanations of the Midianite/Ishmaelite alternation in ch. 37, and of Jacob/Israel as the name of the patriarch, are among the least convincing parts of the book.

R. J. COGGINS

McEVENUE, S.: *Interpreting the Pentateuch* (Old Testament Studies, 4). 1990. Pp. 194. (Liturgical Press, Collegeville, Minnesota. Price: $12.95. ISBN 0 8146 5654 4)

This book is only incidentally about the Pentateuch. Its main purpose is to defend historical-critical study and interpretation of the Old Testament over against literary and canonical approaches, and to suggest a method for making historical-critical reading available for theology. The core of the argument derives from reflection on the processes of writing and maintains that, in each writer, there is a foundational stance which can be felt by readers even though this foundational stance is almost never directly expressed in texts. 'It is felt through the gaps, through the edges of the text, through what is missing in the text, through the reader's sense that he or she would have approached this subject matter differently' (p. 59). Biblical writers expressed themselves in particular situations or contexts (e.g. war, liturgy) which have to be taken into account, but the foundational stance of each was centred upon expectations about revelation and salvation.

This thesis is illustrated by discussions of the Yahwist (a contemporary of Solomon), the Elohist, the Priestly writer, and the Deuteronomist, and the work concludes with a sketch of how Lonergan's theological method can integrate the findings of 'foundational-stance interpretation' into theology. The book does not make for easy reading and is occasionally marred by irritating errors such as Gerald (*sic*) Manley Hopkins, and George Elliot (*sic*). The page numbers given in the index are consistently inaccurate in references to the end-notes. The chapters on the foundational stance of writers are of considerable interest but the theory, if correct, is surely of limited value. Can it be used to read Psalms or prophetic texts? Further, it is a hostage to fortune at a time when the old certainties of pentateuchal criticism are more and more questioned. However, the author is to be commended for his attempt to argue that Old Testament texts address and challenge readers in their contemporary world, and that historical-critical methods cannot be ignored in the interpretative enterprise.

J. W. ROGERSON

McKENZIE, S. L.: *The Trouble with Kings. The Composition of the Book of Kings in the Deuteronomic History* (Supplements to Vetus Testamentum XLII). 1991. Pp. xii, 186. (Brill, Leiden. Price: fl. 98.00; $50.26. ISBN 90 04 09402 4; ISSN 0083 5889)

This book seeks to reaffirm in a modified form the view of the 'Cross School' in relation to the composition of the Deuteronomistic History,

LITERARY CRITICISM AND INTRODUCTION 79

namely that it was initially written during the reign of Josiah and later expanded. To that end, the books of Kings are subjected to a fresh literary- and text-critical examination. A significant proportion of the monograph (chapters 1–5) is, in fact, given over to the analysis of the various prophetic narratives of Kings. McKenzie finds no evidence here of any pre-Deuteronomistic prophetic 'work' of the kind proposed by Campbell. Many of the narratives are post-Deuteronomistic additions (e.g. 1 Kings 17–19). The remainder are either Deuteronomistic compositions, some of which have been glossed by later editors (e.g. 1 Kings 11:29–39), or isolated stories used by the author (e.g. 1 Kings 21). In 2 Kings 18–19 we find both types of material combined, the B1 narrative of Sennacherib's invasion being a reworked older story, and the B2 narrative being composed by the Deuteronomist himself. In the Josiah narrative of 2 Kings 22–23, the oracle of Huldah (22:15–20) is to be seen as a Deuteronomistic composition which has been glossed by an exilic hand. This brings McKenzie to the question of dating (chapter 6). Recent attempts to take Hezekiah as the 'hero' of Kings, and to date the first Deuteronomistic edition either in his reign or early in Josiah's (e.g. Provan), are first considered and rejected. The case for a later Josianic date is then rehearsed and reaffirmed in the face of objections from scholars dissatisfied with source-critical and redactional theory (e.g. Long, Van Seters). Chapter 7, however, rejects attempts by supporters of this kind of dating for the initial history to find any systematic redaction by one later editor within Kings or the Deuteronomistic History as a whole. The process by which the Josianic Deuteronomistic History grew to its present dimensions was a long and complex one. Noth was therefore correct in his original model of 'unified composition with many unconnected supplements', though mistaken in his exilic dating for the basic work.

This is an important monograph, with both strengths and weaknesses. Its main weakness lies in its reiteration (with no perceptibly new additions or emphases, in spite of recent criticism) of the arguments of the Cross School for a pre-exilic and Deuteronomistic Kings which from the first ended with the story of Josiah, a king 'like David' who reforms the cult. When it is recognized that 2 Kings 18:1–8, by its choice and use of language, so clearly identifies Hezekiah as the second, reforming David of Kings, and that the 'Deuteronomistic composition' of 2 Kings 23, by contrast, so signally fails to pick up the earlier thematic threads of the book in a similar way; when the case for a pre-exilic version of the Josiah account is seen to depend so greatly upon a hypothetical early oracle of Huldah which it has always proved impossible to reconstruct (pp. 111–12); and when the ground for nevertheless believing in this oracle is stated to be the all-pervading optimism of 2 Kings 22–23 (p. 115), which proves as elusive as the oracle itself when one actually tries to find it in the text; then it becomes no easier than it was before to believe in the existence of this kind of Josianic version of Kings. The great strength of the monograph, however, lies in its refusal in general to oversimplify the 'trouble' in Kings for the sake of any overarching theory about the composition of the books. There is a keen awareness throughout of the need to deal with each aspect of the question on its own terms, interacting both with the text- and literary-critical work of scholars like Trebolle on detailed section of Kings, as well as with the broader critique of the redactional model by scholars like Van Seters. A consequence of this wide interaction with the secondary literature, and of McKenzie's concomitant openness to differing perspectives on individual texts, is that readers who happen to disagree with his overall solution to the riddle of the books' composition will still find much of interest and value here, particularly if they are interested in the history of the various prophetic narratives now to be found in Kings.

I. W. PROVAN

80 LITERARY CRITICISM AND INTRODUCTION

MASON, R.: *Micah, Nahum, Obadiah* (Old Testament Guides). 1991. Pp. 116. (JSOT Press, Sheffield for the Society for Old Testament Study. Price: £5.95 ($9.95). ISBN 1 85075 702 X; ISSN 0264 6498)

This successful series continues with a contribution on three of the Minor Prophets. The purpose of this series is to assist students approaching each of the books of the Old Testament for the first time, and this volume achieves this goal admirably. Naturally, Micah, at the head of the trio, gets more space than the others. After a brief introduction, Mason sketches the contents of the book before giving the historical background according to the dates of the kings mentioned in the superscription. He then attempts a character sketch of Micah before two chapters on the history of criticism and the post-exilic message of the book, both of which take the reader forward into the more complicated world of Old Testament scholarship. Mason is more brief in his treatment of Nahum. After introductory remarks on the unusual nature of the 'prophet', he describes the historical background, the contents and the history of criticism, concluding with a chapter on the function and message of the book. A similar approach is offered on Obadiah which, though short, has many problems, and Mason makes this clear at the outset and concludes with remarks on the function and theology of the book. These three books are sensitively handled and, while some of the 'further reading' will be too difficult for the beginner, the latter will be well served by this volume and stimulated to further study.
R. B. SALTERS

MATTIES, G. H.: *Ezekiel 18 and the Rhetoric of Moral Discourse* (SBL Dissertation Series, 126). 1990. Pp. xi, 244. (Scholars Press, Atlanta GA. Price: $24.95 (member price: $14.95); paperback price: $14.95 (member price: $9.95). ISBN 1 55540 458 8; 1 55540 459 6 (pbk))

This is a Vanderbilt University doctoral dissertation completed in 1989 under the supervision of Douglas A. Knight. It presents a detailed rhetorical analysis of Ezekiel 18 and explores what the author calls the 'shape of moral discourse in the book of Ezekiel'. After a brief discussion of the relationship of Ezekiel to Israelite tradition, especially the Priestly and Deuteronomistic traditions, the author moves to a form-critical and traditio-historical analysis of the text of Ezekiel 18 and its 'suasive' potential. The dissertation then goes on to explore three major moral issues raised by Ezekiel 18. The first of these is the question of individual responsibility and the community. Matties discusses the nature and identity of 'moral agency' and he explores in detail 'Corporate Personality' and related concepts as they bear on discussion of Ezekiel. The second major issues discussed is that of the function of Law, and of legal language and conceptions, within moral discourse, whilst the third concerns the relationship between ethics and theodicy. Matties closes by presenting Ezekiel's ethics as the envisioning of a 'community of character' with a renewed identity and mission, a community which forms itself through the self-conscious acts of individuals, within the context of divine moral enablement. In using the notion of a 'community of character', and also in other respects (e.g. the particular use of the term 'moral agent'), the work reflects the influence of Stanley Hauerwas.

This dissertation provides a very detailed treatment of a short text, but it avoids the danger of narrowness of perspective, since the author's chosen text is handled in the light of Ezekiel as a whole, and indeed within the broad context of the theology and ethics of the Hebrew Bible. It is a well-informed and workmanlike dissertation. It is a pity that it lacks indexes; in a published work of this kind this is a real drawback. Also Matties fails to provide an adequate treatment of questions of unity, authorship, and redaction in Ezekiel as a whole; such references as there are are brief and tend to the cryptic (e.g. 'I shall follow Boadt and Greenberg, who favour a synchronic

LITERARY CRITICISM AND INTRODUCTION   81

analysis, while recognizing the possibility of diachronic development'); one forms the impression that this issue has not been fully thought through. Moreover, whilst the author's use of categories from the ethical work of Hauerwas is stimulating and fruitful, it would be good to have some reflection on the methodological and hermeneutical issues raised by this. Notwithstanding these reservations, however, Matties has given a thorough and insightful exegesis of Ezekiel 18, and — beyond this — he has provided a theologically sophisticated handling of questions of ethics in the broader Hebrew Bible, which constitutes a valuable contribution to a still relatively neglected field.

P. M. JOYCE

MORI, A.: *Seisho no Shuchukozo (jo) Kyuyaku hen (Concentric Structure in the Bible*: (I) *Old Testament*). See p. 142.

MOWVLEY, H.: *The Books of Amos & Hosea* (Epworth Commentaries). 1991. Pp. xix, 168. (Epworth, London. Price: £7.50. ISBN 0 7162 0475 4)

Here is an excellent short commentary suited to a wide readership, based on the *REB* as is the practice in this series. The exegetical comments are clear and balanced, and despite its brevity the author finds room for additional discussion of important topics such as 'word of the Lord', 'day of the Lord', and 'righteousness' (Amos); 'knowledge of God' and 'the covenant at Shechem' (Hosea). Of particular interest is the interpretation of Hosea 3 as a later Judean story, based on the facts of Hosea's marriage, showing Judah (the 'adulteress') to be more guilty than Israel (the 'unchaste woman' of ch. 1; cf. Ezekiel 23:11ff.), yet to be eventually the recipient of salvation. The message of both Amos and Hosea is regarded as one of unmitigated judgment. Expressions of hope for the future belong entirely to the later Judaean redaction, but both strands alike are to be treated seriously. In Amos, and to some extent in Hosea, the restoration envisaged depends not on the nation's repentance but solely on Yahweh's love.

G. I. EMMERSON

NAUMANN, T.: *Hoseas Erben. Strukturen der Nachinterpretation im Buch Hosea* (Beiträge zur Wissenschaft vom Alten und Neuen Testament, Siebente Folge 11). 1991. Pp. 198. (Kohlhammer, Stuttgart. Price: DM 69.00. ISBN 3 17 011579 0)

Interest in the redactional history of the book of Hosea has characterized a number of recent commentaries and monographs. Naumann's work limits itself to chapters 4–14 and so does not attempt to tell the full story. In its general approach to Hosea it draws heavily (but not slavishly) on the views of Jörg Jeremias. An analytical section reviews each passage in order, defining later additions and examining their effect on the context. This attention to the context is a valuable and distinctive feature of the book. A shorter synthetic section then groups the additions broadly as pre-exilic or exilic/post-exilic, recognizing the importance in the former group of the series of Judaean actualizations of Hosea's oracles. But no evidence is found of systematic redactional activity and only one case (8:1b, which many would dispute) of deuteronomistic editing. There are few surprises in the passages identified as secondary, except perhaps that there are not more of them. The value of this work lies, on the whole, in its careful attention to individual texts rather than in any major new insights.

G. I. DAVIES

NIELSEN, K.: *Satan — den fortabte søn?* 1991. Pp. 162. (Anis, Frederiksberg. Price: DKr 168.00. ISBN 87 7457 11 7)

The title of this book, 'Satan — the prodigal son?', gives some idea of the span of its contents, especially because the two bodies are normally not placed

82   LITERARY CRITICISM AND INTRODUCTION

next to each other; in a subtitle, found on the page with the colophon, it is called 'Biblical and pseudepigraphical conceptions of Satan as one of the sons of God', and these conceptions have been found by the author in more texts than the reader expects from the outset. Taking her point of departure in modern literary theories, she looks for potential meanings in a network of texts in which the root metaphor, a father's quarrel with two sons, is found. Among the texts in which God is the father, and Satan could be understood as one son of God in conflict with another, are notably the Book of Job read in its totality, the temptation in the wilderness (Matth. 4), the parable of the prodigal son (Luke 15: the elder son), and the fourth vision of Zechariah (ch. 3).

K. JEPPESEN

O'BRIEN, J. M.: *Priest and Levite in Malachi* (SBL Dissertation Series, 121). 1990. Pp. xiv, 164. (Scholars Press, Atlanta GA. Price: $22.95 (member price: $14.95); paperback price: $14.95 (member price: $9.95). ISBN 1 55540 438 3; 1 55540 439 1 (pbk))

The immediate aim of this work is to examine the use of the terms *kōhēn* and *lēwî* in the book of Malachi. However, this is done in a wide context, giving attention to issues which may well affect our decisions, such as 'The Form of the Book', the 'Sources' utilized by Malachi and the broader development of ideas of priesthood after the exile. An introductory chapter briefly but comprehensively surveys the history of scholarly study of the development of the priesthood.

Broadly speaking there are those who have always seen the two terms as synonymous, but those also who have, with Hanson, seen a deliberate contrast intended between the official priests and the Levites, a contrast much to the disadvantage of the priests. O'Brien will have none of it. She is convinced that in every case the reference is to the priests, a conclusion largely based on the fact that 3:3 recognizes the need for the Levites to be cleansed and purified. O'Brien notices, but does not really take into account, the views of those of us who believe that 3:1b–4 is intrusive in its present position. At the very least the extreme confusion between who is being spoken about, the 'messenger', the 'Lord' (*hā'ādôn*) and 'the messenger of the covenant' suggests later exegetical tampering with the text. 3:3 therefore remains a hazardous verse on which to base so important a conclusion. O'Brien believes that the Priestly Writing was one of the sources known to the author, who thus was familiar with, but did not accept, P's differentiation between priest and levite.

Among the most interesting implications of the study raised in a concluding chapter are the lack of any support for the idea of a conflict between priestly groups after the exile; the uniqueness of Malachi's contribution to the understanding of the priesthood; the formation of the canon, hinted at by Malachi's extensive use of other biblical sources; the dual role of the priest as expert in sacrifice but also teacher of Torah; and the fact that, for all his criticisms of the institution of priesthood, Malachi seeks its reform, not its abolition. This welcome book combines meticulous and careful scholarship with imaginative flair to a degree which makes one eager for future work from its author.

R. A. MASON

OSUMI, Y.: *Die Kompositionsgeschichte des Bundesbuches Exodus 20, 22b–23, 33* (Orbis Biblicus et Orientalis 105). 1991. Pp. 273. (Universitätsverlag, Freiburg (CH); Vandenhoeck & Ruprecht, Göttingen. Price: SwFr 75.00. ISBN 3 7278 0744 X (Universitätsverlag); 3 525 53738 7 (Vandenhoeck & Ruprecht))

This book is the revised form of a thesis presented at the Kirchliche Hochschule, Bethel, in 1989 by the author, a lecturer at the Tokyo Union

LITERARY CRITICISM AND INTRODUCTION 83

Theological Seminary and graduate in law from the University of Tokyo (and protégé of long-time *Book List* reviewer K. K. Sacon). The work begins from the criticism of Alt's form-critical categorization of 'apodeictic' and 'casuistic' law in B: Alt not only separated formally two varieties of law which had been deliberately combined by the compilers but compounded that separation by tracing them back to two distinct *Sitze im Leben*. Osumi, by contrast, so far from wishing to divorce these materials seeks to illuminate them from their context — not so much their postulated historical, political, and social, as their literary context within their present legal framework: they have been deliberately arranged according to recognizable literary principles and techniques. B is the end product of a long history of literary composition, beginning from two smaller collections, the book of religious law in Exod. 34:11–26 and the casuistic lawcode Exod. 21:1, 12–22:18* (19). The large part of B is composed of a work, recognizable from its use of the second person sg, which bound these two corpora together: in the process, the casuistic lawcode was scarcely affected but the religious laws were completely recast. The casuistic lawcode presents a systematic consideration of the legal principles governing two areas — delicts against life and delicts against property — which were the especial responsibility of the Jerusalemite courts. The theologizing 2 sg. material has integrated that 'secular' material with a concern for social justice. As might be anticipated in a thesis presented under the supervision of F. Crüsemann, it is argued that that collection reflects conditions post-721 in the period of Hezekiah or thereafter and probably stands under the influence of Amos. The 2 pl. material stems from Jerusalemite Temple circles of the late monarchical, but still pre-Deuteronomic, period, and is designed to give B the function of a book of instruction for a religious community. The epilogue to B, which reflects varying attitudes within Israel to the indigenous population, shows the influence of both 2 sg. and 2 pl. phases, as well as that of Deut. 7. Only after its completion was B inserted into the Sinai pericope. The book concludes with the author's own translation and analysis of B and with a full index of citations from the Hebrew Bible and ancient near eastern legal texts.

W. JOHNSTONE

OTTOSSON, M.: *Josuaboken. En programskrift för davidisk restauration* (Acta Universitatis Upsaliensis. Studia Biblica Upsaliensia I). 1991. Pp. 300. (Almqvist & Wiksell, Stockholm. Price: SKr 174.00. ISBN 91 554 2782 0; ISSN 1101 878 X)

For those who do not read Swedish, the author provides a comprehensive fifteen page English summary, although the full force of the argument of this important and well-documented study can only be appreciated by reading the whole book. It has long been recognized that the presentation of the conquest in the book of Joshua is an ideal and programmatic Deuteronomic construction, a view which Ottosson convincingly underlines in his chapter 'Conquest and Archaeology', which shows that there is no archaeological evidence for such a conquest in the period between the Late Bronze Age and the Iron Age. Ottosson's particular contention is that the book of Joshua is a Deuteronomic programme for the restoration of the Davidic kingdom, with Joshua as prototype of the perfect Israelite king, inspired by Josiah's reformation when such a restoration seemed possible. The Deuteronomic author employed and re-interpreted old local traditions to achieve his object and here especially interesting is Ottosson's claim that so-called 'P' passages are not later insertions in an existing Deuteronomic work but that these were taken over by the Deuteronomist from existing collections made in 'P' circles. The geographical indications are discussed in detail to show how they reflect the ideal extent of the Davidic kingdom, but

84 LITERARY CRITICISM AND INTRODUCTION

also reveal awareness of the Divided Kingdom, portray Judah as the leading tribe, and, in the book's attitude to the tribe of Benjamin, look back to the hostility between David and Saul. The Deuteronomic author was also concerned to ensure the permanence and stability of the restored kingdom, which for him could only be guaranteed by a faithful observance of the Law. This concern is seen in the last three chapters of Joshua, culminating in the assembly at Shechem in Jos. 24, the relation of which to the rest of the book has often posed a problem for commentators but which Ottosson views, through the people's pledge of obedience to Yahweh, as actualizing the promise of the land to Abraham there in Gen. 12:6–7. Many other stimulating and original suggestions in Ottosson's work could be noted but his most impressive achievement is to present, better than has ever been done previously, the book of Joshua as a unified whole, with all its parts cohering in a single purpose.

J. R. PORTER

PAUL, S. M.: *Amos. A Commentary on the Book of Amos.* Edited by Frank Moore Cross (Hermeneia — a Critical and Historical commentary on the Bible). 1991. Pp. xxvii, 409. (Fortress Press, Minneapolis. Price: $44.95. ISBN 0 8006 6023 4)

Hermeneia already has a commentary on Amos, within Wolff's volume on Joel and Amos (*B.L.* 1978, pp. 57f.). The volume under review will join rather than replace Wolff's in the series. Shalom Paul brings 'several decades of research and teaching' of Amos to the preparation of his commentary; and it is clear that it will find a place on reading lists for students of this perennial favourite for courses on Hebrew and/or the prophets.

A short first part of the Introduction (pp. 1–7) allows us to sample the author's approach to the main issues, and prepares us for his repeated defence of 'the integrity of the book'. Most issues are handled within the unfolding exegesis; however, some 'causes célèbres' merit detached essays whose varied styling causes some surprise at the final editorial work on the commentary. An Excursus on the doxologies follows the exegesis of 4:4–13; Introductory Comments immediately follow the translations of 5:1–17; 5:18–20; 5:21–27; and 9:11–15; an Excursus on the visions precedes the commentary on 7:1–9; while the structure and unity of the opening two chapters are uniquely discussed at length within the remainder of the Introduction (pp. 7–30).

The classified Bibliography is compendious, with upwards of two thousand items. The range of information made available within the discussion is often impressive, perhaps especially in two areas where we expect our Israeli colleagues to excel: familiarity with Ancient Near Eastern languages and thought, and the Mediaeval Jewish interpretative tradition. And yet, despite the detail involved and the level of interaction with alternative opinions, the argument is quite taut, and not discursive or even diffuse like that of this commentary's major recent competitor, Andersen and Freedman (*B.L.* 1990, p. 49f.).

And yet — there are some odd gaps. It is simply asserted without argument that the nominal clauses in 7:14 can refer as well to past and present. And in the midst of the most detailed discussion of all, while attractive points both old and new are made in favour of the literary unity of the oracles against the nations, not a word is said about the chief argument for a group of four: short complaint, extended threat, and concluding 'says Yahweh'. On the other side, it is surprising that Paul had to excerpt the doxology of vv.8ff from the chiastic structure in 5:1–17. Paul is an impressive debater, who so regularly anticipates his opponent's arguments that one has to be alert to notice the few occasions when he goes silent at crucial points. But he has certainly helped the discussion onwards.

A. G. AULD

LITERARY CRITICISM AND INTRODUCTION 85

PREWITT, T. J.: *The Elusive Covenant. A Structural-Semiotic Reading of Genesis* (Advances in Semiotics). 1990. Pp. x, 146. (Indiana University Press, Bloomington. Price: £13.50. ISBN 0 253 34599 5)

In a very short book (131 pages) Terry Prewitt, a professor of Anthropology at the University of West Florida, offers a splendid reading of the book of Genesis. I finished the book wondering why conventional biblical scholarship (especially that of my undergraduate days) does not produce this kind of work which illuminates the text as it exercises the grey cells. Of his own approach Prewitt writes: 'A structural reading of Genesis can be rather like encountering geometry. The premises are relatively few, but the combinations of premises yield complex and ordered arguments. What could not happen, or would not likely happen, occurs purely, offering a *mimesis* rich in possibilities. We experience the story, take hold of the signs, concatenate them, and *know* the law of the group which creates their transformations. We are not surprised, then, as we would be in the informal reading based upon unconscious traces of connection, when the narrative turns to the very possibility we have already generated. Structural analysis is incapable of unlocking anything beyond this, yet we should not lack appreciation for a process which brings the artefacts of a reading into conscious representation. The formal experience of Genesis involves us in poetics and mythscape in such a way that we more precisely apprehend how the richness of text is created, even as we deprive ourselves of its effect.' (p. 130; emphases the author's).

The tenuous or elusive covenant of the title is that between writer and listener, as well as that which is represented in the Genesis stories. The book is essentially about the book of Genesis in terms of its genealogies and its narrative structures. There are the usual complex graphs and diagrams typical of semiotic analysis, but there are also very good close readings of the text which yield most useful analyses of what is going on in the narratives of Genesis. Prewitt does not see Genesis as providing appropriate material for reconstructing events or actual systems operative at the time during which the patriarchs are supposed to have lived. The data yielded by Genesis relate to a particular view of the world far removed from the time it represents, but very much related to the community which created that representation. Working my way through this book I encountered a very sophisticated approach to myth and history, to structural hermeneutics, and to the cultural production of meaning. As *a* reading of Genesis I think this is a brilliant book, though its argument is too complex for me to summarize here. Read it for yourselves.

R. P. CARROLL

PRICKETT, S. and BARNES, R.: *The Bible* (Landmarks of World Literature). 1991. Pp. xii, 141. (Cambridge University Press. Price: £20.00 ($27.95); paperback price: £6.95 ($10.95). ISBN 0 521 36569 4; 0 521 36759 X (pbk))

In this contribution to the series 'Landmarks of World Literature', the authors reject a split into Old Testament and New Testament, preferring to describe the bible as a single unit. The introduction covers briefly and competently such topics as the canon, literary form, and history. Chapter two goes through the bible, book by book, with brief indications of content. Next come eleven 'leading themes' of the bible which include God, of course, as well as creation, covenant, law and righteousness, sacrifice and expiation, and wisdom. In the chapter on interpretation the point is made 'that any idea of a clear distinction . . . between the original literal meaning and a later process of commentary and interpretation is historically quite

86 LITERARY CRITICISM AND INTRODUCTION

misleading. Right from the beginning . . . the biblical writings were inseparably intertwined with interpretation and comment' (p. 81). The final chapter deals principally with translations, from the Targums to current versions, and closes with a section showing how the bible has influenced English literature. There is a time chart and suggestions for further reading are provided. For anyone totally unfamiliar with the bible this is the book to read; for others, although the aspect of appraising the bible as literature may not be novel it is refreshingly presented.

W. G. E. WATSON

RAABE, P. R.: *Psalm Structures* (Journal for the Study of the Old Testament Supplement Series 104). 1990. Pp. 240. (Sheffield Academic Press. Price: £30.00 ($50.00); sub. price: £22.50 ($37.50). ISBN 1 85075 262 1; ISSN 0309 0787)

The poetic structure of six Psalms (42/3, 46, 49, 56, 57, 59) is here subjected to detailed analysis, with 39, 67, 80, and 99 given more cursory attention; the particular concern is to advance the study of Hebrew poetry, through an analysis of the techniques employed in these Psalms. Raabe focuses especially on the 'building blocks' isolated by the use of refrains and the patterns that emerge thereby. Syllables are counted, stanzas defined and described, and a number of literary artifices noted. Whether at the end of the book there will be a 'better understanding of how to read a psalm' must remain open to question; for many readers the Psalms have more and different things to offer than an analysis of their structures.

R. J. COGGINS

DE REGT, L. J.: *A Parametric Model for Syntactic Studies of a Textual Corpus, Demonstrated on the Hebrew of Deuteronomy 1–30* (Studia Semitica Neerlandica). 1988. Pp. ix, 138 with a 91-page supplement. (Van Gorcum, Assen/Maastricht. Price: fl. 46.50. ISBN 90 232 2381 0)

This book supplies in its Supplement frequency and percentage tables for all sorts of syntactic phenomena in its chosen sample (e.g. verb form, subject, object, clause type, etc.), these being called *parameters*. The main volume is concerned with how to choose a corpus and why Deuteronomy 1–30 is sufficiently homogeneous to be used as such; with how the parameters may be formally identified for counting purposes and their functions differentiated and described; and with a commentary on the tables. The results are sometimes unremarkable, sometimes new and surprising, but could have been presented more simply. It is clear that the book is more concerned with making out a case for the parametric method than with helping the student of Deuteronomy. That the method is potentially fruitful there can be no doubt, and the linguists among us will be well advised to close with it and learn from it. Others can wait for the practical sequel which must surely follow if de Regt's claims are to be substantiated. It is a pity that the book is not only densely written but densely printed and that its English is sometimes deficient (e.g. 'intension' for 'intention'; 'foregoer' for a verb in a previous clause); these weaknesses will make it more difficult for it to receive the attention it merits.

J. C. L. GIBSON

RENAUD, B.: *La Théophanie du Sinaï. Ex 19–24: Exégèse et Théologie* (Cahiers de la Revue Biblique 30). 1991. Pp. 219. (Gabalda, Paris. Price: Fr 348.00. ISBN 2 85021 049 8; ISSN 0575 0741)

The book divides into two sections. The first is concerned with the literary history of Exod. 19–24. Without prejudice to the possible validity of

LITERARY CRITICISM AND INTRODUCTION 87

the traditional documentary hypothesis elsewhere in the Pentateuch, not least in Genesis, Renaud seeks, without using it as an *a priori* assumption in connection with *this* pericope, to work back from the final edition of the text by a process of 'subtraction'. In the process he comes to the conclusion that something approximating a fragment and supplementary hypothesis is more appropriate: there is a major edition of this material, Dtr 1 (19:3b–8; 24:4–8), which has passed through two subsequent theological editions, Dtr 2 (19:9, 11b, 18; 20:18a, 19, 21; 24:3) and Rp, the final redaction of the Pentateuch (19:12, 13a, 20–25; 24:1–2, 9–11), which includes a fragment of Pg (19:1, 2a and possibly 19:20). Beneath these redactions there lie early 'Elohistic' traditions (not to be regarded as comprising a unified E document), concerning theophany (ch. 19), and aspersion and sanctuary meal (ch. 24). The Decalogue and the Book of the Covenant, which no doubt have their own literary histories, have been located in their present positions by Dtr 1 and Dtr 2, respectively (20:11, however, is the work of Rp). The second half of the work expounds in detail and with considerable acuteness the theologies contained in the sources and editions so identified.

The present reviewer finds the approach congenial. Inevitably, discussion on detail will continue: I am not convinced that the distinction between Dtr 1 and Dtr 2 can be maintained (Renaud himself is not entirely consistent in the date he assigns to Dtr 1: in one place he describes it as late exilic, while in another as early post-exilic, thus bringing it close to the date he assigns to Dtr 2), nor am I sure that the 'noyau ancien' is to be pursued through literary history rather than through the history of institutions which the writers are freely exploiting. The distinction between P and Rp is also problematical. None the less, this book is to be welcomed as marking a further stage in the development of something approaching a procedural agreement with regard to this part of Exodus. In this connection the work of, for example, T. B. Dozeman, might have been mentioned.

W. JOHNSTONE

ROFÉ, A.: *Storia di Profeti. La narrativa sui profeti nella Bibbia ebraica: generi letterari e storia*. Italian edition by P. G. Borbone (Biblioteca di storia e storiographia dei tempi biblici 8). 1991. Pp. 269. (Paideia Editrice, Brescia. Price: Lire 38,000. ISBN 88 394 0461 9)

This Italian translation has been made from the English edition of Rofé's work, which was noted in *B.L.* 1989, p. 91 (the original Hebrew edition was reviewed in *B.L.* 1984, pp. 80f) but there are a number of variations. Chapters 1 and 10 have undergone some revision and amplification and a section has been added to chapter 4, dealing with Elisha and the usurpation of Hazael. The discussion of the story of Micaiah ben Imlah in chapter 8 has been considerably extended. Lastly, there is appended an Italian translation of Rofé's article *The Vineyard of Naboth* which appeared in *VT* 38 (1988), pp. 91–104. It is anticipated that these new features will be incorporated in future editions of the work in other languages.

J. R. PORTER

ROGERSON, J.: *Genesis 1–11* (Old Testament Guides). 1991. Pp. 87. (JSOT Press, Sheffield for the Society for Old Testament Study. Price: £5.95 ($9.95). ISBN 1 85075 274 5)

This is a welcome addition to the Old Testament Guides. It provides a useful introduction to recent approaches to Genesis 1–11, including literary, liberation, and feminist readings. It is particularly helpful in leaving many questions open and challenging the reader to think the issues through to a responsible conclusion. There is an excellent bibliography of studies in Genesis 1–11 since 1980.

R. DAVIDSON

88   LITERARY CRITICISM AND INTRODUCTION

RÜGER, H. P.: *Die Weisheitsschrift aus der Kairoer Geniza. Text, Übersetzung und philologischer Kommentar* (Wissenschaftliche Untersuchungen zum Neuen Testament 53). 1991. Pp. ix, 176. (Mohr, Tübingen. Price: DM 98.00. ISBN 3 16 145618 1; ISSN 0512 1604)

This book carries exactly the same main title as one published in 1989 by Klaus Berger (Francke Verlag, Tübingen). Both books claim to present us with an edition, translation and commentary on a wisdom text from the Cairo Geniza which was partially edited by Schechter and Harkavy at the beginning of the century and then almost totally ignored by scholars since. The text itself is extremely interesting, presenting itself, as it does, as a clear continuation both in style and content of the biblical wisdom literature (especially the Book of Proverbs). But far more interesting, perhaps, is the radically different conclusions reached by these two scholars as to its nature and origin. For Berger WKG (as he always abbreviates it) represents the last attempt to bind together the dualistic approach of hellenistic philosophy with the traditional dualism of the Jewish wisdom literature. He dates it to *c*. 100 CE and sets its place of origin in Alexandria. He relates it to the kind of dualistic, ascetic, philosophically inclined Judaism about which Philo writes when he discusses the Essenes and the Therapeutae. It is thus a text of immense interest to a professor of New Testament Theology at the University of Heidelberg.

For Rüger (also a New Testament scholar, but in his case from Tübingen) Berger's book is basically nonsense which is why he felt the need to completely redo the edition, translation and commentary of this text. Rüger accuses Berger of having misread the Geniza manuscript and hence of having produced a seriously defective translation. Rüger dates WKG 1,000 years later than Berger — in the twelfth century and close to the probable date of the Geniza manuscript. He places its 'Sitz im Leben' among the Karaite section of the 'mourners for Zion' in Palestine. This is a remarkable example of scholarly disagreement.

Who is right and which is the best book? Interested scholars will, I am afraid, have to work with both books. Judging from the photographs of the manuscript Rüger's transcription of it is much superior to Berger's, indeed almost faultless except for one or two details. But his introduction is short and his commentary (as the subtitle says) is mainly confined to philological observations. The use of transliteration throughout the book is most irritating. There is surely no need, in this age of computerized book production, to have a work with an edition of a Hebrew text with no Hebrew text in it! Berger's book is, by contrast, easier to use, and has a much fuller introduction and commentary, but is marred by too frequent inaccuracy in transcription and translation and by the constant urge to make his text relevant to New Testament studies. As to who is right, Rüger seems to me to get the better of the debate, but he does use arguments which are less conclusive than he thinks they are, especially when dating texts from the type of Hebrew they contain. Unfortunately, the dialogue between these two scholars cannot continue. Rüger died at the age of 57 in November 1990.

A. P. HAYMAN

SACCHI, P.: *L'Apocalittica Giudaica e la sua Storia* (Biblioteca di Cultura Religiosa 55). 1990. Pp. 374. (Paideia Editrice, Brescia. Price: Lira 47,000. ISBN 88 394 0446 5)

With self-confessed reluctance, Sacchi adopts the entrenched term 'apocalyptic' to designate a 'current of thought' which begins with the Enochic 'Book of the Watchers' (1 Enoch 6–36), whose essential characteristics according to Sacchi are belief in the heavenly origin of evil and in immortality/resurrection. The history of 'apocalyptic' traced in Part One of

LITERARY CRITICISM AND INTRODUCTION 89

the book falls into four stages, of which the first three are characterized by portions of the Enochic corpus. The second part of the book deals with other themes of apocalyptic — calendars, messianism, and the devil.

An attempt, such as this, to describe rather than define 'apocalyptic' in more precise literary and historical terms is understandable, and here we have a stimulating study. But the approach tends to divorce Jewish apocalyptic from its cultural and historical milieu — what of non-Jewish apocalypses? Are they a quite independent phenomenon? Further, Sacchi's use of the Dead Sea Scrolls is dated; the book of Daniel is not really dealt with adequately, and his treatment of Second Temple Judaism presupposes a degree of knowledge which this book itself calls into question: after all, should not the bible, from the purely historical point of view, be regarded as literary tradition rather than cultural norm? If there is an 'Enochic tradition', which Sacchi does much to establish, maybe it would have been better to call it such and leave 'Jewish apocalyptic', whatever *that* is, undefined!

P. R. Davies

Schmid, H.: *Die Gestalt des Isaak. Ihr Verhältnis zur Abraham- und Jakobtradition* (Erträge der Forschung 274). 1991. Pp. 122. (Wissenschaftliche Buchgesellschaft, Darmstadt. Price: DM 26.80. ISBN 3 534 10414 5; ISSN 0174 0695)

The presentation of Isaac in Genesis is notoriously little more than a bridge between the fuller accounts of Abraham and of Jacob, but there is no scholarly agreement whether this bespeaks an ancient, now overlaid, tradition or is merely a late literary device. These and many related issues are fairly discussed by Schmid, whose book is both a supplement to and an up-dating of Westermann's treatment of Genesis 12–50 in the same series (cf. *B.L.* 1977, p. 76). Literary criticism (new style), source criticism, and tradition-history are treated; detailed attention is paid to Gen. 26, the only chapter in which Isaac appears as the primary figure; the particular theological significance of Isaac is assessed, with special attention to Gen. 22; and an appraisal offered of understandings since Alt of the 'God of the Fathers'. Nearly all is reportage of the views of others; Schmid allows his own assessment to come to the fore only in the concluding chapter, where he is sceptical about the current tendency to date everything in the Second Temple period. The whole is rounded off by a very useful bibliography.

R. J. Coggins

Schmidt, W. H.: *Exodus, Sinai und Mose. Erwägungen zu Ex 1–19 und 24* (Erträge der Forschung 191) 2., bibliographisch erweiterte Auflage. 1990. Pp. viii, 176. (Wissenschaftliche Buchgesellschaft, Darmstadt. Price: DM 35.00. ISBN 3 534 08779 8; ISSN 0174 0695)

The text is unchanged from the first edition (for which see *B.L.* 1984, pp. 81f) but twelve further pages of bibliography of relevant works up to 1989 have been added.

W. Johnstone

Schwienhorst-Schönberger, L.: *Das Bundesbuch (Ex 20, 22–23, 33). Studien zu seiner Entstehung und Theologie* (Beiheft zur Zeitschrift für die alttestamentliche Wissenschaft 188). 1990. Pp. xiii, 468. (De Gruyter, Berlin. Price: DM 168.00. ISBN 3 11 012404 1; ISSN 0934 2575)

The work stands in the 'Münster' tradition of studies in Exodus associated with such names as E. Zenger, P. Weimar, F.-L. Hossfeld, and C. Dohmen.

90 LITERARY CRITICISM AND INTRODUCTION

The author is concerned with three major issues regarding the Book of the Covenant: the relation between divine and secular law within B; the relationship between B and the ancient near eastern tradition; and how far B may be regarded as having passed through a Deuteronomistic edition. His conclusion is that an original secular casuistic law-code with Ancient Near Eastern antecedents (21:12, 18–22:14*) has passed through proto-Deuteronomic (20:24–26*; 21:2–11*, 13–17, 20f., 22aβbβ, 23f., 26f., 30; 22:1f., 9*, 15–19a, 20aα, 22b, 24a*, 25–29; 23:1–7, 10–12, 14–19*, 20–33*) and Deuteronomistic (20:23, 24aβ; 21:1, 2aα*, 6aβγ, 8b, 25; 22:19b, 20aβb, 21, 22a, 23, 24aα*, 5, 30; 23:8f., 13, 15aα*, 20–33*) editions and a final priestly redaction (22:22aβb). For the proto-Deuteronomic circles, cf. the priestly figures alluded to in Hos. 4–7. The Deuteronomistic edition brings B within the compass of a theological narrative stretching from Genesis 2:4b to 2 Kings 25.

This is a valuable discussion. The exegetical work alone, which accounts for well over half of the book, is constantly informative about the state of scholarly discussion, stimulating in its proposals and independent in its judgement. The book is clearly organized: there is an elaborate table of contents and full textual and subject indexes; each part of the argument is prefaced by a preliminary statement, tabulation or diagram, so that the thread of the argument can be readily followed through the often close exegetical discussion. With its clear German and methodical approach I have found it a useful seminar text for postgraduate students.

W. JOHNSTONE

SEYBOLD, K.: *Nahum Habakuk Zephanja* (Zürcher Bibelkommentare). 1991. Pp. 134. (Theologischer Verlag, Zürich. Price: DM 28.00. ISBN 3 290 10134 7)

Seybold has published a number of earlier articles dealing with various aspects of these prophetic books so that it is good now to have this small, but valuable commentary. His approach is firmly along the lines of redaction criticism but this serves his wider interest in the theological significance of the books and the way they have been interpreted in later tradition. Typical is his approach to the book of Nahum. This is made up of an early tradition of Nahum's words in the poem of 3:8–19a which arises from the conquest of Thebes by the Assyrians in 663 BCE. Nahum's words are also enshrined in the 'woe' poem of 3:1, 4a and the poems of 3:2 and 2:2–13 which, since they concern the fall of Nineveh, must be dated shortly before 612. Nahum himself prophesied about the middle of the seventh century. Later, in the time of the exile, promises of salvation for Judah were added (1:12ff) while a final level of redaction (*c.* 400) extended the whole message onto a cosmic scale (1.2f). His analysis of the book of Habakkuk is the most controversial part of his commentary. He solves the problem of the exact relation to each other of the various parts of cc. 1 and 2 and of those to whom they refer, by following Schmidt's analysis of the book into three literary layers, all from different times. First were the prophecies and visions going back to Habakkuk (*c.* 630), but these were gathered after his life about 550 when, combined with the hymn of *c.* 3, Habakkuk's words which had been related to the Babylonians were applied to the hopes raised by the advance of the Persians. Finally, psalm material which sought an answer to questions of theodicy was added by a post-exilic editor in the fourth century. Similarly, while Zephaniah prophesied during the time of the minority of Josiah, again an exilic editor found fulfilment of his threats in the exile and looked for hope beyond it while, in a much later apocalyptic-type editing, 3:11–20 was added.

One can certainly question the confidence of much of the alleged 'source' division and the dates to which the various material is assigned while admitting that *some* such process of growth clearly did take place. And even

LITERARY CRITICISM AND INTRODUCTION 91

when doubting some conclusions the reader is always in Seybold's debt for the literary and theological perception of his work.

R. A. Mason

SHERWOOD, S. K.: *Had God Not Been on My Side. An Examination of the Narrative Technique of the Story of Jacob and Laban, Genesis 29, 1–32, 2* (Europäische Hochschulschriften, Reihe XXIII, Bd. 400). 1990. Pp. 433. (Lang, Frankfurt (Main)–Bern–New York–Paris. Price: SwFr 42.00. ISBN 3 631 43092 2; ISSN 0721 3409)

This dissertation is something of a model of its kind, a narratological analysis in which plot, narrator, reader response, and style are systematically considered in the five episodes of this narrative. Particularly attractive are the author's analyses of focalization (point of view) and of the way the narrator either shares information with the reader or else withholds it. Sherwood makes us read as slowly and lingeringly as possible; at the mention of a 'well' in 29:2, for example, we have to stop in order to reflect that a well is a place of meeting (as it has been in ch. 24) and to allow ourselves time to wonder whom Jacob will meet at the well. 'If men, we may expect conflict. If a woman, romance. Which way will the plot go?' (p. 36). And at 29:4 when Jacob says, 'My brother, where are you from?', we must pause to learn that this is the only place where such a question is addressed to people already at a place rather than to someone arriving at a place, and register the effect this reversal of the customary speech makes on our construction of the character of Jacob as a man of initiative and activity (p. 39). We may hope that the author of this study, formalist through and through, having now read the text in slow motion, will read it all over again in other more dynamic post-structuralist modes.

D. J. A. Clines

SIMON, U.: *Abraham Ibn Ezra's Two Commentaries on the Minor Prophets: An Annotated Critical Edition*. Vol. 1: *Hosea–Joel–Amos* (in Hebrew). 1989. Pp. 332. (Bar Ilan University Press, Ramat-Gan. Price: $30.00. ISBN 965 226 103 3)

The recent interest in editing and publishing the works of the medieval Jewish commentators on the text of the Hebrew Bible is to be welcomed, though it does come as a surprise to find Ibn Ezra's commentary on Hosea edited in 1988 (see *B.L.* 1990, pp. 57f) followed so soon by this work. But, apart from the fact that this volume is number one in a series covering all twelve minor prophets, the title testifies to the actual concerns of the author. He is concerned not only with the traditional commentary as published in *Mikraoth Gedoloth* but also with Ibn Ezra's *šîtâ ăḥeret*, another commentary based on other manuscripts in Paris etc. What Simon does is to edit the traditional commentary (pp. 21–265) and to follow this with the edited and annotated second commentary, which has never before been published (pp. 269–313). There is an introduction explaining the sources and method, and a good bibliography. The result is a substantial and satisfying contribution to medieval studies in general and to Ibn Ezra studies in particular; in addition it is to be welcomed by all students of the exegesis of the Old Testament.

R. B. Salters

SKLBA, R. J.: *Pre-Exilic Prophecy. Words of Warning, Dreams of Hopes, Spirituality of Pre-Exilic Prophets* (Message of Biblical Spirituality 3). 1990. Pp. ii, 183. (Liturgical Press, Collegeville, Minnesota. Price: $9.95. ISBN 0 8146 5569 6)

The author is Catholic Bishop of Milwaukee. Contributing to a series planned to provide 15 volumes on the spiritual message of the Bible, he has

92 LITERARY CRITICISM AND INTRODUCTION

drawn on all kinds of prophecy up to the Exile to expound prophetic themes. The themes are many and include visions, group ecstasy, the call to prophecy, zeal, faith, the voice of the poor, worship, judgment, salvation, and images for God. Since there is also a great abundance of illustrative reference to the biblical texts, it may be that readers who already have acquaintance with the flow of the Old Testament will profit most. Otherwise the book is pitched at a fairly simple level and would be useful to groups reflecting on the relevance of the prophets to life today. The style is direct and clear, and there are questions for reflection at the end of each chapter.

J. H. EATON

SMITH, M. S.: *The Laments of Jeremiah and their Contexts: A Literary and Redactional Study of Jeremiah 11–20* (SBL Monograph Series, 42). 1990. Pp. xxi, 92. (Scholars Press, Atlanta GA. Price: $24.95 (member price: $14.95); paperback price: $14.95 (member price: $9.95). ISBN 1 55540 460 X; 1 55540 461 8 (pbk))

Yet another monograph on those poems in Jeremiah 11–20 commonly known as 'the confessions of Jeremiah'. But this is a superior piece of work which has the added virtue of being brief (less than eighty pages of text). It is not so much a monograph as a series of different lectures held together by a common focus on the laments in Jeremiah 11–20. It is also an excellent review of the scholarly literature on the subject, as well as being a brief examination of the various poems constituting the laments of Jeremiah. Mark Smith steers a careful course between the differing viewpoints expressed by many recent scholarly works on Jeremiah, while commenting on the biblical text in the company of these works. While it would be very unwise not to read all the recent writers on Jeremiah, especially Diamond, O'Connor, and Polk on the laments, Smith's little book would be an excellent place to start. Apart from its brevity, it has the additional virtue of functioning as an Ariadne's thread in the labyrinth of contemporary Jeremiah studies.

R. P. CARROLL

SOLL, W.: *Psalm 119: Matrix, Form and Setting* (Catholic Biblical Quarterly Monograph Series 23). 1991. Pp. vii, 192. (Catholic Biblical Association, Washington D.C. ISBN 0 915170 22 1)

Here is a massive psalm, adjudged by the Fathers 'a paradise of all fruits' and by Duhm 'the most empty product that ever blackened paper'. Soll has a positive view of its value and works through the main critical questions with lucid style and level-headed judgment. The acrostic form, which he thinks has nothing to do with memory-aids, is usefully discussed in the context of Babylonian analogies and other Hebrew examples. Likewise, the outstanding feature of constantly recurring words for 'law' is studied with a search for analogies which makes good headway. The synonyms and the acrostic make an interlocking scaffolding set up, not for affixing any maxim about Torah which came to mind, but to serve the building of an elaborate prayer. The classification of the psalm, therefore, should be as a Lament of the Individual, and not as a medley of all the types. A reasonable case is made for regarding the voice as that of Jehoiachin in the Exile. Altogether this is a commendable contribution to the study of the Psalms.

J. H. EATON

SPERLING, U.: *Das theophanische Jahwe-Überlegenheitslied. Forschungsbericht und gattungskritische Untersuchung der sogennanten Zionlieder* (Europäische Hochschulschriften Reihe XXIII Theologie Band 426). 1991. Pp. 472. (Lang, Frankfurt (Main)–Bern–New York–Paris. Price: SwFr 35.00. ISBN 3 631 43804 4; ISSN 0721 3409)

The appropriate classification of the so-called 'Songs of Zion' (Pss. 46, 48, 76, 84, 87 and 122) is the main concern of this study. More than 300 pages

LITERARY CRITICISM AND INTRODUCTION   93

are devoted to an analysis of earlier work, with special attention being paid first to the interpretation of the *Gattung* by Gunkel, Mowinckel, Weiser and Kraus, and then to the various themes (holy mountain, dwelling-place of God, etc.) which have been identified as characteristic of these Psalms. Sperling claims that too often imprecise links have been accepted where specific analysis was needed, and he supports his point with a series of tables designed to bring out exactly which features are found in which Psalm. His conclusion is that we have inadequate evidence to posit a specific festival as did Mowinckel and others, or to claim that a particular historical event shaped the genre, or that ancient Jebusite forms have been taken over and reused. Indeed the classification as 'Songs of Zion' is misleading; rather Pss. 46, 48, and 76 should be seen as songs which proclaim Yahweh's supremacy revealed by a theophany, a genre with which 87 and 122 share some characteristics; 84 stands somewhat apart. The point could have been made more briefly, but the clear analysis is a valuable antidote to the vague assertions sometimes made about these Psalms.

R. J. COGGINS

STRÜBIND, K.: *Tradition als Interpretation in der Chronik. König Josaphat als Paradigma chronistischer Hermeneutik und Theologie* (BZAW 201). 1991. Pp. xiii, 220. (De Gruyter, Berlin, New York. Price: DM 98.00. ISBN 3 11 012791 1; 0934 2575)

This Berlin dissertation falls into two equal parts. The first is a survey of critical work on the books of Chronicles, including both introductory questions and attempts to define their major ideological and theological concerns, together with a discussion of some of the critical issues raised by the study of the historical books in the OldTestament as a whole. This is all competently handled, though there are some notable gaps in the coverage of the secondary literature. The second half is then devoted to a detailed analysis of the Chronicler's treatment of Jehoshaphat (2 Chron. 17–20). Strübind broadly follows P. Welten in denying the existence of written sources other than those already known to us from elsewhere in the Old Testament and T. Willi in maintaining that the Chronicler was concerned principally to offer an interpretation of his canonical *Vorlage*. The results are then briefly related back to the questions seen in the first part still to be open. While some of Strübind's conclusions are open to question, this is a valuable work. Unwary readers should be warned, however, that the citation of Biblical references is not always accurate. With the coming of age of the modern period of Chronicles studies, there have been several such detailed analyses of particular sections of the work, and this is a trend which we may expect to see continued.

H. G. M. WILLIAMSON

UEHLINGER, C.: *Weltreich unde 'eine Rede'. Eine neue Deutung der sogenannten Turmbauerzählung (Gen. 11, 1–9)* (OBO 101). 1990. Pp. xvi, 627, and XXII plates. (Universitätsverlag, Freiburg (CH); Vandenhoeck & Ruprecht, Göttingen. Price: Sw Fr 155.00. ISBN 3 7278 0697 4; 3 525 53733 6)

The first part (pp. 9–290) of this book was a dissertation (1989) at Fribourg. It begins by discussing the versions of Gen. 11:1–9 and offering a translation, and then surveys its interpretation in Jewish tradition. Uehlinger next turns to the theory that the Tower of Babel was a ziggurat and finds its origin in Jewish and Islamic traditions. After examining the archaeological evidence for the stages of construction of Etemenanki, the ziggurat of Babylon, and their dating, he challenges the widely-accepted view that it is to be identified with the tower of Gen. 11:1–9. The first part of the book ends with an account of the interpretation of the story as a condemnation of human hybris, and G. von Rad's theory of a series of stories of growing human sin in

94 LITERARY CRITICISM AND INTRODUCTION

Gen. 1–11; and the validity of such interpretations is questioned. The second part (pp. 291–584) offers a new interpretation of the passage. The composition and themes of the story are discussed, and it is maintained, among other things, that 'one lip' means 'eine Rede' rather than 'eine Sprache', and that 'tower' here denotes a citadel. The idea of 'eine Rede' is then studied in comparison with Mesopotamian texts speaking of 'one mouth', and the phrase's political implications are explored. Finally, four stages in the history of the passage are reconstructed. (1) The original story (c. 700 BC) is found in verses 1 (apart from 'and the same words'), 3a^a, 4 (apart from 'and they said'), 5–7, 8b; it is understood as an allusion to Dur Sharrukin, a city whose building was begun by Sargon II but abandoned after his death. (2) The story was expanded by the addition of 'and the same words' in verse 1, and verses 3a^b–4a^a, 9a. The additions show an interest in language and word-play and introduce a reference to Babylon. The date cannot be earlier than the time of Esarhaddon, under whom brick and bitumen were used for building in Babylon (and in whose reign the additions to Etemenanki using those materials were made) and was more probably in the exile after the death of Nebuchadnezzar II. (3) Verse 4 was added when the story was incorporated into the primeval story at a stage before the Priestly writing. (4) Verses 4b, 8a and 9b were added later; and an attempt is made to relate their theme of the scattering of people to ideas current in the Achaemenid period. The book has a list of abbreviations, a bibliography, indexes (of biblical and other ancient texts, words, subjects, and authors), a synopsis setting out the stages of composition of the passage (in German and Hebrew), and brief summaries of the argument in German and English. A short review cannot do justice to the rich detail of this long book, which is obviously a major contribution to the subject and a basis for further discussion, whether in agreement or in disagreement.

J. A. EMERTON

VAWTER, B. and HOPPE, L. J.: *A New Heart. A Commentary on the Book of Ezekiel* (International Theological Commentary). 1991. Pp. xi, 218. (Eerdmans, Grand Rapids MI; Handsel, Edinburgh. Price: $15.95. ISBN 0 8028 0331 8; 1 871828 09 0)

By the time of his death in 1986, Bruce Vawter had completed the first draft of the introduction to this volume, and the commentary on chapters 1–24. Leslie J. Hoppe of the Catholic Theological Union, Chicago, has brought the volume to completion. It follows the general pattern of the International Theological Commentary, with an emphasis on theological questions (with a Christian theological context explicitly acknowledged) and a fairly popular style.

In spite of the history of the volume, it is remarkably consistent in both content and style. In most respects the commentary as a whole adopts what one could risk describing as a 'standard' view on the main critical questions. Thus Ezekiel is regarded as having lived and worked at the beginning of the Exile and to have spent the whole of his prophetic ministry in Babylonia. The basic material in the book is traced to the historical Ezekiel, but much evidence of redaction is found; the book itself is described as 'a product of the faith community that treasured the memory and message of the prophet'. (For the most part, no attempt is made in the commentary to separate primary and secondary material.) The book's continuities with the classical prophetic tradition are emphasized, whilst its distinctive features (e.g. affinities with pre-classical prophecy) are also acknowledged. Perhaps the most original section, and as it happens the most questionable, is that on the history of the priesthood.

LITERARY CRITICISM AND INTRODUCTION   95

There is evidence of considerable learning, but it is worn lightly, as befits the series. References to secondary literature are included (albeit sparingly) in brackets within the text. All Hebrew is transliterated. There are no indexes, but there is a select bibliography of books and articles. The comments on the text are brief, indeed at one or two points they seem too brief to be viable. There are a few minor errors and occasional obscurities in expression. Nevertheless, the volume largely fulfils the stated aims of the series.

P. M. Joyce

WESTERMANN, C.: *Basic Forms of Prophetic Speech*. Translated by H. C. White, with a new foreword by G. M. Tucker. 1991. Pp. xvi, 222. (Lutterworth, Cambridge; Westminster/John Knox, Louisville KY. Price: £9.95. ISBN 0 7188 2842 9; 0 664 25244 3)

The *Book List* carried a warm review of this work when it was first made available in English (*B. L.* 1968, p. 45; *Bible Bibliog.*, p. 99). To this welcome paperback reprint of the 1967 original, Gene M. Tucker has added an appreciation of the significance of the work in a short foreword (pp. ix–xvi).

A. G. Auld

WESTERMANN, C.: *Forschungsgeschichte zur Weisheitsliteratur 1950–1990* (Arbeiten zur Theologie 71). 1991. Pp. 51. (Calwer, Stuttgart. Price: DM 22.00. ISBN 3 7668 0789 7)

This brief historical survey is both wider and more restricted in scope than the title suggests. It is concerned almost entirely with the Book of Proverbs, and in particular with the individual proverbs found in Prov. 10–22 and 25–29. On the other hand, it begins with a substantial section on works published *before* 1950, going as far back as Eissfeldt's work on the *māšāl* (1913). The method employed is to present a series of short critical reviews of some thirty representative works arranged mainly in chronological order and interspersed with general comments on the nature of the problems involved and on the general directions in which the study of the subject has moved. A final section summarizes what Westermann considers to be the main results of the investigation. It is important to make a sharp distinction between the *Spruchweisheit* of chapters 10–22 and 25–29 and the *Lehrweisheit* of chapters 1–9 and parts 22–24. The individual proverbs in the former have an oral background and closely resemble the proverbs of modern non-literate peoples; they are not concerned with abstract concepts such as an universal 'Order' but with the manifold situations encountered by ordinary men and women in daily life. The latter belong to the didactic tradition of the school-texts of Egyptian and Mesopotamian wisdom literature, and are concerned with more abstract concepts. As an introduction to the complexities of the proverb literature of Proverbs this study, despite its brevity, is immensely valuable and will fulfil a pressing need. It would have been even more valuable if the concluding bibliography — of some seventy items — had been more comprehensive.

R. N. Whybray

WHITE, H. C.: *Narration and discourse in the Book of Genesis*. 1991. Pp. xiii, 312. (Cambridge University Press. Price: £35.00. ($49.50). ISBN 0 521 39020 6)

Hugh White's book is a beautifully structured combination of text and theory in the pursuit of a functional theory of narrative as applied to the narratives of Genesis. The book consists of three parts: a functional theory of narrative (pp. 1–91), the structure of the Genesis narrative (pp. 93–112), and

96   LITERARY CRITICISM AND INTRODUCTION

an analysis of the Genesis narratives, with an excursus on sacrifice in religion and literature (pp. 113–275). The bulk of the book is given over to the analysis of the biblical text and that produces a just proportion of text to theory. Notes, bibliography, and indexes complete a very handsomely produced book by CUP (the dust-jacket is very attractive and features a detail from The Pantheon Bible, Rome).

On the theory side White discusses semiotics in general, taking up the Saussurian distinction between the signifier and signified in conjunction with the work of Seymour Chatman, Mieke Bal, and Gérard Genette. Further discussions involve the work of Mary Louise Pratt and J. L. Austin with special attention to Eugenio Coseriu's refutation of Saussurian linguistics. Coseriu and the work of Angel Medina contribute to the establishing of the primacy of intersubjectivity (communicative fusion). Among other theoreticians considered Derrida and Shklovsky also figure, but the dominant influence is that of Edmond Ortigues. Typologies of narrative functions developed by Norman Friedman, Franz Stanzel, Dorrit Cohn, and Gérard Genette are examined and the work of Mikhail Bakhtin and Lubomir Doležel utilized in the discussion. In the final section on narrative types White examines representative, expressive, and symbolic narrative. The great virtue of the section on theory for biblical scholars will be the amount of analytical work done on many of the major literary theorists (Bakhtin's work is a major area of analysis worthy of study by the Guild). Narrative structure is constituted by narrator's discourse plus character's discourse (DN + DC); it is these discourse modes which structure White's analysis of the Genesis narratives. In what I would regard as being among the finest readings of the Genesis narratives with which I am familiar White offers a superb reading of these (virtually inexhaustible) narratives. This book is also the most mature 'first book' by a biblical scholar which I have ever read. Thoroughly recommended, it will enhance the reader's knowledge of theory while also increasing their appreciation of the narratives in Genesis.   R. P. CARROLL

VAN WOLDE, E. J.: *A Semiotic Analysis of Genesis 2–3. A Semiotic Theory and Method of Analysis Applied to the Story of the Garden of Eden* (Studia Semitica Neerlandica, 25). 1989. Pp. 244. (Van Gorcum, Assen/ Maastricht. Price: fl. 42.50. ISBN 90 232 2433 7)

Ellen van Wolde's dissertation is the first fruit of study spent with Umberto Eco in Bologna and at the Pontificium Institutum Biblicum in Rome. As a semiotic study of Genesis 2–3 it moves away from the diachronic study of the text and conventional biblical scholarship's obsession with the prehistory of the text in order to find what is decisive for meaning in the textual elements in their interrelationship with each other and the reader. One third of her book analyses the semiotics of Greimas and Peirce in order to produce a homologated and operationalized approach to narrative texts (analysis of the expression forms, narrative analysis, semantic analysis, discursive analysis, communicative analysis). The other two thirds analyse Genesis 2–3 in accordance with her developed semiotic approach. There are many diagrams, sketches, and much technical jargon in the book, but the arguments can be followed with no difficulty by the intelligent reader. The footnotes provide a constant conversation with the secondary literature on Genesis. Throughout the book there is a strong development of the strategies involved in the reading of texts process — 'the text steers the reader by means of strategic designs, while at the same time the reader's own influence on this process of meaning generation increasingly grows' (p. 210) — and this will prove one of the real benefits of studying this book. One of the other most positive features of her book is her reading of Genesis 2–3 as a discursive network in which 'the reader interprets Gen 2–3 as a creation story in which

LITERARY CRITICISM AND INTRODUCTION   97

man himself is not central, one in which the development of a total of correlations forms the nucleus. Within the correlation, the one between YHWH God, man, and earth is the central one and the development of the other correlations which define man is analogous but subordinate.' (p. 229) That reading of Genesis 2–3 is a distinct improvement on the more conventional Augustinian one of the story as the 'Fall' of man. An interesting, even fascinating, analysis of an ancient story and therefore a book worth reading.

R. P. CARROLL

ZUCKERMAN, B.: *Job the Silent. A Study in Historical Counterpoint*. 1991. Pp. viii, 294. (Oxford University Press, New York, Oxford. Price: £26.00. ISBN 0 19 505896 8)

This book is a *tour de force*, an impressive achievement and a good read. Zuckerman ranges over many of the critical problems in the study of Job from the vantage point of a nineteenth-century Yiddish short story about a Job-like figure, 'Bontsye Schvayg' ('Bontsye the Silent') by Y. L. Perets. This is the principal 'historical counterpoint' of the title. Bontsye suffers perpetually without complaining all his life long, and the reader becomes convinced that he is the most pious man on earth — as also the heavenly court after his death thinks. But in the last five words of the story it is revealed (if you believe Zuckerman) that Bontsye is not the most pious of men but the most stupid, the ultimate *schlemiel*, and the story becomes a 'parody of piety'. Likewise the poet of Job created a parody of the traditional prose tale of Job, turning him from a patient silent sufferer into an impatient and vocal challenger of God. The irony is that, as with Bontsye, who became an archetypal and paradigmatic Jewish sufferer, the parody of Job went unrecognized by later readers (as in *The Testament of Job* and the Epistle of James) and the moralistic interpretation won out. In a way, Zuckerman's whole thesis rests on his reading of the heavenly prosecutor's laugh in the last words of 'Bontsye Schvayg'; but even if you read it not as a laugh of triumph but (as I did) as an expression of chagrin, not bitter, perhaps even affectionate, the voyage Zuckerman takes us on s still a rewarding one.

D. J. A. CLINES

7. LAW, RELIGION, AND THEOLOGY

ACHENBACH, R.: *Israel zwischen Verheissung und Gebot* (Europäische Hochschulschriften Reihe XXIII Theologie Band 422). 1991. Pp. ix, 442. (Lang, Frankfurt (Main)–Bern–New York–Paris. Price: SwFr 35.00. ISBN 3 631 43847 8; ISSN 0721 3409)

This dissertation was presented in 1989 to the Faculty of the University of Göttingen, where the author's research was supervised by Professor L. Perlitt. It contains a detailed and well-documented literary critical analysis of Deuteronomy 5–11. After an introduction discussing the pre-history and the literary history of the section, the analysis is based on a breakdown of the seven chapters into five main parts. In the first (4:45–49; 5:1–6:3), called the aetiology of deuteronomic law, particular attention is paid to the Horeb covenant and the Decalogue. God's exclusive demand upon Israel is the subject of Deut. 6, and there is a comparison between parts of this chapter and Josh. 24:1–28. The section on Israel and the nations, which is the title given to Deut. 7, focuses on the ban, the war tradition, and Israel's election. The analysis of Deut. 8, dealing with Israel between the desert and the promised land, is accompanied by an excursus on Israel in the wilderness period in the light of Jeremiah and Hosea. In the final part on Israel and law there is an

98 LAW, RELIGION, AND THEOLOGY

analysis of Deut. 9–11 with an excursus on the Levites. The various strings are brought together in a final short chapter which gives the book its title. Although the detail of the analysis and the rather heavy dissertation format of the work make it tedious to read, the author has given a well-structured and meticulous presentation and has been careful in drawing his conclusions.

G. H. Jones

ADDINALL, P.: *Philosophy and Biblical Interpretation. A Study in Nineteenth-Century Conflict*. 1991. Pp. xii, 330. (Cambridge University Press. Price: £35.00 ($54.50). ISBN 0 521 40423 1)

This book is based on Peter Addinall's doctoral thesis done at Sheffield under the supervision of Professor John Rogerson. The central focus of the book is the conflict between religion and science in Britain in the nineteenth century, and in particular the various responses to David Hume's critique of religion, especially those influenced by William Paley. Addinall's thesis, stated in the simplest of terms, is that British apologists for religion made a serious mistake in following Paley's apologetics. They would have been much better served if they had followed Kant's response to Hume. The substance of the book then is a 'history of ideas' approach to a period of serious ideological conflict. Much attention is paid to Hume's critique, Paley's attempted rebuttal of it in his *Natural Theology*, various Paleyesque writings of the period (esp. the Bridgewater treatises), and Kant's critical philosophy of religion. There is a wealth of information and informed discussion of 'battles long ago' in this book which will make it a most useful reference work for theologians and biblical scholars wishing to find out more about the history of their subject. Figures such as Thomas Chalmers and Hugh Miller (well-known to Scots and those who work in Scotland) appear here, as well as fine treatments of conservative and liberal attitudes to natural theology. Addinall sees the response to Hume as having been an inadequate metaphysical one which made critical scholarship the enemy rather than a necessity in the conflict. This came about because 'British natural theology was flawed and inadequate, and weakness on this front involved the desperate attempt to preserve inherited notions of revelation on the other, and the implicit obligation to preserve the text, the whole text, and nothing but the text.' (p. 137) Addinall offers a lengthy analysis of Kant's critical philosophy, especially in terms of his moral and religious philosophy and his thinking on religion. Kant's thought reflects 'paradoxes woven inextricably into the fabric of human experience' (pp. 260f) and the development of Kantian insights into the nature of moral experience in the direction of a genuinely critical philosophy would, according to Addinall, have aided in the construction of a strong case for religion against the serious weakness of an empirically based scepticism. A very interesting, informative book which should be read by all biblical scholars, though personally I'm inclined to think that Addinall is far too optimistic in imagining that many British scholars are going to read (let alone understand) Kant.

R. P. Carroll

ALONSO SCHÖKEL, L. and ARTOLA, A. M. (eds): *La Palabra de Dios en la Historia de los Hombres. Comentario Temático a la Constitución "Dei Verbum" del Vaticano II sobre la Divina Revelación*. 1991. Pp. 702. (Ediciones Mensajero, Bilbao; Universidad de Deusto, Bilbao)

This volume was published to commemorate the twenty-fifth anniversary of the promulgation of the Constitution DEI VERBUM, delivered at the Second Vatican Council in 1965. The Constitution presented the Catholic Church's approach to the scriptures and this volume contains the latin text in its progressive versions, its Spanish translation and an exhaustive commentary

LAW, RELIGION, AND THEOLOGY   99

on its contents with excellent bibliographies, and references. Although there are numerous references to historical and critical study, the writers are much more concerned to examine the Catholic theology of revelation and the place of the scriptures in the thought and practice of Catholic Christianity. Hence the unity of the testaments is seen as resulting from the centrality of Christ and his place in Salvation History.

So far as the Old Testament is concerned, emphasis is placed upon the historic character of the revelation and due regard is paid to a progressive understanding of god's nature and purpose. The books of the Old Testament are not considered so much in their own historical contexts as in their preparatory character, looking for fulfilment or completing in Christ, seen as the Mediator and Plenitude of revelation. As a result stress is laid upon the typological use of the Old Testament. There is an interesting section of the communication of the scriptural message through preaching and the paranetic character of Deuteronomy is given as a paradigm — with the call to repentance seen as a leading theme. In a book of this kind, clearly the most valuable material is that devoted to the New Testament, introducing, as it does, many modern critical and hermeneutical approaches   R. HAMMER

ASSMANN, J. and SUNDERMEIER, T. (eds): *Das Fest und das Heilige. Religiöse Kontrapunkte zur Alltagswelt* (Studien zum Verstehen fremder Religionen 1). 1991. Pp. 253. (Gütersloher Verlagshaus (Gerd Mohn), Gütersloh. Price: DM 78.00. ISBN 3 579 01783 7)

The first two chapters and the last chapter in this volume are concerned with the nature of a religious festival as such, seeing it as the counterpart to the life of every day and as the setting through which human beings enter a different sphere of existence and a different time-dimension. In between, various experts discuss aspects of festivals in diverse cultures, ancient Egypt, first-century Christianity, Greece and Rome, Persia, Africa, and India. A distinct section considers anti-festival tendencies in Gnosticism, among the Puritans, and in contemporary fundamentalist Iran. All these contributions are worth reading but the main concern of the *Book List* is represented by two essays under the heading 'Theologie des Festes', one by Rolf Rendtorff on ancient Israel, the other by Matthias Klinghardt on the Sabbath and Sunday in early Judaism and Christianity. The former is somewhat disappointing given the particular scope of the book as a whole: it deals solely with the historical development of the Old Testament festival calendars; it says little that is unfamiliar and hardly considers at all the real significance of festivals in Israel's life and religion, which has been so prominent a theme in much recent scholarship. Klinghardt's chapter, on the other hand, surveys a wide range of not easily accessible material and provides a comprehensive and original account of both the similarities and differences between Jewish Sabbath and Christian Sunday at this particular period.   J. R. PORTER

BARBIERO, G.: *L'Asino del Nemico. Rinuncia alla vendetta e amore del nemico nella legislazione dell'Antico Testamento (Es 23, 4–5; Dt 22, 1–4; Lv 19, 17–18)* (Analecta Biblica 128). 1991. Pp. xi, 418. (Editrice Pontificio Istituto Biblico, Roma. Price: Lire 40,000. ISBN 88 7653 128 9)

The principal topic of this very detailed study is non-violence in interpersonal relationships as expressed in the concrete forms of giving up revenge and loving one's enemy. B. combines a sociological approach with a close reading of the texts involved. He also cites and discusses a whole range of relevant passages from the literature of ancient Egypt, Mesopotamia, Anatolia, and Syria, as well as from the writings of Qumran. The author demonstrates that the exilic passage Lev. 19:17–18 is dependent on Deut. 22:1–4

4*

100 LAW, RELIGION, AND THEOLOGY

which, he shows, derives from Exod. 23:4–5. He concludes that the three passages in question show the development of Old Testament legislation concerning personal enemies. Also, each in turn reflects the type of society outlined in the Code of the Alliance, in Deuteronomy, and in the Holiness Code. In the final chapter he extends his findings to the New Testament. There are two brief excursuses, on the Israelite village in the period before the monarchy and on juridical immunity in segmentary societies. Indices and a bibliography are provided. The author's findings should lead to a re-evaluation of the traditional view of Old Testament ethics.

W. G. E. Watson

BARKER, M.: *The Gate of Heaven. The History and Symbolism of the Temple in Jerusalem.* 1991. Pp. 198. (SPCK, London. Price: £10.99. ISBN 0 281 04510 0)

Here is an example of that unfortunately rather rare genre among scholarly works — the 'good read'! There are aspects of the detective story here as Margaret Barker follows clues in Old Testament, Intertestamental, and New Testament literature, extra-biblical sources (primarily Jewish and Christian), and Christian hymnody. It is her claim that What gave life to the New Testament and shaped the early Christian liturgies was the mythology of the Old Testament centred on the temple (p. 179).

After a brief survey of the history of the Jerusalem temple, its construc-tion, furnishings and cult, the mythology associated with the temple is discussed under three main headings (the Garden, the Veil, the Throne), and its influence on subsequent Jewish and early Christian thought is traced, and it is suggested that imagery derived from this mythology continued to affect the language of some familiar hymns. The temple, representing the Garden of Eden, was a place of creation and renewal. Its veil symbolized the boundary between the natural and spiritual worlds, so it was a place of meditation and atonement. The temple was a place where some would pass beyond the veil to experience the vision of the throne of God. As an illustration of the type of connection made by Barker, the example of the Tree of Life can be cited. Links are traced between the tree, the *menorah*, the lamp as symbol of God and king (was Isa. 42 using the imagery of a broken *memorah* to describe a king's fate?), Wisdom as a tree, Jesus as light and vine, and the cross sometimes depicted as combined with a lamp in early Christian art (pp. 90–95).

It is perhaps not surprising that some of the connections are clearer, and therefore some of the paths easier to follow (from the point of view of convincingness of argument rather than clarity of presentation) that others. It is sometimes necessary to allow the possibility that some premises may be correct, before going on to subsequent stages of an argument. There are claims which not all will find easy to accept, e.g. that Jeremiah was a priest (p. 47), or that the ancient cult believed the king to be both an earthly king and a heavenly patron, an angelic being (p. 73). While there may be some speculation there is much stimulation here. The reader will tread some paths which are familiar and some which to the writer of this notice were quite unfamiliar. It was a worthwhile journey! A. H. W. Curtis

BARTH, C.: *God with Us. A Theological Introduction to the Old Testa-ment.* Edited by Geoffrey W. Bromiley. 1991. Pp. x, 403. (Eerdmans, Grand Rapids MI. Price: $29.95. ISBN 0 8028 3680 1)

This is an edited version by G. W. Bromiley of a theological introduction to the Old Testament published in Indonesia between 1970 and 1990. It makes no claim to wrestle with methodological problems. The material is presented

LAW, RELIGION, AND THEOLOGY 101

in nine sections following the order in the Old Testament: God Created Heaven and Earth, God Chose the Fathers of Israel, God brought Israel out of Egypt, God led his People through the Wilderness, God Revealed Himself at Sinai, God Granted Israel the Land of Canaan, God Raised up Kings in Israel, God Chose Jerusalem, God Sent His Prophets. A brief conclusion points to the links with the New Testament. The supreme value of this book lies in its rich quarrying of material under each heading. The discussion of texts is lucid and often illuminating. It is arguable that the material cannot be so easily integrated as this approach suggests, but here is the raw material which in one way or another must be shaped into an Old Testament theology. It is a fitting memorial to the pastoral concerns and the academic integrity of its author.

R. DAVIDSON

BORI, P. C.: *L'Interpretation Infinie. L'hermeneutique chrétienne ancienne et ses transformations.* Translated from Italian by F. Vial. 1991. Pp. 148. (Cerf, Paris. Price: Fr 120.00. ISBN 2 204 04156 4)

This mature and intelligent essay on hermeneutics ranges from Greek antiquity to modern times, but its main focus is on the key figure of Gregory the Great. Bori traces the pre-history of Gregory's hermeneutics (notably in Philo and Origen), and also the subsequent history of his underlying principles. His aim is to show that it is erroneous to regard hermeneutics in the contemporary secular sense as something that originates in the Enlightenment and has no earlier roots. The book was published in Italian in 1987; an English translation would be welcome.

· N. R. M. DE LANGE

BRETT, M. G.: *Biblical Criticism in Crisis? The impact of the canonical approach on Old Testament studies.* 1991. Pp. xiii, 237. (Cambridge University Press. Price: £30.00 ($44.50). ISBN 0 521 40119 4)

Childs's canonical approach has been compared with various modern intellectual trends, but no book ranges more widely in so doing than this one: New Criticism, synchronic linguistics, intratextual theology, critique of ideology, anti-foundationalist philosophy, you name it, it's in here. How does all this bear upon Childs? His own statements about his approach are here subjected to severe criticism for vagueness, self-contradiction, and equivocation. Not all criticisms of Childs, however, have been justified. In fact there is a path which may lead to a more 'charitable' view: that path leads through Gadamer's view of 'the classic', corrected by Popper, transmitted through Jauss, associated with Lindbeck's intratextual theology, accepting a close relatedness with the many 'literary' approaches now current, and all this will validate the canonical approach so long as it works in a pluralistic context as one approach among others. If this is so, then the question asked in the book's title is answered: there is no crisis after all. This may indeed be the way in which canonical criticism will develop, and salutarily. The author's critical sense is keen, and he writes very well, or would have done so if he had avoided the neologisms *emic* and *etic* which most readers will find annoying and obfuscating. For biblical scholars interested in the impact of these modern trends, this is an informative work, with rich bibliography, including a special listing of Childs's own publications.

Is there anything negative to be said? Well, there is. Remarkably, Brett seems to do nothing to prepare his readers for the most likely eventuality, namely that Childs, presented with this charitable proposal, will say no to the whole thing. If he does, it must mean that the problems lie at a deeper level than Brett's careful analysis has reached. On the one hand, with some minor exceptions Brett seems to accept too readily the general world-picture upon which the canonical movement was built. Some of his discussion is heavily

102   LAW, RELIGION, AND THEOLOGY

derivative and some goes back over well-trodden ground. And he misreads some things: he devotes much space to arguing that, when this reviewer points to the absence of a 'scripture' in the biblical period and the consequent 'anachronism' of later attitudes to the Bible, this is not a serious criticism of Childs's work. I never said, or thought, that it was. Unlike many others who have tried to adapt Gadamer's ideas to biblical interpretation, Brett perceives that they are liable to criticism, but he gives these criticisms little room (brushing aside, for instance, the important discussion by Oeming) and, like most of these others, proceeds as if Gadamer's views are self-evidently valid. Similarly, his analysis of particular statements of Childs is good, but he does not explain the deeper interrelations so well. Thus, though Karl Barth is mentioned, nothing is said about him in depth. What makes Childs appear confused, equivocating, impatient, and totalitarian (all terms actually used by Brett)? Is it just a personal weakness or is there some principle behind it all? Why, when Lindbeck's intratextuality comes so close to the canonical approach, is Childs so against it (pp. 164 and especially 180 n. 24)? And, most important: is Childs willing that his approach should depend upon the support of postmodern intellectual tendencies, however influential; or will he feel that such a support will actually do damage to his own ultimate convictions? Does canonical thinking rest upon divine revelation, or is it like liberal theology before it, a distillation of our end-of-century Zeitgeist?

J. BARR

BROOKS,R. and COLLINS, J. J. (eds): *Hebrew Bible or Old Testament? Studying the Bible in Judaism and Christianity* (Christianity and Judaism in Antiquity 5). 1990. Pp. xiv. 242. (University of Notre Dame Press, Indiana. Price: £18.95. ISBN 0 268 01900)

Nicely the outer cover of this important collection of essays interposes between the English title and sub-title the Hebrew words of Psalm 62:12 — 'One thing has God spoken, these two things have I heard . . .'. The papers, first presented at a conference in 1989 at the University of Notre Dame where seven of the thirteen contributors teach, are organized in three sections, with the mostly large-scale programmatic essays in the first two, and shorter worked examples in the third. Under What's in a Name? The Problem of What We Study, R. E. Murphy gives a useful lead in his discussion of 'Old Testament/ *Tanakh* — Canon and Interpretation', though he presupposes that the theologian believes, while the historian (of religion) interprets 'with empathy no doubt'. J. M. Ford develops three of his themes in 'The New Covenant, Jesus, and Canonization': she parallels the Qumran sect and Christianity as new covenant communities, reports her interest in Wyschogrod's contention that Paul remained an Orthodox Jew, and notes the importance of liturgy in shaping canon. J. A. Sanders, writing one of the fullest articles, offers a wealth of text-historical information in his 'Hebrew Bible *and* Old Testament: Textual Criticism in Service of Biblical Studies'. And E. Ulrich, offering 'Jewish, Christian, and Empirical Perspectives on the Text of our Scriptures', urges that as with the New Testament and the *textus receptus* so the Masoretic text is no longer the best we can provide.

In the Section, The Theological Costs of Historical-Critical Study, R. Rendtdorff writes 'Toward a Common Jewish-Christian Reading of the Hebrew Bible'; J. D. Levenson, 'Theological Consensus or Historicist Evasion? Jews and Christians in Biblical Studies'; J. Blenkinsopp, 'Theological Honesty through History'; and D. Levenson, 'Different Texts or Different Quests? The Contexts of Biblical Studies'. Rendtorff pleads for a common reading of a Hebrew Bible which was prior to both Judaism and Christianity, and for a step by step discussion of texts and topics rather than general hermeneutical questions. However, Jon Levenson insists in the longest and most powerful piece in the volume that such a neutral meeting ground may

LAW, RELIGION, AND THEOLOGY 103

encourage each tradition to vanish 'into the past in which neither had as yet emerged'. Blenkinsopp is closer to Rendtorff's position; and David Levenson, while warm about the value of grappling with the meaning of a text within the open academy, doubts the virtue of basing common theology for individual communities on historical meanings of the Hebrew Scriptures.

Finally, Reading Religious Texts in Community heads seven mostly shorter pieces, illustrating some of these issues and introducing still more: 'Cain and Abel in Fact and Fable: Genesis 4:1–16' (J. L. Kugel), 'Humanity in God's Image: Rabbinic Biblical Theology and Genesis 1:26–28' (Brooks), 'The Historical-Critical and Feminist Readings of Genesis 1:26–28' (A. Y. Collins), 'The Suffering Servant: Isaiah Chapter 53 as a Christian Text' (A. Y. Collins), 'A Christological Suffering Servant? The Jewish Retreat into Historical Criticism' (Brooks), 'Divine Love Poetry: The Song of Songs' (C. Kannengiesser), and 'The Song of Songs in Comparative Perspective' (A. Y. Collins).

A. G. AULD

BRUEGGEMANN, W.: *Abiding Astonishment; Psalms, Modernity, and the Making of History* (Literary Currents in Biblical Interpretation). 1991. Pp. 94. (Westminster/John Knox Press, Louisville, Kentucky. Price: $8.95. ISBN 0 664 25134 X)

This work has developed from a lecture on the 'historical psalms' (Psalms 78, 105, 106, 136). These are seen as rhetorical acts which shape the past and exclude rival shapings. They mediated the past to the present, the past as it was so shaped and remembered. The 'history' in these texts is a mode of rhetoric, and modern use still participates in its exercise of power.

It is valuable to have Brueggemann's theological mind focused on this small part of the Psalter. He sees the recital of these psalms as making a world which is 'intergenerational, covenantly shaped, morally serious, dialogically open, and politically demanding'. An indispensable ingredient is the element of miracle, the new and awesome ingressions of God, evoking 'abiding astonishment', the creative reaction perpetuated by the recitals.

The book proceeds to consider the contrast with the modern 'histories of Israel' and, at the other extreme, the 'complacent insiders' who fasten on to the shaped history to support certain kinds of human domination. Old questions of history and faith are considered in a modern context. This is a thoughtful, stimulating, and well-documented little discussion.

J. H. EATON

BURKE, D.: *Genesis to Jesus: Making sense of the Old Testament.* 1991. Pp. 96. (Frameworks, Leicester. Price: £3.25. ISBN 0 85111 219 6)

This is a résumé of Old Testament history for the beginner, written from a semi-fundamentalist Christian perspective. The English is readily intelligible, and the diagrams and maps clear; but at least every second statement is of questionable accuracy.

B. P. ROBINSON

CARROLL, R. P.: *Wolf in the Sheepfold. The Bible as a Problem for Christianity.* 1991. Pp. xi, 159. (SPCK, London. Price: £9.99. ISBN 0 281 04525 9)

The theme of this passionately and pungently written study is 'the ecclesiastical captivity of the Bible' (p. xi). Carroll wants to liberate the Bible from the Philistines (p. 31), to wit theologians, so that it can be read critically, not as a sacred text but as literature with life-changing possibilities. Down the centuries believers have taken the metaphorical language of the Bible in a

104 LAW, RELIGION, AND THEOLOGY

substantive sense, and have imposed a bogus unity on the Bible's discrete and contradictory parts. As for evangelical claims to have a 'Biblical Christianity', they are a dangerous chimera. Many of the problems that Carroll identifies are real enough, and have too often been glossed over, but many readers will feel that he too often spoils a good case by overstating it. Thus while it is true that the method of classical theology owes much to Greek philosophy the claim that theology 'does not need the Bible in order to do its work' (p. 56) is very questionable. There is also a degree of repetition in the book, and the language tends at times to lurch from the academic and technical to the demotic and back.

B. P. ROBINSON

DARR, K. P.: *Far More Precious than Jewels. Perspectives on Biblical Women* (Gender and the Biblical Tradition). 1991. Pp. 223. (Westminster/ John Knox Press, Louisville. Price: $15.95. ISBN 0 664 25107 2)

The four women whose stories are told here are Ruth, Sarah, Hagar, and Esther; the three perspectives chosen are the modern critical approach, the rabbinical, and the feminist, and a useful first chapter describes the methods and significance of each. The author argues that for the enrichment of ideas and judgments 'literary interpretation — including biblical interpretation — must be a dialogue among members of more than a single constituency'. The discussion is well presented and is suited to a wide readership including those not already familiar with the biblical narratives. Something of the flavour of the book is seen in the summary of the chapter on Ruth: 'Who is Ruth? A Paradigm of faithfulness, a puppet in the service of patriarchy, or a radical call to inclusiveness?' The discussion of Esther well illustrates the diversity of feminist views; is Esther simply 'the stereotypical woman in a man's world' (Laffey) or was her conduct 'a masterpiece of feminine skill' (White)? The bibliography is particularly useful as a guide to feminist writings.

G. I. EMMERSON

DEISSLER, A.: *Was wird am Ende der Tage geschehen? Biblische Visionen der Zukunft.* 1991. Pp. 112. (Herder, Freiburg–Basel–Wien. Price: DM 16.80. ISBN 3 451 22190 X)

This very readable, straightforward paperback surveys Old Testament material relating to Israel's ultimate hopes for the world, the people, and the individual. It summarizes the content of passages one by one in the light of mainstream German traditio-historical convictions and against the passages' presumed historical background. This inevitably involves rather brief explanations of often controverted critical questions; similarly the book has to take up positions on matters such as the interpretation of the Psalms which there is hardly space to argue. It sometimes notes points at which the New Testament takes up Old Testament passages, but does not otherwise seek to get under the surface of their theological implications and eschews the attempt to interrelate them, in the conviction expressed in the conclusion that they are better treated as imaginative variations on the one theme that Yahweh is the God of the future.

J. GOLDINGAY

EBACH, J., MARQUARDT, F.-W., PAULY, D., SCHELLONG, D. and WEINRICH, M.: *Die Bibel gehört nicht uns* (Einwürfe 6). 1990. Pp. 207. (Kaiser, München. Price: DM 32.00. ISBN 3 459 01867 4)

This volume, sixth in an almost annual series which began in 1983, contains five essays linked only by their attempt to open new approaches to biblical texts and by the conviction of their authors that understanding the

LAW, RELIGION, AND THEOLOGY

Bible requires to be liberated from our expectations of it. D. Schellong enquires further about the quest of the historical Jesus: 'why do you look for the living among the dead ?' M. Weinrich's 'humble victors' reports two case studies on fundamentalist and evangelical biblical interpretation. D. Pauly studies Luke 16:1–13 under the title 'God or Mammon: the reinstatement of the economy'. F.-W. Marquardt reports on a biblical way of reading the Bible: Frans Breukelman's Biblical Theology. But the essay of perhaps most interest to readers of the *Book List* is J. Ebach's thoughtful triple passage through Qohelet 3:1–15 under the title '. . . and a time for exposition of Qoh. 3: on the links between exegesis and time'.

A. G. AULD

GALEY, J.-C. (ed.): *Kingship and Kings*. 1990. Pp. v, 280. (Harwood Academic Publishers, Chur (CH) — London–Paris–New York. Price: $54.00. ISBN 3 7186 5066 5)

One essay from this collection of seven will be of direct concern to *Book List* readers: that by A. Caquot on Kingship in ancient Israel. This is an analysis of the development and distinctive features of the institution in Israel and Judah within the cultural context of the Levant, influenced as were all the petty local monarchies by the elaborate ideologies of the great powers of the age. Caquot invites a reassessment of various common views. The so-called 'anti-royalist version' in the conflate 1 Sam. 8–12 is rather positively disposed towards kingship, and it is only the later incorporation of certain deutero-nomistic asides into the text, at 8:7c; 10:18, 19a and 12:12c, following the discontinuation of the monarchy, and resulting in the transference of the idea of monarchical rule to Yahweh, that any devaluation of the older view took place. Anti-monarchical sentiments alleged among the prophets are to be traced back to Hosea, who objected not to the institution but to its schismatic northern form, his ideal being expressed in Hos. 3:5. The law on kingship in Deut. 17:14–20 is directed not against Solomon and his excesses, but is concerned that a foreign dynast might seize power, and thus implicitly endorses the davidic line. Caquot thinks that scholars have overreacted against the myth-and-ritual theories of Hooke et al., and thus tended to underestimate the extent of royal imagery in the Psalms and other poetical texts. The study concludes with some observations on the problem of the coronation, and on the transference of royal motifs in the hellenistic period to the high priest and the Hasmonean rulers, and the rise of messianic aspirations.

N. WYATT

HASEL, G. F.: *Old Testament Theology. Basic Issues in the Current Debate*. 4th edition, revised and expanded. 1991. Pp. x, 262. (Eerdmans, Grand Rapids MI. Price: $14.95. ISBN 0 8028 0537 X)

This is a further update of the work which originally appeared in 1972 (*B.L.* 1974, pp. 68f) and now is enlarged by more than fifty pages from the third edition (1982). It is essentially concerned with the methodology of Old Testament theology and begins with a survey and critique of the major attempts to present such a discipline. It singles out three main areas of contention, the first of which is the history of tradition, focusing on the interpretation of a saving history by which Israel is related to God. The second looks at efforts to define a centre to the Old Testament. The third examines the extent to which the relationship between the Old and New Testaments can properly be taken into account in an Old Testament theology. As a biblio-graphical essay the volume is a valuable text-book, although it does not move

106 LAW, RELIGION, AND THEOLOGY

far in resolving the more strongly debated areas which it notes. It has evidently met a real need for a study explaining why the subject has elicited such markedly different approaches.

R. E. CLEMENTS

HEYMEL, M.: *Zur Verherrlichung Israels. Vorträge und Predigten.* 1990. Pp. 204. (Lang, Frankfurt (Main)–Bern–New York–Paris. Price: SwFr 26.00. ISBN 3 631 42793 X)

The lectures and sermons collected in this book represent an attempt at Christian apologetic which takes seriously the Hebrew scriptures and Jewish exegesis of them. They express a concern to recognize the Christian debt to Israel; to acknowledge the common debt of both communities to the Torah; to recognize the divine election of the descendants of Abraham and to see in the Messiahship of Jesus a confirmation of this election, the one in whom God's 'glorification' of Israel finds its climax. It thus urges Christians to recognize their common bond with the Jewish people. With the re-emergence of signs of anti-Semitism in many parts of the world it is particularly good to see such concerns being expressed by a German minister. He is pleading for Christians and Jews to discover together how much they have in common while he does not seek to plane down the hard edges of difference.

R. A. MASON

Ho, A.: *Ṣedeq and Ṣedaqah in the Hebrew Bible* (American University Studies Series, VII: Theology and Religion, Vol. 78). 1991. Pp. 212. (Lang, Bern, New York. Price: DM 24.00. ISBN 0 8204 1349 6; ISSN 0740 0446)

This book examines the two Hebrew words of the title in detailed contextual study of their occurrences in the Hebrew Bible, concluding that their meanings, often taken to be synonymous, differ in certain respects. An introduction describes methods of study commonly used for such examinations, and judges contextual study to be preferable by far to comparative philology. After surveying treatments of both words in research, she examines them separately on each occurrence in narrative (including Deuteronomy), wisdom (including Psalms), and prophets. Then twenty-one 'main conclusions' are offered. Hebrew type is used which is not always clear: such vowel points and dageshes which do appear are strangly random and sometimes wrong.

Bibliographical coverage seems wide: 152 works are cited including eighteen in Hebrew; it seems strange that in such 'in-depth philological research' neither D. W. Thomas nor G. R. Driver appear. Comparative philology and etymology are here subordinated to contextual study too much.

J. G. SNAITH

HOUTMAN, C.: *Het altaar als asielplaats. Beschouwingen over en naar aanleiding van Exodus 21:12–14* (Kamper Cahiers, 70). 1990. Pp. 89. (Kok, Kampen. Price: fl. 19.90. ISBN 90 242 3250 3; ISSN 0923 120 X)

Houtman has already published two large volumes of a commentary on Exodus, which cover chapters 1–19 (see *B.L.* 1987, p. 50; 1990, p. 56), and this monograph (the annotated text of his inaugural lecture at Kampen) gives a foretaste of what can be expected from his treatment of the legal texts in the third volume. He holds that in Exodus 21:12–14 asylum is provided for a person who kills someone while not in full control of himself (e.g. because of a fit of passion or through drunkenness), rather than as a result of a chance encounter, as some others have thought; and he thinks that those seeking asylum would have been investigated by a local (lay) court rather than by

LAW, RELIGION, AND THEOLOGY 107

priestly divination. Re-entry into the community may have been achieved by negotiations with the victim's family. There are also illuminating comparisons with the related passages in Numbers 35, Deuteronomy 19, and 1 Kings 1–2, an interesting discussion of the (once again topical) practice of using churches as places of asylum, and a select bibliography.

G. I. DAVIES

KAISER, W. C.: *Hard Sayings of the Old Testament*. 1991. Pp. 259. (Hodder and Stoughton, London. Price: £7.99. ISBN 0 340 54617 4)

This study of 73 hard sayings in the Old Testament, for which no explanation seems to be given or which seem to contradict other portions of Scripture, will no doubt satisfy those who share the author's conservative approach to the Bible. Others may wonder whether the hardness does not lie rather in the author's critical assumptions, the discussions of where Cain got his wife from (pp. 38–39) and of Psalm 81:1 providing classic examples.

R. DAVIDSON

KLEIN, H.: *Leben neu entdecken; Entwurf einer Biblischen Theologie* (Calwer Taschenbibliothek 23). 1991. Pp. 246. (Calwer, Stuttgart. Price: DM 29.80. ISBN 3 7668 3138 0)

This outline of a biblical theology by a Rumanian New Testament professor has several noteworthy features. It has the street credibility of a reflection on the nature of human life written about the time of the Rumanian revolution. It illustrates the way in which a study of a specific biblical theme can provide a vantage point which illumines the whole Bible from one angle. And it is interestingly laid out: the pages have a wide margin which is used to provide brief summaries of the text, relevant biblical passages, and occasional scholarly quotations. It begins with the good observation that uncertainty over method in biblical theology ought not to be allowed to hold us back from writing biblical theology, because people will in any case operate with an implicit framework of biblical theology and will interpret scripture in the light of it. I was disappointed that Professor Klein nevertheless still sometimes confines himself to juxtaposing what the various biblical witnesses say and does not quite attempt to state what are the implications of the Bible as a whole for his subject; and I am unhappy with the antithesis 'Old Testament — life, New Testament — new life'.

J. GOLDINGAY

KOCH, R.: *Der Geist Gottes im Alten Testament*. 1991. Pp. 147. (Lang, Frankfurt (Main)–Bern–New York–Paris. Price: SwFr 15.00. ISBN 3 631 43885 0)

The first part of this study considers the fundamental significances of *ruaḥ*, and looks at passages referring to the activity of Yahweh's spirit in Israel's history; the second part considers the exegesis of prophetic passages which refer to Yahweh's spirit, taking up the theme of the author's *Geist und Messias* (Vienna, 1950). The blurb's declaration that 'the texts of the Old Testament speak often and explicitly of the Holy Spirit' raises eyebrows but alerts the reader to the fact that Professor Koch's study is consciously a piece of Christian theology; it is, indeed, consciously a piece of Roman Catholic theology, though works by other writers are taken into account. It is, however, primarily an exegetical study rather than a theological one in the

108 LAW, RELIGION, AND THEOLOGY

sense of a work which goes on to ask what it is that allusions to the spirit actually refer to. The transliteration falters (*racah* and *'äbäd* commonly appear where one expects *ra'ah* and *'äbäd*).

J. GOLDINGAY

LOHFINK, N.: *The Covenant Never Revoked. Biblical Reflections on Christian–Jewish Dialogue.* Translated by John J. Scullion. 1991. Pp. v, 96. (Paulist Press, New York. Price: $7.95. ISBN 0 8091 3228 1)

The German original of this book *Der niemals gekündigte Bund: Exegetische Gedanken zum christlich-jüdischen Dialog*, published in 1989, has already been reviewed in *B.L.* (see 1990, p. 107). The English translation now makes it widely accessible.

R. B. SALTERS

LOHFINK, N.: *Violencia y pacifismo en al Antiguo Testamento* (Coleccion Cristianismo y Sociedad). 1990. Pp. 111. (Desclee de Brouwer, Bilbao. ISBN 84 330 0818 8)

This is a Spanish translation of the two contributions of Lohfink to the composite volume which he edited, *Gewalt und Gewaltlosigkeit im Alten Testament*, and which was commended in *B.L.* 1984, p. 99.

J. R. PORTER

MOLLENKOTT, V. R.: *Gott eine Frau? Vergessene Gottesbilder der Bibel.* Translated by C.-M. Knirck from *The Divine Feminine*. 3rd edition (Beck'sche Reihe 295). 1990. Pp. 139. (Beck, München. Price: DM 14.80. ISBN 3 406 34783 5)

Originally published in the USA as *The Divine Feminine: The Biblical Imagery of God as Female* (1983; not noticed in *B.L.*), the American title gives a fairer idea of the contents of this modest paperback than does that of the translation. After a brief survey showing the persistence of the use of feminine imagery for God throughout the history of the Christian church, a series of short chapters explores a variety of biblical pictures, from both Old and New Testaments, whose implications involve the divine feminine. Elisabeth Moltman-Wendel contributes a brief 'After-word', outlining for German readers three different types of feminist biblical and theological study. Much here is interesting and thought-provoking, though books of this kind tend to be read only by those who already accept the views propounded, and not all of the images are likely to have universal appeal (Jesus as mother?).

R. J. COGGINS

NIEHR, H.: *Der höchste Gott. Alttestamentlicher JHWH-Glaube im Kontext syrisch-kanaanäischer Religion des 1. Jahrtausends v. Chr.* (Beiheft zur Zeitschrift für die alttestamentliche Wissenschaft 190). 1990. Pp. x, 268. (De Gruyter, Berlin. Price: DM 98.00. ISBN 3 11 012342 8; ISSN 0934 2575)

The title of this very important book fails to do justice to the way in which it suggests new answers to some of the most central questions of the history of Israelite and Old Testament religion. Basically, it is an attack on the 'Jerusalem cult-tradition' theory, according to which Israelite religion was influenced by the El religion by way of Jebusite Jerusalem. The author's counter thesis is that Israelite religion developed in the general context of Canaanite religion and that it was the grim experience of Canaanite religion during the reign of Manasseh that inspired the deuteronomic movement to postulate a Canaanite-free origin for Israel's faith. In the post-exilic period two seemingly opposing tendencies shaped Israelite religion and literature: the monotheism

LAW, RELIGION, AND THEOLOGY

of Deutero-Isaiah and the use of Canaanite mythic motifs to articulate belief in Yahweh as the supreme God. The result was the ambiguity in the Old Testament whereby it is both monotheistic and to some extent polytheistic.

The argument is based upon a painstaking study of the religion of Israel's neighbours, with special reference to inscriptions. The Ugaritic evidence is regarded as untypical of Canaanite religion, and close similarities are perceived between the god Baalshemaim who becomes a supreme god in Syria in the first millennium and Yahweh. These developments are considered under the themes of the heavenly judge, the dwelling-place of the supreme god, the lord of creation and chaos, and the relation between the sun god and the supreme god. There are many discussions of Old Testament passages, especially the Psalms. Although in such an ambitious work there are many assertions that one might wish to question, this is a book which cannot be ignored. It draws together some of the newer suggestions about the origin of Israelite religion, it challenges many older, established opinions, and raises questions that future research will have to address.

J. W. ROGERSON

PERDUE, L. G.: *Wisdom in Revolt; Metaphorical Theology in the Book of Jacob* (Journal for the Study of the Old Testament Supplement Series 112; Bible and Literature Series 29). 1991. Pp. 296. (Almond Press, Sheffield. Price: £30.00 ($52.50). ISBN 1 85075 283 4; ISSN 0309 0787; ISSN 0260 4493)

In this substantial study of the Book of Job, Perdue argues that it moves on two mythic levels. The internal structure enacts the tradition where the central metaphor is humanity as slave to the gods, but the pattern also includes creation, revolt against the gods, fall, judgment, and redemption. The external structure of the book expresses the tradition of conflict between the creator and the monstrous chaos. The two mythic traditions interact and intersect; the creator's battle with the monster is mythically transferred to the struggle with Job.

Working through the main parts of the drama, Perdue vividly draws out the nature of the sweeps of metaphor. Searching for knowledge of God and the meaning of existence, Job is found to move through a series of collapsing and emerging worlds, but after the last great deconstruction of mythic reality there emerge the promising beginnings of new creation. Perdue's work is an instructive example of the application of modern literary insights to biblical interpretation. *Job* is an ideal text in which to search with the keys of the science of metaphor. He has made a good exploration, which will stimulate fresh thinking and discussion.

J. H. HEATON

PREUSS, H. D.: *Theologie des Alten Testaments*. Band 1: *JHWHs erwählendes und verpflichtendes Handeln*. 1991. Pp. viii, 330. (Kohlhammer, Stuttgart. ISBN 3 17 011074 8)

It is now more than thirty years since G. von Rad published his Old Testament theology and, in spite of many shorter surveys and publications, no treatment of comparable length has appeared. This gap is now filled by H. D. Preuss, whose work on the subject is planned in two volumes and which endeavours to offer a fully comprehensive treatment. It both promises to be a most valuable study, sharing some perspectives with those of both W. Eichrodt and von Rad, but with full updating of the literature. More especially there is an awareness that critical approaches to the Old Testament have undergone major changes in recent years which require to be taken fully into account.

By giving a summary outline of what is to be included in volume 2 it is possible to form a broad idea of how the finished presentation will appear. The approach is introduced by a survey of the history of the discipline down to

110   LAW, RELIGION, AND THEOLOGY

von Rad. Volume 1 is then divided between two major parts, the first of which presents an overview of the central assertion of the Old Testament that Yahweh has chosen Israel to be his people. The second part then turns its attention to the variety of affirmations and concepts through which the biblical testimony describes the being and activity of God. Accordingly the God–Israel relationship, which Eichrodt focused in the concept of covenant, and which von Rad explored through the tradition of a saving history, is here retained. Preuss presents this feature less narrowly than his predecessors, however, by speaking simply of the elective will of God and of Israel's response. What material is placed where is then left to a rather open series of individual preferences. God's elective will is primarily seen to be focused on the Decalogue, the land, and the divine leadership in war, all of which are themes which require to be referred to again later in the volume. It is not that undue attention is thereby given to such themes, but rather that such a proceeding inevitably tends to hold apart features which belong more closely together. The ark, for instance, is dealt with quite separately from both war and Decalogue, to both of which the Old Testament relates it very closely.

Such points, however, should be regarded as little more than minor quibbles with a very impressive and comprehensive achievement. Any attempt at systematic classification and analysis is forced to make such choices, unless the theology is to be merely a commentary upon the text. The great merit of Preuss's presentation is to have achieved a remarkable degree of comprehensiveness, without forcing the Old Testament material into a straitjacket. Also the larger systematizing headings are sufficiently broad and flexible so as not to intrude too forcefully upon the material they are designed to introduce and explain. That certain topics have to be dealt with in more than one setting is a negative consequence of this.

The need for an Old Testament theology of some kind appears to remain deeply felt among biblical and theological scholars, in spite of the difficulties that its exponents have encountered in trying to sort out methodological issues. Such a discipline provides a desirable text-book for theological studies, bringing out the rich variety of the faith of ancient Israel, which no formal history of the community can provide. Preuss includes valuable bibliographies to each section and gives particular attention to the foundations of Old Testament faith in the life of the ancient Near East. Volume two promises to deal in detail with the cultus and the different agents of divine revelation and administration.

This is clearly a very important book, which must take its place as a major attempt to present the theological content of the Old Testament in the context of its Near Eastern background, without too much discussion of complex hermeneutical issues. It deserves close attention and well merits an English translation.

R. E. CLEMENTS

REITERER, F. V. (ed.): *Ein Gott — Eine Offenbarung. Beiträge zur biblischen Exegese, Theologie und Spiritualität. Festschrift für Notker Füglister OSB zum 60. Geburtstag.* 1991. Pp. 620. (Echter, Würzburg. Price: DM 78.00. ISBN 3 429 01363 1)

These essays by numerous contributors in honour of Notker Füglister cover a wide field, but offer most on the Psalms. The first group contains studies of seven-fold patterns in Deuteronomy, Job's encounter with God, God as king in the call and preaching of Isaiah, the concept of power in the Psalms, the 'new' in Deutero–Isaiah etc., Ben Sira's attitude to work, the theology of giving and receiving in the Psalms, the priestly redaction of Exodus 7–14, canonical exegesis of the Psalms, along with essays on Psalms 26, 48, 50, 87, 93, 120, 127; Isaiah 42:18–25; 51:7; Jeremiah 13:1–11. The second group consists of three essays on New Testament exegesis, including

LAW, RELIGION, AND THEOLOGY   111

Hellenistic analogies to the parables. The third group contains three essays on the Psalms in Benedictine spirituality, including one on the influence of Ps. 22 on Benedictine life. This large collection reflects a tradition of careful and devout scholarship and is provided with useful bibliography.   J. H. EATON

RINGGREN, H.: *Le Religioni dell'Oriente Antico* (Biblioteca di cultura religiosa 58). 1991. Pp. 284. (Paideia Editrice, Brescia. Price: Lire 39,000. ISBN 88 394 0463 5)

This is an Italian translation of the author's *Die Religionen des Alten Orients*, reviewed in *B.L.* 1981, p. 109. It appears to be a straight reproduction of the 1979 German edition: no attempt has been made to up-date the bibliographies.   J. R. PORTER

SCHENKER, A.: *Text und Sinn im Alten Testament: Textgeschichtliche und Bibeltheologische Studien* (Orbis Biblicus et Orientalis 103). 1991. Pp. 302. (Universitätsverlag, Freiburg (CH); Vandenhoeck & Ruprecht, Göttingen. Price: SwFr 75.00. ISBN 3 525 53735 2 (Vandenhoeck); 3 7278 0730 X (Universitätsverlag))

This is a collection of fourteen articles and studies issued by Schenker throughout the late 70s and 80s. They cover a formidable range of interests and texts and show enviable knowledge of many branches of Old Testament and related studies. The most substantial is the first, a study of the 'biblical metaphor' of the Fatherhood of God. Others include a note on popular elements in Old Testament religion (although Schenker is no Morton Smith); the new covenant prophecy of Jeremiah 31 compared with Deuteronomic teaching on covenant; expiatory sacrifice and the significance of 'blood'; the Decalogue and the teaching of the pre-exilic prophets on judgement.

These studies are characterized by erudition but also, in the way of Freiburg, by theological, almost devotional concerns and interests. They range beyond the Old Testament to the use of its language and imagery in the New. Aesthetically it is unfortunate that the individual articles have been reproduced photographically. When it comes to its print system and format this book's name is Legion.   R. A. MASON

SCHÜSSLER FIORENZA, E.: *Bread Not Stone. The Challenge of Feminist Biblical Interpretation*. 1990. Pp. xxv, 182. (T. & T. Clark, Edinburgh. Price: £9.95. ISBN 0 567 29184 8)

This is a carefully argued and challenging approach to the question of feminist biblical interpretation in both church and academic circles. Against those feminists who would discard the biblical tradition as irretrievably patriarchal the author seeks to demonstrate that the Bible is to be seen as a powerful feminist resource. It has functioned not only to legitimatize the subordination of women but to empower those who have struggled against exploitation and oppression in many spheres. Historical criticism is not obsolete, but there is a need for theologians to develop a critical hermeneutics rather than a 'hermeneutics of consent'. There is much useful discussion of various methods of biblical interpretation. The author argues that '*the* litmus test for invoking Scripture as the Word of God must be whether or not biblical texts and traditions seek to end relations of domination and exploitation'. Feminist biblical hermeneutics does not focus on *text* as revelatory word but

112 LAW, RELIGION, AND THEOLOGY

on the story of women as the people of God. Though there is little which relates in any specific way to Old Testament studies, the work is undoubtedly of importance for the whole question of biblical interpretation.

G. I. EMMERSON

SMITH, M. S.: *The Early History of God. Yahweh and the Other Deities in Ancient Israel*. 1990. Pp. xxxiv, 197. (Harper & Row, San Francisco, distributed by T. & T. Clark, Edinburgh. Price: $26.95 (£17.95). ISBN 0 06 067416 4)

The title of this work is somewhat odd and its subject is better indicated by the sub-title. In his Introduction and first chapter, Smith emphasizes the cultural identity of Canaanites and Israelites during Iron Age I and argues that, at this period, Israel's religion included the worship of El, Baal, and Asherah, as well as Yahweh. He rejects the idea that such worship was the product of syncretism with Canaanite religious practices: rather it was 'an instance of old Israelite religion'. But since he regularly speaks of Israel's Canaanite 'heritage' and also considers that at this period Israel possessed its own non-Canaanite Yahwistic traditions — though he does not discuss the significance of these — one wonders how far the distinction is really valid. The second chapter deals with the relationship between Yahweh and Baal and the assimilation of much of the imagery associated with the latter by the former. In the next chapter, 'Yahweh and Ásherah', Smith, following other scholars, sees the asherah in the Yahweh cult as no longer representing a goddess but as an expression of maternal aspects in Yahweh, to which the female imagery occasionally used of him also witnesses. Two further chapters examine the solar imagery employed for Yahweh and practices with regard to the dead and the *mlk* sacrifice. These chapters are rather brief and one notices some important omissions: for instance, in considering Yahweh and the Sun, Smith does not discuss LXX I Kings 8:53 or the theme of Yahweh's help 'in the morning'. Perhaps the most interesting chapter is the one on the development of Israelite monotheism, which the author charts through a chronological process of both convergence of Yahweh with other deities and differentation from them. A final short postscript argues that Yahweh was never a dying god or one who had sexual relationships.

Many of Smith's specific arguments and conclusions are not particularly new. What his work contributes is an overall view of the topic with which he is concerned and a valuable presentation of the most recent archaeological and epigraphical evidence, backed up by very full references to the relevant literature. Detailed discussion sometimes detracts from the clarity of the general argument but this book provides a useful quarry for all students of Israel's early religion.

J. R. PORTER

SUGIRTHARAJAH, R. S.: *Voices from the Margin. Interpreting the Bible in the Third World*. 1991. Pp. ix, 454. (SPCK, London. Price: £15.00. ISBN 0 281 04506 2)

This reader brings together a good range of examples of biblical interpretation emanating from the Third World. The last section ('People, as Exegetes') should be read first; it gives fascinating instances of the repossession of the Bible by ordinary folk in various contexts. Particularly striking is the study of Matt. 26:5–13 tape-recorded by Ernesto Cardenal in a peasant community in Nicaragua. Earlier chapters present a range of ways in which critical scholarship may be put at the service of the people's use of scripture, among which Clodovis Boff's piece on hermeneutics and Itumeleng Mosala's essay on 'The Use of the Bible in Black Theology' are particularly impressive and stimulating. Of special interest to Old Testament specialists are Gustavo

LAW, RELIGION, AND THEOLOGY 113

Gutierrez on Job, and the section on various interpretations of the Exodus. All in all this is a very useful textbook, which puts biblical study today in a broad context and contains many unusual insights.

D. B. FORRESTER

SYKES, S. W. (ed.): *Sacrifice and Redemption. Durham Essays in Theology*. 1991. Pp. xi, 339. (Cambridge University Press. Price: £35.00 ($54.50). ISBN 0 521 34033 0)

Seventeen essays are here gathered together; all the authors have past or present Durham links; and not only is an extremely wide range of topics discussed, but also an equally wide range of opinions is offered as to the centrality and abiding value of the theme of sacrifice. In the contributions of most immediate relevance to *B.L.* interests, D. R. Jones claims that despite the lack of specific Hebrew or Greek words meaning 'sacrifice' the term is rightly frequently found in English versions as reflecting a basic characteristic of the human situation (a view widely challenged elsewhere in the book). R. Hayward, writing about Ecclesiasticus, notes the similarities between the portrayal of wisdom in ch. 24 and of Simon in ch. 50, and suggests that the two pictures illustrate the way in which *torah* incorporates both ritual and ethical requirements. The Hebrew Bible is also referred to by E. Hulmes in an essay rather puzzlingly entitled 'The Semantics of Sacrifice', which sketches comparisons between attitudes to sacrifice in different religious traditions. Other topics discussed in the book include Paul and Hebrews; Athanasius and Augustine; eucharistic language in Syria, the Western Middle Ages, and the Counter-reformation; Puritan usage; Kierkegaard; the Dublin Easter Rising of 1916; Anglican social ethics; Simone Weil; and finally two sharply contrasted doctrinal assessments. It is important, therefore, to recognize that this is a collection of a very different kind from the essays gathered by M. F. C. Bourdillon and M. Fortes under the title *Sacrifice*. Most of the essays here seem to have been completed by *c.* 1983, and the attractive presentation is somewhat marred by curious lapses — the proof-reader seems in places not to have been aware of the names of some of the contributors.

R. J. COGGINS

THEISSEN, G.: *The Open Door. Variations on Biblical Themes*. Translated by John Bowden. 1991. Pp. xii, 191. (SCM, London. Price: £9.95. ISBN 0 334 02510 9)

The first four of these twenty-five sermons to university students were preached from Old Testament texts. Cain and Abel are the subject of what is perhaps the outstanding *tour de force* of the whole collection, as the biblical critic, the sociologist, and the philosopher are called as witnesses at the trial of Cain. But scarcely less telling is the updating of Jeremiah's letter to the exiles into messages for our time, and Theissen's reading of the Jacob and Esau saga and of Isaiah 7:10–16 also abound — as do all these sermons — in wit, surprise, and cogency. An apparently cavalier disregard for traditional exegesis conceals an observant and imaginative hermeneutic closely similar to reader-response criticism. Theissen revels in the richness of the text and then makes it speak incisively to our condition.

C. J. A. HICKLING

TSCHUGGNALL, P.: *Das Abraham-Opfer als Glaubensparadox. Bibeltheologischer Befund — Literarische Rezeption — Kierkegaards Deutung* (Europäische Hochschulschriften, Reihe XXIII, Bd. 399). 1990. Pp. 208. (Lang, Frankfurt (Main)–Bern–New York–Paris. Price: SwFr 23.00. ISBN 3 631 42835 9; ISSN 0721 3409)

The first section conducts a critical exegesis of Genesis 22 and briefly reviews theological and traditio-historical interpretations. The second section

114   LAW, RELIGION, AND THEOLOGY

surveys the reception of the story in philosophy and literature (including, of course, Holocaust writings). The third and longest section deals with the treatment of the Akedah in Kierkegaard's pseudonymous (significantly choosing the name Johannes De Silentio) *Fear and Trembling*, which emphasizes so much Abraham's love for his son (against most modern literary readings, which find the absence of reference to emotion so compelling), and expresses Kierkegaard's notion of belief as existential and paradoxical. A final section reflects on the three preceding lines of interpretation; the theological approach, according to Tschuggnall, viewing the story as one about Abraham's faith, the literary as one of provocation (*Anstoss*) and vexation (*Ärgernis*), and Kierkegaard's as one about the paradox of faith. As a summary of approaches to Genesis 22 this is quite wide-ranging, though the book's emphasis on Kierkegaard unbalances it. A decent dissertation, but a book without an obvious argument or audience.   P. R. Davies

WERBICK, J. (ed.): *Offenbarungsanspruch & fundamentalische Versuchung* (Quaestiones Disputatae). 1991. Pp. 245. (Herder, Freiburg in Breisgau. Price: DM 49.00. ISBN 3 451 02129 3)

Six essays, together with an extended introduction by the editor, deal with fundamentalism, perceived not in the strict sense of Protestant Christian groups with a particular view of the fundamentals of their faith, but in the broader popular sense of rigidly conservative tendencies discernible in many religious traditions. The overall theme is the use of 'revelation' language in significantly different ways. Two essays are of particular relevance to the *Book List*. M. Peek-Horn takes as her starting point Gen. 28:10–22, goes on to other 'revelation' material in the Hebrew Bible, and warns against the attempt to freeze the insights gained therefrom in one particular context; they must be re-applicable to new situations. J. Maier offers an interesting survey of fundamentalist tendencies in Judaism, including some controversial statements relating to the modern state of Israel and the causes and consequences of the Holocaust. Other contributions deal with the New Testament, Church history, relations between Christianity and Islam, and with problems inherent in the communication of religious truths.   R. J. Coggins

WÖLLER, H.: *Vom Vater verwundet. Töchter der Bibel* (Tabus des Christentums). 1991. Pp. 137. (Kreuz, Stuttgart. Price: DM 19.80. ISBN 3 7831 1072 6)

A vigorous denunciation of patriarchy in the biblical and the contemporary world is the main theme of this lively paperback. Its first section reads the stories of women in Genesis and of Jephthah's daughter in terms of the loss of a 'matrizentrisch' culture, involving for women the loss of sexual rights and of choice of partner and the deprivation of legal rights and of priestly duties to the goddess. Later biblical women are seen as betraying their sex by being content to carry out their role according to masculine perceptions; Esther is here interestingly compared with Mrs M. Thatcher. Reading Ezek. 16 in the light of the demands of a 'jealous God' brings out the theme of an incestuous relationship, and this is further explored through various legends and in the light of particular psychological theories, to show how the independent creative gifts of women have been thwarted. At times an infuriating book, whose aggressiveness makes it less compelling than, for example, Phyllis Trible's *Texts of Terror*; but there is food for thought here.   R. J. Coggins

LAW, RELIGION, AND THEOLOGY 115

WRIGHT, C. J. H.: *God's People in God's Land. Family, Land and Property in the Old Testament*. 1990. Pp. xx, 284. (Eerdmans, Grand Rapids MI; Paternoster, Exeter. Price: $16.95. ISBN 0 8028 0321 0; 0 85364 396 2)

This is a revised and updated rewriting of the 1977 Cambridge thesis which laid the foundation for Wright's work in the field of Old Testament ethics that culminated in *Living as the People of God* (1983, title of American edition: *An Eye for an Eye*, *B.L.* 1985, pp. 114–15). In several ways it is a more satisfactory work. Theory is no longer imposed so extensively upon the Old Testament. There is a greater recognition of historical development and a fuller awareness of critical positions. Although the presentation remains at a fairly high theological level and it assumed that the laws reflect the Israelite ethic, an attempt is made to relate the discussion to the social life of ancient Israel. Some features from the earlier book remain, however, in particular the conservative stance and the proposal to apply the ethics to the modern world by way of 'paradigms'.

The book is in three sections: 'The Centrality of the Family in the Social, Economic, and Religious Life of Israel', 'Land and Property Ethics', and 'Dependent Persons as Property'. Some of the discussions needed to be widened. For example, it is a pity that the discussion of 'wives' is limited almost entirely to a refutation of the view that they were regarded as the property of their husbands, with little interaction with feminist writers. Scholars will find useful discussions of several matters, while the easy style makes the book accessible to ordinary readers.

C. S. RODD

8. THE SURROUNDING PEOPLES

ASSMANN, J.: *Ma'at. Gerechtigkeit und Unsterblichkeit im Alten Ägypten*. 1990. Pp. 319. (Beck, München. Price: DM 68.00. ISBN 3 406 34667 7)

A typically dense and original treatment in nine survey-chapters, in which Assmann (still inventing his own terminologies) deals at length and in (as ever) stimulating fashion with the ancient Egyptian concept *maat*, often circumscribed by a catena of concepts (truth, right, justice, good order), all facets of this entity. He stresses the need to weigh the nature of ancient sources available (how far central and fundamental, or peripheral), putting wisdom–literature at the centre, while fully using other categories of written evidence (private biographical texts, royal inscriptions, funerary composi- tions, other religious literature, etc.). *Maat* is the bond binding individuals together within 'society'; it stands at the heart of moral and religious values in ancient Egypt. While not every detail or viewpoint will command assent, this book can be warmly recommended for thoughtful reading by all who are involved with the emergence and impact of moral and religious values in the biblical world, using as it does data from three millennia of well-documented society.

K. A. KITCHEN

BUTTERWECK, C., DELSMAN, W. C., DIETRICH, M., GUTEKUNST, W. KAUSEN, E., LORETZ, O., MÜLLER, W. W. and STERNBERG-HOTABI, H.: *Religiöse Texte. Rituale und Beschwörungen* II (Texte aus der Umwelt des Alten Testaments, Bd. II/Lfg 3). 1988. Pp. 293–452. (Gütersloher Ver- lagshaus Gerd Mohn, Gütersloh. Price: DM 118.00. ISBN 3 579 00068 3)

The first part of this two-part section of *TUAT* (*B.L.* 1987, p. 121) dealt with Sumerian, Akkadian, and Hittite rituals and incantations, this second part with Ugaritic (Dietrich and Loretz) and Egyptian (Gutekunst, Kausen, and Sternberg-Hotabi) for the most part. There are many fewer Old South

116 THE SURROUNDING PEOPLES

Arabic texts (Müller), and one Aramaic (Delsman), and one Phoenician incantation (Butterweck). The Ugaritic material has received much attention from specialists over the last few decades, and it is good to have selections presented here for all Old Testament scholars to study. The poetic myths and legends from Ras Shamra have long been accorded the importance they deserve as part of the Old Testament cultural background, but the rituals have not yet received the attention they deserve as possible antecedents to later Israelite and Phoenician cult. All the material in this fascicle is well presented for its intended readers and is on a high level of scholarship.

W. G. LAMBERT

CRAWFORD, H.: *Sumer and the Sumerians*. 1991. Pp. x, 182. (Cambridge University Press. Price: £27.50 ($44.50); paperback price: £11.95 ($14.95). ISBN 0 521 38175 4; 0 521 38850 3 (pbk))

This is a survey intended for university students of the current state of knowledge of southern Mesopotamia (Sumer and Akkad) from about 3800 to 2000 BC, in technical terms from the beginning of the Uruk period to the end of the Neo-Sumerian (Third Dynasty of Ur) period. It begins with the Uruk period because it is the first which is identifiably Sumerian (the author does not go into the question of Sumerian origins or the possibilities of their arrival in Mesopotamia at an earlier date), and concludes with the time when Sumerian was displaced as the predominant language. For the student of the Old Testament this monograph draws attention to evidence which may be considered in the study of the Biblical accounts of Eden, Shinar, and Ur of the Chaldees.

The author deals with the physical environment, summarising the available evidence on the geographical history of the Mesopotamian plain, the changing courses of the rivers, and the varying patterns of settlement at different periods. The archaeological material is then presented thematically: town planning; the architecture of temples, public buildings, and private houses; burial practices; manufacture of textiles, pottery, metal, and stone objects; trade; seals; and writing. She concludes with a sketch of the main changes over the nearly two millennia dealt with, as deduced from the available evidence. The author makes use of evidence from the texts but concentrates mainly on the environment and the material remains, so this study brings a useful view to periods which have been dealt with rather unevenly by earlier scholars, many of whom have concentrated on political history as far as it could be derived from the texts, but were not able to make much of the prehistoric periods. There is a six-page bibliography.

T. C. MITCHELL

GRIFFITHS, J. G.: *The Divine Verdict. A Study of Divine Judgement in the Ancient Religions* (Studies in the History of Religions LII). 1991. Pp. xviii, 410. (Brill, Leiden. Price: fl. 180.00; $92.31. ISBN 90 04 09231 5; ISSN 0169 8834)

This wide-ranging study, discussing conceptions of divine judgement in various Old-World cultures, falls into two parts, concerned respectively with the present life and the hereafter. While Israelite and Jewish matters constitute only a fraction of the whole, one of the strengths of the study is its emphasis on mutual influence, a case being made for key themes commonly regarded as distinct to one culture or another being intellectual common property, the debt being not always one-way. In the first section, among other discussion, Bentzen's thematic linking of the execration texts and the oracles of Amos 1–2 is reassessed, the theme of divine control over history is touched on, Job is mentioned, and themes in the deuteronomistic history treated and compared with other ancient historiographical and theodicial writings. The

THE SURROUNDING PEOPLES 117

strongly eschatological bias of the New Testament is noted, explaining why present and future treatments of divine judgment are often inseparable, and after sections on classical and oriental matters, the first part concludes with a useful survey of current assessments of kingship in Egypt.

The second part begins with an exhaustive treatment of Egyptian eschatology, followed by a treatment of its relationship with Judaeo-Christian ideas, a consideration of Iranian influences in the same areas, and Greek receptiveness to such ideas. A short section tries unconvincingly to read eschatological concern into Job (notably 19: 25–27), and the study concludes with some remarks on the mystery-cults.

This kind of study, taking for granted the free flow of ideas throughout the ancient world, and recognizing that no culture was in principle impervious to these intellectual currents, may disconcert some biblical scholars who would wish to see the Bible unsullied by such influences. But to those with eyes to see, such comparative studies as the present one immeasurably enrich our understanding of its real intellectual and spiritual climate. N. WYATT

HOFFNER, H. A. (transl.); BECKMAN, G. M. (ed.): *Hittite myths* (Society of Biblical Literature Writings from the Ancient World). 1990. Pp. xi, 92. (Scholars Press, Atlanta GA. Price: $19.95; paperback price: $12.95. ISBN 1 55540 481 2 (cloth); 1 55540 482 0 (paper))

This is the first of a planned series of *Writings from the Ancient World* which is intended to cover much the same ground as J. B. Pritchard's *Ancient Near Eastern Texts*, 1969 (in which the Hittite texts were translated by A. Goetze). Inevitably in such a project everything will depend on the choice of translators of the ancient texts and for the Hittite myths no more authoritative figure could have been found than Hoffner. (The title page indicates that G. M. Beckman had some role in the production of the book, though what his role was is nowhere made clear). Hoffner provides a most useful introduction followed by translations of Old Anatolian myths (principally the Illuyanka–Serpent texts and texts concerned with disappearing deities), myths which had a Hurrian origin (the Kumarbi cycle which has close connections with Greek texts), a miscellaneous group of tales involving deities and mortals and the Elkunirsha myth, which is Canaanite in origin and closely related to the Ugaritic mythology. There are useful bibliographies and a glossary. This book should provide a reliable guide to these texts, but unfortunately most of the texts remain extremely fragmentary and are frequently incoherent. The *content* of the Hittite myths, in so far as it can be determined, is less relevant to the Old Testament than Hittite rituals, but the clear evidence of a link between myth and cult is undoubtedly instructive at the comparative level. The series is much to be welcomed and further volumes can be expected which *will* have more interest for *B.L.* readers. J. F. HEALEY

KLEIN, J. and SKAIST, A. (eds): *Bar-Ilan Studies in Assyriology dedicated to Pinhas Artzi* (Bar-Ilan Studies in Near Eastern Languages and Culture). 1990. Pp. 294 and xvi plates. (Bar Ilan University Press, Ramat-Gan. Price: $44.00. ISBN 965 226 100 9)

Twelve papers are presented in this volume, four, by S. N. Kramer, R. Kutscher, Y. Sefati, and J. Klein, on aspects of Sumerian Literature. Kutscher writes briefly but importantly on the early stages of the Dumuzi/Tammuz cult in Sumer. The Amarna archive and period is covered by four contributors. Artzi himself surveys the scholarly texts available to the Amarna cuneiform scribes. A. Demsky collects evidence for the education of Canaanite scribes of the period in cuneiform learning. A. F. Rainey argues that in the Amarna letters the Akkadian preposition *ana* is used as a reflection

118   THE SURROUNDING PEOPLES

of the West Semitic *l*. S. Vargon builds a case for continuing to identify Mu'rašti in Amarna letter 335 with the prophet Micah's birthplace. Other Assyriological contributions of relevance here are those of A. Altman on the 'Historical Prologue' of the treaty between Šunaššura and the Hittites; P. Ling-Israel's publication of a new duplicate of the famous Sennacherib prism, now in the Israel Museum, but with no changes for the campaign against Palestine; and J. Fleishman's note on debt slavery in a law of Hammurabi.

W. G. Lambert

LONGMAN, T. III: *Fictional Akkadian Autobiography: A Generic and Comparative Study*. 1991. Pp. xi, 274. (Eisenbrauns, Winona Lake IN. Price: $29.50. ISBN 0 931464 41 2)

This work comes from an author with biblical training and a biblical scholar's approach, but who has some Assyriological learning and guidance from W. W. Hallo. It strives to assert the existence of an Akkadian literary genre characterized by a tripartite structure. Each text begins with the claimed author's self-identification, proceeds by giving autobiographical material in the first person, and concludes with one of the four: blessing or curse, donation, instruction, or predictive prophecy. There are a handful of Akkadian texts which fit these requirements, though one or two may not be fictional in the sense intended, and several are so damaged that not all three parts are present. The alleged authors, when their names are preserved, were mostly kings. Longman asserts that all these texts are prose, but some are in fact poetry. The difficulty with the thesis advanced is that while the criteria used do indeed occur in some texts, in themselves these criteria do not always provide an adequate classification of the work. In looking at possible Hebrew parallels, the author finds Qoheleth, after the first and last few verses have been dispensed with, fictional autobiography. However, there is nevertheless much of interest and value in this book. The Appendix brings together in up-to-date English translation a fascinating group of Akkadian texts, autobiographical and prophetic, which are not elsewhere easily accessible. There is also a long discussion on possible relationships between these prophetic texts and Hebrew predictive prophecy and apocalyptic.

W. G. Lambert

MATTHEWS, D. M.: *Principles of Composition in Near Eastern Glyptic of the Later Second Millennium B.C.* (OBO, Series Archaeologica 8). 1990. Pp. iv, 166, and 626 line drawings and 614 b/w reproductions. (Universitätsverlag, Freiburg (CH); Vandenhoeck & Ruprecht, Göttingen. Price: SwFr 75.00. ISBN 3 7278 0698 2; 3 525 53658 5)

This is a revised form of a Cambridge PhD thesis supervised mainly by J. N. Postgate and D. Collon. It is technical art history and not a book for beginners in the field. It uses cylinder seals and impressions of them on clay tablets since these are the only art objects surviving in sufficient quantity and from most periods and areas. The period covered is roughly the second half of the second millennium BC, since there arose then a variety of new styles: several Cassite styles in Babylonia, the first genuinely original Assyrian style, and Mitanni styles in north Mesopotamia, Syria, and Palestine, to name the most important. Unlike the thesis, the book also deals with Old Babylonian (first half of second millennium) because that style underlies much of the later developments. The author has done himself much credit by bringing a keen open mind to a field hitherto largely dominated by intuitive and impressionistic research. Material was systematically gathered and computerised so that conclusions are based on a full body of evidence. Much progress has been

THE SURROUNDING PEOPLES 119

made in classifying and explaining developments, but the author's lack of knowledge of texts means that there is no serious attempt to explain scenes, and remarks on history and general culture are not up to par.

W. G. LAMBERT

MATTHEWS, V. H. and BENJAMIN, D. C.: *Old Testament Parallels. Laws and Stories from the Ancient Near East*. 1991. Pp. vii, 276. (Paulist Press, New York. Price: $14.95. ISBN 0 8091 3182 X)

The production of this book was spurred by the realization that such a work as J. B. Pritchard's *Ancient Near Eastern Texts* is unsuitable as an undergraduate textbook or for general readers. This volume is meant to serve such a readership with matter simply presented. It is arranged according to the Christian Bible, and each appropriate book, from Genesis to Daniel in fact, serves as the title heading under which the apposite ancient Near Eastern texts are briefly introduced, and are then presented in translation, usually excerpts. There are many black and white illustrations with explanatory captions, and the book concludes with too brief summaries of Mesopotamian, Egyptian, and Israelite history, a selected bibliography of each text, and finally a list of selected verses of the Old Testament with the numbers of preceding pages on which parallels can be found. The idea of the book is a good one, but as produced it cannot be recommended. The translations are called 'responsible paraphrases' and 'reader-centered translations' by their authors, but they are unreliable and even at times introduce things not present in the original languages. For example, the birth legend of Sargon tells of his being placed on a river, like Moses, without offering any explanation of his mother's action. Her title, however, indicates a priestess not permitted to bear children. This new paraphrase baselessly states, '(she) would be expected to offer her children as sacrifices'. The explanatory sections are no more reliable and the captions also contain serious errors. W. G. LAMBERT

PATRICH, J.: *The Formation of Nabataean Art. Prohibition of a Graven Image among the Nabataeans*. 1990. Pp. 231. (Magnes, Jerusalem; Brill, Leiden. Price: fl. 95.00. ISBN 90 04 09285 4)

This finely illustrated work based on an M.A. thesis from the Hebrew University covers a topic which has long cried out for attention. The main concern of the author is with the way the Nabataeans showed an ideological aversion to the figurative representation of their gods. This is examined in detail in a principal chapter which considers the typology of Nabataean stelae representing deites, as well as external evidence such as comments on this matter in Greek and Latin sources. Another chapter looks at Nabataean art in more general terms, from funerary architecture to jewellery. (For architecture note may now be taken of the monumental work of J. McKenzie, *The Architecture of Petra*, 1990). Again the Nabataean resistance to figurative art is evident, for example, in the designs of tomb facades and in the distinctive local painted pottery. As in neighbouring Judaea, high society and the court offered less resistance to Hellenization. Hence some concessions to external influence. A third chapter sets these features in a wider context, giving an account of the worship of stone stelac outside Nabataea and making comparisons with Judaism and Islam. The main conclusion, however, is that religious aniconism was a deeply rooted part of the Arabian heritage of the Nabataeans. This book is, therefore, of obvious importance in the history of religions, particularly in relation to aniconic attitudes in contemporary and earlier Judaism on the one hand and in Islam on the other. Patrich would

120 THE SURROUNDING PEOPLES

ascribe some of the signs of iconoclasm at Petra to the Nabataean, not the Islamic period. Given the first century AD date of most of the Nabataean material and known contacts between Nabataea and Palestine, this subject is also of great interest as reflecting part of the environment of Christian origins.

J. F. HEALEY

RÖMER, W. H. P. and HECKER, K.: *Religiöse Texte. Lieder und Gebete* I (Texte aus der Umwelt des Alten Testaments, Bd. II/Lfg 5). 1989. Pp. 641–783. (Gütersloher Verlagshaus Gerd Mohn, Gütersloh. Price: DM 118.00. ISBN 3 579 00070 5)

ASSMANN, J., CONRAD, D., DELSMAN, W. C., DIETRICH, M., LORETZ, O., ÜNAL, A., and WESSELIUS, J. W.: *Religiöse Texte. Lieder und Gebete* II (Texte aus der Umwelt des Alten Testaments, Bd. II/Lfg 6). 1991. Pp. 785–938. (Gütersloher Verlagshaus Gerd Mohn, Gütersloh. Price: DM 108.00. ISBN 3 579 00071 3)

These two fascicles complete the second of *TUAT*'s three planned volumes. The first of the two parts offers Sumerian (Römer) and Akkadian (Hecker) hymns and prayers, the second presents Hittite (Ünal), Ugaritic and from Meskene/Emar (Dietrich and Loretz), Egyptian (Assmann), and in conclusion are given the recently found seventh-century silver *tefillin* with the Hebrew priestly blessing (Conrad), extracts from Amherst Papyrus 63 (Aramaic in Demotic script, Delsman, and Wesselius) and the Aramaic prayer of Nabonidus from Cave 4 (Delsman). The greater part of this material has not appeared in previous works of this kind, such as *A.N.E.T.*, so that with its undoubted scholarly quality it supplies a real need. The introductions supply necessary information, but in some cases (the Sumerian especially) the notes are for Sumerologists, not for Old Testament scholars. The occurrence of Meskene (ancient Emar) can serve to draw attention to the large find of cuneiform tablets, roughly contemporary with the Ras Shamra tablets, which include very important rituals reflecting Anatolian religion, but those are not included here. The translators of the Amherst Papyrus hold that it comes from either the Jewish colony at Elephantine or a close relative of it, and that it offers (among other things) three psalms which were originally Hebrew and have been only slightly dressed up with an Aramaic veneer. The first, if correctly rendered, is certainly related to the canonical Psalm 20.

W. G. LAMBERT

ROSATI, G.: *Libro dei Morti. I papiri torinesi di Tachered e Isiemachbit* (Testi del Vicino Oriente antico, 1: Letteratura egiziana classica). 1991. Pp. 118. (Paideia Editrice, Brescia. Price: Lire 18,000. ISBN 88 394 0466 X)

Following a short history of the *genre*, this short study gives an annotated Italian translation of two papyri of the Book of the Dead from the Egyptian Museum in Turin: catalogue Nos. 1793 and 1794, belonging to two women, respectively Isi(em)achbit and Ta(che)red. The two papyri are translated in tandem, so that where both have preserved the same chapters the reader may see at a glance typical examples of recensional differences. The vignettes are described, but not reproduced: at least monochrome photographs would have been of advantage for iconographic comparison. The book concludes with a glossary.

N. WYATT

THE SURROUNDING PEOPLES 121

SCHLÖGL, H. A. and BRODBECK, A.: *Ägyptische Totenfiguren aus öffentlichen und privaten Sammlungen der Schweiz* (OBO, Series Archaeologica 7). 1990. Pp. 354, incl. many illustrations. (Universitätsverlag, Freiburg (CH); Vandenhoeck & Ruprecht, Göttingen. Price: SwFr 124.00. ISBN 3 7278 0675 3; 3 525 53657 7)

Well-produced on high-quality paper, this volume published a virtual corpus of the better-quality Egyptian *shabti*-figures in various Swiss collections, both public and private. Such little figures were intended, magically, to relieve their deceased owners of all irksome work in the afterlife; the series published here (over 250 items) are ranged in chronological order from the twelfth/thirteenth Dynasties (*c.* 1750 BC) to the Ptolemaic period, third century BC. This catalogue is prefaced by a well-illustrated introduction to the various types of figure, and followed by indexes of names and titles. A work of undoubted value to Egyptologists, less so to biblical scholars, except for examples of very special enquiry.

K. A. KITCHEN

STEIBLE, H.: *Die neusumerischen Bau- und Weihinschriften* (Freiburger Altorientalische Studien, 9, 1 & 9, 2). 1991. Pp. xv, 430, vii, 359 and xxiv plates. (Franz Steiner, Stuttgart. Price: DM 146.00. ISBN 3 515 04250 4; ISSN 0170 3307)

This is an up-to-date, scholarly edition of the Sumerian royal inscriptions from southern Iraq from, roughly, the last century of the third millennium BC. The two main dynasties are the second of Lagash and the third of Ur. Gudea is the main figure of the former, and all his statue inscriptions are included, but not the two large cylinders because they are works of literature. Old Testament scholars will not usually have occasion to refer to such texts, but they form an important part of the intellectual heritage of ancient Mesopotamia and are presented here in a reliable form, available for use if needed.

W. G. LAMBERT

WERNER, R.: *Kleine Einführung ins Hieroglyphen-Luwische* (Orbis Biblicus et Orientalis 106). 1991. Pp. xii, 101. (Universitätsverlag, Freiburg (CH); Vandenhoeck & Ruprecht, Göttingen. Price: SwFr 34.00. ISBN 3 7278 0749 0 (Universitätsverlag); ISBN 3 525 53739 5 (Vandenhoeck & Ruprecht))

One of the most picturesque, yet enigmatic scripts of the biblical world is the 'Hittite Hieroglyphs', virtually undeciphered until recent decades, and even so not completely. They were the first used on official seals and occasional formal stone monuments during the Hittite Empire of the fourteenth-thirteenth centuries BC — in that sense, they are culturally 'Hittite'. But the language so written is not Hittite proper (strictly, Nesite), but its sister-tongue, Luvian (or Luwian). Hence the language of these hieroglyphic texts is 'Hieroglyphic Luvian', to distinguish it from the cuneiform variety. Along with Palaic, all these go to form the Anatolian group of Indo-European languages. Lycian is in effect a later form (or very close relative) of Luvian. The main body of these hieroglyphic texts belongs to the north-Syrian and south-Anatolian states of the twelfth-eighth centuries BC, 'the kings of the Hittites' of Kings, and set up by rulers of such states as Hamath.

The author of this compact volume here provides a clear, elementary introduction to Hieroglyphic Luvian: general introduction, essential bibliography, a summary of the best-attested grammatical forms and syntactic usages, and then presents thirty-six sample documents. Half of these are seals and short texts of the Empire period, the rest are from the later period, including royal building texts from Hamath, items from Carchemish, etc. All are given in actual drawings (usually from the publications), plus transcription

122 THE SURROUNDING PEOPLES

and translation, and brief notes. Only the last, the celebrated Karatepe bilingual, is given without hieroglyphs (first sixteen clauses only). These enable the reader to see the language and script at work, and to taste a little of their flavour — but the full corpus of course (to be issued by D. J. Hawkins in due course) is very much richer and more extensive than the handy sample given here. The work ends with a list of about 150 of the most important signs and values (out of 497 in Laroche's corpus), and other useful indexes. A beginner's guide (and reliable) to a little-used resource for biblical background.

K. A. KITCHEN

9. APOCRYPHA AND POST-BIBLICAL STUDIES

AALEN, S.: *Heilsverlangen und Heilsverwirklichung. Studien zur Erwartung des Heils in der apokalyptischen Literatur des antiken Judentums und im ältesten Christentum* (Arbeiten zur Literatur und Geschichte des Hellenistischen Judentums XXI). 1990. Pp. xxi, 70. (Brill, Leiden. Price: fl. 55.00. ISBN 90 04 09527 9)

This slender monograph is a revised version of Aalen's Franz Delitzsch Lectures of 1974. It is essentially a study of the development of the belief in the resurrection in the Jewish apocalyptic literature of the last two centuries BC and the first century AD. It also includes a discussion of the Old Testament passages in addition to Dan. 12 which are held to have been influential in the development of this belief (Ezek. 37; Isa. 24–27; 65–66) and a brief statement of Early Christian writings which deal with this subject. One of the main concerns of the author was to argue that in Jewish literature prior to AD 70 the setting of the life of blessedness to which the righteous rise was a renewed earth, and that the idea of the righteous dwelling in heaven after death was a later development. Aalen had more or less completed the revision of his work by the time of his death in 1980, but, for reasons indicated by K. H. Rengstorf in his Foreword, publication was delayed for a considerable time. The study inevitably has a slightly dated appearance now, but even in terms of 1980 some aspects of the discussion would have seemed questionable. The volume includes an appreciation of Aalen's scholarly work by E. Baasland.

M. A. KNIBB

ALEXANDER, L. (ed.): *Images of Empire* (JSOT Supplement Series, 122). 1991. Pp. 316. (Sheffield Academic Press. Price: £35.00 ($57.50); sub. price: £26.00 ($42.95). ISBN 1 85075 312 1)

The thirteen essays in this collection are the conference papers of a Sheffield colloquium of classicists, orientalists, and biblical scholars, on perceptions of Roman power among subject peoples. Three of the essays are on topics of direct concern to readers of this *Book List*. P. R. Davies, ranging beyond the immediate Roman concerns of most of the papers, suggests that attitudes to empire in the book of Daniel are more subtle and ambiguous than has sometimes been supposed; T. Rajak offers a reassessment of Josephus' presentation of Agrippa, and speculates how far the attitudes expressed are those of Josephus himself; and G. J. Brooke warns against attempting to discern too directly historical allusions in the references to *kittim* in the Dead Sea Scrolls. Other contributions deal with Luke — Acts and Revelations, and with the church fathers, as well as with various classical authors. Overall a most interesting collection on a highly topical theme.

R. J. COGGINS

APOCRYPHA AND POST-BIBLICAL STUDIES 123

ATTIAS, J.-C.: *Le Commentaire Biblique. Mordekhai Komtino ou l'herméneutique du dialogue* (Patrimoines Judaïsme). 1991. Pp. 204. (Cerf, Paris. Price: Fr 120.00. ISBN 2 204 04261 7; ISSN 0762 0829)

Mordecai Khomatiano (1402–1482) occupies a major position among Jewish scholars of his century, not only in his native Constantinople but on a world-wide stage. Astonishingly, this is the first full-length study of his biblical exegesis. Jean-Christophe Attias discusses the reasons for this history of neglect in his introduction, before proceeding to a general account of Khomatiano's life and work. Khomatiano's important commentary on the Pentaeuch forms the basis for the succeeding chapters, which investigate with clarity and authority the nuances of his relationship with Karaism and his debt to his great predecessor Abraham Ibn Ezra. This is a masterly treatment of a compelling subject, well documented, necessarily detailed in places, yet written in such a way that it is accessible to a wide readership. I have only one serious cavil: having conceded early on that the correct name of his subject was 'more than probably' Khomatiano, who does Attias persist in calling him 'Komtino'? The book deserves to be translated into English.

N. R. M. DE LANGE

BELLEVILLE, L. L.: *Reflections of Glory. Paul's Polemical Use of the Moses–Doxa Tradition in 2 Corinthians 3.1–18* (Journal for the Study of the New Testament Supplement Series 52). 1991. Pp. 351. (JSOT Press, Sheffield. Price: £40.00 ($70.00); sub. price: £30.00 ($52.50). ISBN 1 85075 265 6; ISSN 0143 5108)

Pages 26–79 of this study are devoted to an exhaustive survey of Exodus 34:28–36 in Jewish tradition, from a slender crop of alleged allusions in the Apocrypha and Pseudepigrapha through the Targums, Philo, Pseudo-Philo and Josephus, Qumran ('the language of "shining", "glory", "face", "light" and "covenant"' in 1QH 'is clearly reminiscent of Exod. 34:28–35'), to the Samaritan and Mandaean texts, the Rabbis and the Kabbalah. The author claims that several motifs in Paul's use of the Exodus narrative in 2 Cor. 3 have parallels in three or four of the sources examined.

C. J. A. HICKLING

ELLIS. E. E.: *Paul's Use of the Old Testament* (Twin Brooks). 1991 (reprint). Pp. xii, 204. (Baker Book House, Grand Rapids MI. Price: $10.95. ISBN 0 8010 3368 3)

The third printing of this classic study (*B.L.* 1959, p. 26, *Decade*, p. 162) is an exact replication of the second (*B.L.* 1983, p. 63).

C. J. A. HICKLING

DE JONGE, M.: *Jewish Eschatology, Early Christian Christology and the Testaments of the Twelve Patriarchs. Collected Essays* (Supplements to Novum Testamentum LXIII). 1991. Pp. xix, 342. (Brill, Leiden. Price: fl. 180.00; $92.31. ISBN 90 04 09326 5; ISSN 0167 9732)

Twenty of de Jonge's articles, published over twenty-one years, are reprinted in this collection, which honours his sixty-fifth birthday. Twelve are, predictably, devoted to the *Testaments*. These include three recent studies on the ethics of the *Testaments* as well as the shorter version, published in 1980, of the overview of critical issues in this author's article for *Aufstieg und Niedergang der römischen Welt*. Of the remainder, five are of mainly New Testament interest; the others consider the eschatology of the Psalms of Solomon, Jewish eschatological expectation as reflected in Josephus, and eschatological intermediaries in the Qumran documents. Many will welcome the availability between two covers of this selection from the most important

124 APOCRYPHA AND POST-BIBLICAL STUDIES

of de Jonge's contributions. The editor has appended a full bibliography of his impressive output (the Acknowledgements repeat separately the bibliographical details for the articles here reprinted). Professor de Jonge himself has provided an introduction to indicate the place of each essay in the development of his research. There is a subject index as well as an Index Locorum.

C. J. A. HICKLING

LONGENECKER, B. W.: *Eschatology and the Covenant. A Comparison of 4 Ezra and Romans 1–11* (Journal for the Study of the New Testament Supplement Series 57). 1991. Pp. 318. (JSOT Press, Sheffield. Price: £35.00 ($60.00); sub. price: £26.00 ($45.00). ISBN 1 85075 305 9; ISSN 0143 5108)

Part Two of this Durham (England) thesis, forming just under half of the study as a whole, is a section by section analysis of 4 Ezra, prefaced by an introduction to the book and ending with a concise but informative review of recent work on it. In the course of this review Longenecker gives a useful summary of his own findings (pp. 149f). The narrative of 4 Ezra 'is nothing other than a conversion story': 9:26 to 10:60 — the fourth of the 'episodes' into which Longenecker divides the text — forms 'the dramatic turning point in Ezra's pilgrimage' (p. 111). Thereafter Ezra shows that he has now accepted the teaching of Uriel. Longenecker thus sees 4 Ezra as the work of 'a reluctant liberal' offering 'a new understanding of ... Jewish existence without the temple'. In Part Three he turns to Rom 1:18–11:36, which he studies on a thematic basis. He shows that, like 4 Ezra, this text challenges 'prevalent Jewish perceptions' from within the broad fold of Early Judaism. In his final chapter Longenecker highlights both the similarities and the contrasts between the understandings of Israel and of God's action present in the two texts. By the very fact of their distance from the 'ethnocentric covenantalism' (Longenecker prefers this term to Sanders' 'covenantal nomism') of most Jews during the first century CE, both texts throw light on that 'pattern of religion'. This is an unusual and carefully-argued study which students of Jewish and Christian origins, as well as those working on 4 Ezra, will find valuable.

C. J. A. HICKLING

VAN LOOPIK, M.: *The Ways of the Sages and the Way of the World. The Minor Tractates of the Babylonian Talmud: Derekh 'Eretz Rabbah, Derekh 'Eretz Zuta, Pereq ha-Shalom, translated on the basis of the manuscripts and provided with a commentary* (Texte und Studien zum Antiken Judentum, 26). 1991. Pp. xiii, 389. (Mohr, Tübingen. Price: DM 188.00. ISBN 3 16 145644 0; ISSN 0721 8753)

It is difficult to find anything good to say about this book. The English translation from the author's Dutch is poor to the point of occasional outright obscurity, while the turgid incomprehensibility of the introduction seems to be due as much to the author's muddled thinking as the poverty of the translation. On p. 3 we are told that 'in Derekh 'Eretz we find .... (14) advises and, in certain circles compulsory, aggravations of general standards, a way to express special piety' (!). The discussion in the introduction on the age of Derekh 'Eretz tradition shows no knowledge of the intensive scholarly debate of the last two decades on the problems of dating rabbinic traditions. The claim in the Preface that these traditions 'show us the spiritual and social background of the New Testament and of the rabbinical period of the first centuries and later' is nowhere substantiated in the text. Most scholars would relate this material to the second half of the first millennium CE.

It is difficult to pass a judgement on the reliability of the translations of the texts because the book does not provide us with the Hebrew text on which

APOCRYPHA AND POST-BIBLICAL STUDIES 125

they are based. In each case one manuscript is chosen as the basic text to be translated and though it is claimed that the chosen manuscript contains 'a reliable and complete rendering of the text', we are not told why we should accept such a categorical judgment. The translations are literal and wooden, if not completely obscure. Examples: 'And all these who are prohibited to him, the interdict is not (even) lifted, except in the case of the wife's sister, who is prohibited only during her (i.e. his wife's) lifetime' (DER, I.1); 'Be frightened and rejoice about all the precepts' (DEZ, II.2). Some of the notes to the translations contain useful material, for example, the extensive discussion (pp. 205–18) of the tradition in DEZ I.20 of the nine (ten, eleven, thirteen, fourteen?) people who entered the Garden of Eden alive. But, on the whole, they reflect the procedures of traditional Jewish scholarship and so everything is regarded as relevant with little concern for the date or origin of the material adduced for comparison. Attributions are too often taken at their face value.

Such a book may be of use to those of us who wish to gain a quick insight into rabbinic thinking on ethical issues, but it is of little use for proper ethical work. It is surprising to find such a work in a series as well respected as Texte und Studien zum Antiken Judentum.

A. P. HAYMAN

MCKNIGHT, S.: *A Light Among the Gentiles. Jewish Missionary Activity in the Second Temple Period.* 1991. Pp. x, 205. (Fortress, Minneapolis. Price: $12.95. ISBN 0 8006 2452 1)

The late C. A. Simpson, lecturing on Isaiah 40–55, once observed that, *pace* Isa. 45:22, Judaism was not a missionary-minded religion. McKnight agrees. Noting the universalistic tendency of the biblical belief in Yahweh's sovereignty and the exclusivism of a Judaism which rejected the idolatry and certain ethical practices of paganism, McKnight argues that the Jews did not evangelise Gentiles (though generally favouring their society), but were ready to accept them as converts (though suspicious of their motivations). Partial conversion was not enough; proselytes in effect had to join a new *ethnos*, a new society, which demanded of them full observance of the Jewish law (though the demand of circumcision or baptism by way of *initiation* is not documented until the rabbinic period — indeed, Jewish proselyte baptism might originate in the entrance requirements of Jewish Christianity). God would resolve the problem of universalism by massive conversion of the Gentiles at the eschaton.

McKnight finds virtually no evidence for evangelism or a *kerugma*; hellenistic apologetic literature was written (cf. Tcherikover) for Jewish, not Gentile benefit, and the synagogue, though attended by Gentiles, was not a mission hall. Gentiles were attracted through observing Jewish good deeds, involved through inter-marriage, and occasionally (though unsuccessfully) forcibly Judaised. McKnight argues for different levels of Gentile adherence, from marginal social involvement to intermarriage or to actual conversion. McKnight finds no evidence of widespread Jewish missionary activity in the New Testament, and an analysis of terminology reveals that 'God-fearers' were Gentiles who symphathized with Judaism, perhaps attending synagogue worship; 'proselytes' were actual converts, possibly but not certainly accepting circumcision.

This book is well argued, well documented, well written, and persuasive. In his introduction, McKnight defends his 'synthetic' (as distinct from 'atomistic') method; his method is well justified by the result.

J. R. BARTLETT

126 APOCRYPHA AND POST-BIBLICAL STUDIES

MAGONET, J.: *A Rabbi's Bible*. 1991. Pp. x, 178. (SCM, London. Price: £9.50. ISBN 0 334 02506 0)

Dissatisfied as he is with the coldly academic and narrowly devotional approaches on the one hand and the popular reconstructions beloved of the media on the other, Magonet has set out to apply his own intelligence, experience, and ideas to the texts of the Hebrew Bible in an attempt to achieve some fresh insights. In fourteen brief but informative and thoughtful chapters, the Principal of the Leo Baeck College for training Reform and Liberal Rabbis introduces the reader to the Hebrew original and to the classical Jewish commentators and advises on how best to replace preconceived notions with creative and sympathetic understanding. Drawing on current thought as well as Jewish traditions, the author also offers explanations of revelation, the Garden of Eden narrative, salvation, universalism, prophecy, and the images of God as they are portrayed in the Hebrew Bible. His presentation is lively and entertaining and not without its challenges to standard Jewish and Christian exegesis.

S. C. REIF

MASON, S.: *Flavius Josephus on the Pharisees; a Composition–Critical Study* (Studia Post Biblica). 1991. Pp. xv, 424. (Brill, Leiden. Price: fl. 210.00; $107.69. ISBN 90 04 09181 5; ISSN 0169 9717)

M. offers, against the background of a remarkable and continuing scholarly divergence on almost every aspect of the religious, social and political identity of the Pharisees, a fresh examination informed by a new, more rigorous method, 'composition criticism'. He (rightly) sees Josephus as central, and so focuses the analysis strictly on Josephus; but the old source criticism is replaced by meticulous inspection of the author's overall aims and techniques. The presentation in *Antiquities* emerges as not noticeably more sympathetic to the Pharisees than the earlier one in the *War*, a demonstration which puts paid to the Morton Smith–Neusner–Cohen thesis, that Josephus's late writings exaggerated the power and impact of the Pharisees in the pre-70 period so as to line up with their post-70 ascendency. If the language in *Antiquities* is new, it is because Josephus prizes variation; if anything, his attitude tends to greater hostility. The Smith receives an additional blow from M.'s novel claim that there would have been sense in Josephus's favouring the Pharisees, because the historian himself never claimed to have been a Pharisee: he merely says that he co-operated with them politically. The single sentence in the *Life* from which the common understanding has derived is re-interpreted by M. Whether M.'s rendering of the Greek verb *politeuesthai*, on which everything hangs, will be widely accepted or not, his challenge cannot be ignored in future considerations of the Pharisees. The three extended studies of Josephus's excursuses on the three Jewish 'philosophies' are also a welcome addition to the literature on Second Temple Judaism. On the other hand, the detailed work on those Josephan episodes in which the Pharisees figure, while necessary for the argument, will probably be followed mainly by Josephus specialists or by those concerned with the ins and outs of Hasmonean and Herodian political history.

T. RAJAK

MOMIGLIANO, A.: *Alien Wisdom; the Limits of Hellenization*. 1990. Pp. 176. (Cambridge University Press. Price: £9.95. ISBN 0 521 38761 2)

This is the paperback edition of a work which was first published in 1975. It has already been reviewed in *B.L.* 1976, pp. 92f.

R. B. SALTERS

APOCRYPHA AND POST-BIBLICAL STUDIES 127

NEUSNER, J.: *Judaism as Philosophy, the Method and Message of the Mishnah.* 1991. Pp. 301. (University of South Carolina Press. Price: $39.95. ISBN 0 87249 736 4)

With this volume Neusner completes his trilogy on the Mishnah's religious theory of the social order; already in print are his essays on its politics (1989) and economics (1991). The trilogy forms the first part of Neusner's thesis on the three phases of the Judaic system. Philosophy will give way, in subsequent rabbinic texts, to religion and religion in turn to theology. Part One deals with the reading of a particular tractate (*M. Me'ilah*) as philosophy. Part Two deals with principles and grids of classification, e.g. hierarchical and polythetic; genus and species; mixture and connection. Part Three sets the Mishnah in its contemporary philosophical context, specifically that defined by Aristotle and Neoplatonism. As with these other philosophical systems, the Mishnah is concerned with the logical classification, hierarchical ordering, and systematic unification of all things in the One. (So perhaps Josephus's portrayal of Judaisms as philosophical systems is not inaccurate after all?)

The volume of Neusner's output tends to reduce rather than magnify the impact of his ideas: few scholars find the time to read as much as he writes, and the larger agenda is often hidden in the tidal flow. This book should be noted as concluding another important step in Neusner's redefinition both of rabbinic Judaism and of the methods by which it should be critically studied.

P. R. DAVIES

NEUSNER, J.: *Rabbinic Political Theory. Religion and Politics in the Mishnah* (Chicago Studies in the History of Judaism), 1991. Pp. xxii, 262. (University of Chicago Press, Chicago and London. Price: £39.95 ($57.50); paperback price: £17.95 ($25.95). ISBN 0 226 57651 5)

This is the third of a trilogy of books in which, having completed the process of translating and analysing the Mishnah, Neusner sets out to subject it to a thematic treatment. The first of these works (The Economics of Mishnah) was reviewed in *B.L.* 1991, pp. 139f; the second is his *Judaism as Philosophy* (1991). Not surprisingly, all these works serve to reinforce the conclusions about the nature of the Mishnah reached in Neusner's innumerable other works on the subject. Since for him the Mishnah represents above all a systematic work of philosophy, then whatever question one addresses to it should produce answers which witness to this one ubiquitous system, nowhere explicitly mentioned but everywhere presupposed by the details.

Neusner tackles the subject of the Mishnah's political system exactly as he did its economic system — by means of a comparison with Aristotle. This reveals the striking fact that whereas in Aristotle economics and politics are integrated in the figure of the landowning householder, in the Mishnah the latter has no political role whatsoever. Politics for the Mishnah is a matter of resolving the clash between two conflicting wills — that of God and that of human beings, not the search for the ideal state that will enable the householder–citizen to realize his full potential. Moreover, while Aristotle's system is designed to accommodate realistic political change, the Mishnah presents us with an ideal system (king, priest, scribe, in Jerusalem) that bears no discernible relation to contemporary reality and that exists in an eternal, unchanging present.

For those scholars familiar with Neusner's corpus, this book contains no surprises. As always, where Neusner sees a system others will see only details, and those not particularly interesting ones, for, as he himself admits, politics is only a side interest for the authors of the Mishnah. However, for those interested in the way in which the rabbis preserved Judaism by taking it out of

128   APOCRYPHA AND POST-BIBLICAL STUDIES

the realm of practical politics into 'a state of mind' (the real nature of Jerusalem in the Mishnah according to Neusner) the book makes fascinating reading.

A. P. Hayman

NEUSNER, J.: *The Mishnah: A New Translation*. 1988 (paperback printing 1991). Pp. xlv, 1162. (Yale University Press, New Haven and London. Price: £60.00 ($80.00); paperback price: £22.50 ($35.00). ISBN 0 300 03065 7)

This new 1991 paperback edition is unchanged, apart from ISBN, from the 1988 original reviewed warmly in *B.L.* 1989, p. 141. Since the hardback price has climbed in three years to £60.00 ($80.00), this paperback is all the more welcome.

A. G. Auld

NEUSNER, J.: *Uniting the Dual Torah: Sifra and the Problem of the Mishnah*. 1990. Pp. xii, 233. (Cambridge University Press. Price: £32.50 ($54.50). ISBN 0 521 38125 8)

In this second of his three books on *Sifra*, Neusner argues that this post-Mishnaic halakhic commentary on Leviticus meets the problem of uniting scripture and Mishnah (the two Torahs) by applying a process of hierarchical classification based on scripture, and recasting the programme of the Mishnah accordingly — thus absolishing the independence of Mishnah from scripture but bringing both into a single coherent statement — a method diametrically opposed to the Talmuds, in which the Mishnah provides the base text and the base logic. For Neusner, *Sifra* establishes 'The Torah' as a proper noun, while the Talmuds treat 'torah' as a common noun.

This study includes analyses of several chapters of *Sifra*, a clearly-stated set of propositions, and an explanation of what makes this particular composition different from e.g. *Sifré* or *Leviticus Rabbah*.

P. R. Davies

PAPER, H. H. (ed.): *Hebrew Union College Annual*, Vol. LXI (1990). 1991. Pp. vii, 270 and 46 (Hebrew). (Hebrew Union College, Cincinatti. Price: $30.00. ISSN 360 9049)

This issue maintains the high standards of the journal. L. H. Feldman exploits classical, Jewish, and Christian sources to demonstrate that the area of Jewish settlement in the Holy Land was from 300 BCE called Judaea (following one of its Biblical Hebrew names) and that Palestine originally referred to the coastal area and was later used instead of Judaea (probably at the instigation of Hadrian) with the aim of obliterating the Jewish connections with the land. A wealth of documentary evidence is cited and carefully annotated by S. Greengus in a detailed discussion of the terminology and practice relating to the gifts sent by a bridegroom to the home of his bride in Sumer and their parallels in Semitic marriage customs. Texts containing unattested versions of the Targum to Esther identified in the Cambridge Genizah collection are meticulously introduced, described, and edited by R. Kasher and M. L. Klein and the authors also offer a helpful translation and short bibliography. Following an analysis of dialogue in the Babylonian Talmud, the mediaevel Jewish field is represented by studies of Rashi's commentary on Genesis 1–6 as anti-Christian polemic, Naḥmanides' compositions after the Barcelona disputation of 1263, pre-modern Ashkenazi synagogal chanting and Cambridge Genizah fragments on Ephraim ben Shemarya, and the modern period by essays on Freud's philosophy and R. Shneur Zalman's support for Eretz–Israel.

S. C. Reif

APOCRYPHA AND POST-BIBLICAL STUDIES 129

SCHÄFER, P.: *Übersetzung der Hekhalot-Literatur,* IV (Texte und Studien zum Antiken Judentum 29). 1991. Pp. xlv, 208. (Mohr, Tübingen. Price: DM 98.00. ISBN 3 16 145745 5; ISSN 0721 8753)

This is the final volume of Peter Schäfer's translation of the Hekhalot texts. Volume I is still to appear. This volume covers 598–985 of his *Synopse zur Hekhalot-Literatur.* For a review of volume III see *B.L.* 1991, p. 144. Volume IV contains the works conventionally titled Harba de-Moshe (§§ 598–622) and Merkava Rabba (§§ 623–712). §§ 713–938 are left untranslated since they mainly contain duplicates of material translated in earlier volumes. §§ 938–85 contain the Shiʿur Qoma. As before, the volume contains, in addition to the translations and notes, descriptions of the manuscripts, a summary of current scholarship on the texts, and a survey of the contents of the texts. The introduction to the Shiʿur Qoma is particularly critical of the principles on which Martin Cohen based his edition of this text. But then, the whole production is stamped with Schäfer's well-known caution about drawing any firm conclusions about the origins and dates of these texts in our current state of knowledge about them. Scholars devoted to the view that monotheism is the prime characteristic of Judaism might find the invocations to the sun in §§ 646–48 interesting reading.

A. P. HAYMAN

SCHIFFMAN, L. H.: *From Text to Tradition. A History of Second Temple and Rabbinic Judaism.* 1991. Pp. xvi, 299. (KTAV, Hoboken NJ. Price: $39.50; paperback price: $16.95. ISBN 0 88125 371 5 (cloth); 0 88125 372 3 (pbk))

S. has produced a clearly written survey covering mainly the Second Temple period and the rabbinic period, from about 550 BCE to 600 CE, though an early chapter also looks at the 'Biblical Heritage'. There are no notes and hardly any references to original sources (though original sources and their value are discussed), but a bibliography of further reading is given for each chapter.

In such a span of material, there are bound to be many statements which cause the specialist to raise an eyebrow. But, on the whole, the author shows himself up to date in all areas. The weakness of the book, however, lies in the fact that those for whom it is most directly intended (students and non-specialists) cannot easily follow up or judge the author's statements. That is, even when the author is adumbrating current scholarship, the student can only take his word for it. There are no notes to guide for further discussion or reading, nor specific references to the primary data. The reading for each chapter is no substitute because the student cannot be expected to plough through a dozen or more books or technical articles to find the answer to a specific query. In other words, S. gives his opinion (with which many will often agree), but why he holds that opinion as opposed to some other is not necessarily clear. The student needs to know how we know what we know, if indeed we do know. In the Second Temple and rabbinic periods, we often do not know.

L. L. GRABBE

SCHWARTZ, S.: *Josephus and Judaean Politics* (Columbia Studies in the Classical Tradition). 1990. Pp. xi, 257. (Brill, Leiden. Price: fl. 100.00. ISBN 90 04 09230 7; ISSN 0166 1302)

S. investigates the politics in Judaea in the decades before and after the 66–70 war by using Josephus' own writings and experiences as a platform on which to build. He argues that much can be learned about these politics from a careful study of Josephus' own changing historiography.

130 APOCRYPHA AND POST-BIBLICAL STUDIES

After a look at Josephus' works and his intellectual development, S. considers the priesthood before and after the war (ch. 3), Agrippa II and other Herodians after 70 (ch. 4), and the Pharisees and early rabbinic Judaism in relationship to the *Antiquities* (ch. 5). Among his conclusions are the following: The high priests made a bid for power after 70, supported by Josephus in the *War* and the early part of the *Antiquities*, but were unsuccessful. The *Antiquities*, while not necessarily pro-Pharisaic, shows interest in careful observance of the law and other Pharisaic concerns. S. interprets this to mean that Josephus was propagandizing for a group similar to the Pharisees but not exactly like them. This group is interpreted as the proto-rabbinic movement, a movement made up not only of former Pharisees but also members of the upper priesthood and others.

Similarly, the Herodians attempted to enhance their power after the war. Agrippa II apparently enlisted Josephus' aid in this; however, by the 90s Agrippa's power was in decline, and Josephus ceased to favour him and the other Herodians in his writings.

S. has made a strong case for his main interpretations. In addition, he gives many useful comments on individual points of Josephus' writings. He has made an important contribution to the study not only of Josephus but also first-century Judaism.   L. L. Grabbe

SHATZMAN, I.: *The Armies of the Hasmonaeans and Herod from Hellenistic to Roman Frameworks* (Texte und Studien zum Antiken Judentum 25). 1991. Pp. xiv, 354. (Mohr, Tübingen. Price: DM 178.00. ISBN 3 16 145617 3)

This forms an important companion volume to Bar-Kochva's *Judas Maccabaeus (B.L.* 1990, p. 37) and *The Seleucid Army*. In the first part of the book, S. looks at the army, tactics, and fortifications of the later Hasmonean period. He devotes the second half to the same range of military concerns as they relate to Herod, but there is the additional question of how Herod's military power fitted into the Roman scheme of things. In general, Herod was not in a position to wage war because it would have been against other client kings under the Roman aegis; however, a notable exception was the case of several episodes relating to the Nabateans, even though the latter supposedly owed allegiance to Rome.

In addition to much new information on specifically military questions, S. touches on a range of topics concerning Herod's rule. Some of his conclusions also go against accepted wisdom. For example, he argues that the bulk of Herod's soldiers were Jews, not Idumeans or mercenaries. This is a significant addition to studies on the Second Temple period.   L. L. Grabbe

STRACK, H. L. and STEMBERGER, G.: *Introduction to the Talmud and Midrash*. Translated by Markus Bockmuehl. 1991. Pp. viii, 472. (T. & T. Clark, Edinburgh. Price: £24.95. ISBN 0 567 09509 6)

Günther Stemberger's thorough revision of Hermann Strack's *Einleitung in Talmud und Midrasch* (last edition 1920) was widely acclaimed when it first appeared in German in 1982. Stemberger has taken the opportunity of an English version to make further revisions and to update the bibliographies. The result is that the English translation constitutes, in effect, a new edition of the work. Stemberger is more discursive and readable than Strack, whose style was compressed and whose text, at times, degenerated into a rather cryptic set of notes. However, there are problems with the English rendering which is often stiff and unidiomatic: some paragraphs have to be read carefully several times before they yield their meaning. Stemberger displays a formidable command of the relevant

APOCRYPHA AND POST-BIBLICAL STUDIES 131

literature, and his well-organized discussions of the individual texts are almost invariably better than the corresponding entries in the *Encyclopaedia Judaica*. His listing of the major manuscripts (a methodological imperative nowadays) is welcome, as is his attention to the classic traditional commentaries on Talmud and Midrash. There was a tendency in the nineteenth century, in the white-heat of the new philological approach, to discount the traditional commentaries (though Strack, to his credit, did include some information on them). In fact, the traditional commentaries, despite their pre-modern perspective, are an essential aid to the reading of the literature. This side of the work could well be expanded in future editions. For example, the treatment of the traditional commentaries on *Bere'shit Rabba* is too perfunctory. The Introduction has been totally recast to include new chapters on The Rabbinic School System, on Handling Rabbinic Texts: the Problem of Method, and on the Languages of Rabbinic Literature; and new material has been added to the discussion of the Historical Background and the Oral and Written Tradition. A more exhaustive, analytical listing of the contents (as in the older editions) would alert the reader to the good things on offer in the Introduction. (As it happens, Chap. VII, Languages of Rabbinic Literature, is missing altogether from the Table of Contents.) The disappearance of the brief sections on the mode of citation of Rabbinic texts, and on the definition of terms such as *baraita*, *gemara*, *halakhah*, and *haggadah* (both invaluable to the tiro) is also regrettable. It should also be noted that the omission of any discussion of the Targumim suggests that Stemberger, despite the depth of his revision, has not escaped the conceptual framework of Strack's original work. When Strack first wrote, over one hundred years ago, the Targumim were often seen as highly derivative and, consequently, they were held in rather low esteem. Though this attitude is still found in some quarters, it is increasingly being recognized that the Targumim are as integral a part of early Rabbinic literature as are Talmud and Midrash. Certainly Midrash cannot any longer be meaningfully discussed without reference to Targum and vice versa. Perhaps future editions of the work could include a section of the Targumim. For the present we must express our gratitude to Professor Stemberger for this revision which will extend the life of a classic well into the next century.

P. S. ALEXANDER

TALMON, SH.: (ed.): *Jewish Civilization in the Hellenistic–Roman Period* (Journal for the Study of the Pseudepigrapha Supplement Series 10). 1991. Pp. 269. (JSOT Press, Sheffield. Price: £30.00 ($50.00); sub. price: £22.50 ($37.50). ISBN 1 85075 320 2)

Three essays have appeared previously: internal diversification of Judaism in the early Second Temple period (S. Talmon); Qumran from within (Talmon); and the contribution of the Qumran manuscripts to Old Testament textual criticism (E. Tov). One has been rather overtaken by events: a report on publication (J. Strugnell). Most of the others are important and original contributions and/or a useful summary of scholarship and debate with regard to the Greco–Roman period: material culture (U. Rappaport); religious and national factors in the 66–70 war (T. A. Idinopulos); use of early rabbinic writings for understanding Judaism of the time (G. J. Blidstein); literary typologies and biblical interpretation (D. Dimant); the text of Ben Sira (M. Gilbert); Qumran and rabbinic halaka (L. H. Schiffman; J. M. Baumgarten); purity laws in the Temple Scroll (J. Milgrom); impact of new discoveries and study on university teaching (J. H. Charlesworth); Qumran fragments of 1 Enoch in understanding early Judaism and Christianity; and the Teacher of Righteousness in comparison with Jesus (H. Stegemann). Several writers are already drawing on 4QMMT to rewrite Jewish history. Whether this is wise remains to be seen.

L. L. GRABBE

132   APOCRYPHA AND POST-BIBLICAL STUDIES

TALMON, SH.: *The World of Qumran from Within: Collected Studies.* 1989. Pp. 324. (Magnes, Jerusalem; Brill, Leiden. Price: fl. 140.00; ca. $80.00. ISBN 90 04 08449 5)

It is a risky time to be re-publishing essays on Qumran; so many established views are being overturned and so many new texts have just been published (though not yet transcribed or translated).

Talmon's thirteen essays, dating from 1951–88, are prefaced by one, hitherto unpublished, which brings up to date the author's views on the 'Covenanters of Qumran'. Talmon does not think that any texts published since the mid-sixties have introduced 'new arguments' about issues already debated, nor 'perceptibly affected the insights gained in the preceding period' (p. 19). This is dubious (though revealing from a scholar who is now one of those responsible for the publication of the remaining scrolls!). Did not the *Temple Scroll* reopen the question of whether all the Qumran scrolls were products of one community? Talmon ignores that problem, and appears content to continue the habit of utilizing any Qumran text to form a picture of a 'Qumran community'.

The essays here cover the etymology of *yahad*, transmission of the biblical text, calendrical matters, Qumran 'messianism', and various exegetical notes. Despite his habit of asserting and not arguing, Talmon's views have usually been interesting and often original. This volume shows, too, that he is capable of modifying his opinions (e.g. on identification of the Covenanters with the Essenes, which he once favoured). Recent Qumran research and debate, though, is busy dismantling a great deal of what it has been bequeathed — including quite a bit of this volume.   P. R. DAVIES

TARADACH, M.: *Le Midrash. Introduction à la littérature midrashique (Drš dans la Bible, les Targumim, les Midrašim)* (Le Monde de la Bible, 22). 1991. Pp. 283. (Labor et Fides, Genève. Price: SwFr 45.00. ISBN 2 8309 0616 0)

About two-thirds of this book lists the surviving targums and midrashim, providing in each case notes on provenance and date, the manuscripts, editions and translations, and in some cases a bibliography. This catalogue, drawn up, presumably, for a fairly specialist readership, is somewhat oddly prefaced by a semi-popular introduction on the nature and techniques of midrash, illustrated by a few examples and followed by a few pages of general introduction to the targums. There is a glossary, but — again, surprisingly — no index.   C. J. A. HICKLING

TREBILCO, P. R.: *Jewish Communities in Asia Minor* (Society for New Testament Studies Monograph Series 69). 1991. Pp. xv, 330. (Cambridge University Press. Price: £30.00. ISBN 0 521 40120 8)

This valuable collection, analysis, and discussion of the documentary and particularly inscriptional evidence from a number of sites opens with a chapter on the literary sources, and then presents all the available material about the Jewish communities in Sardis, Priene, Acmonia, and Apamea. Three further chapters discuss the place of women in Jewish communities and in society at large in Asia Minor; the hypothesis that Hellenistic Judaism was syncretistic in its use of the titles Theos Hypsistos and Sabazios (the author denies this); and the identity of the 'God-fearers'. Trebilco's discussion of the latter, though recognizing some exceptions, vindicates the traditional view: the expressions involved indicated a definite status in the life of the synagogue (Trebilco thinks that this status was particularly well-established in the Judaism of Asia Minor). This is an indispensable background study for those

APOCRYPHA AND POST-BIBLICAL STUDIES   133

working on Jewish and Christian origins as well as for historians of late antiquity. Many will find specially suggestive the discussion of *religio licita* (pp. 8–12), of the interpretative stance implied in the use of the curses of Dt. 27–29 (and also of Zech. 5:1–5) in Jewish funerary inscriptions (pp. 60–84), and of non-biblical traditions about Noah (pp. 95–99). On the basis of his occasionally imaginative but always carefully weighed judgements about the evidence he cites, the Jews of these cities are presented as loyal to the Torah and at the same time fully integrated into the society of the cities in which they lived, often holding positions of some prominence. This is an admirable application of sound historical method to problems of wide significance.

C. J. A. HICKLING

WIMBUSH, V. L. (ed.): *Ascetic Behavior in Greco–Roman Antiquity: a sourcebook* (Studies in Antiquity & Christianity). 1990. Pp. xxvii, 514. (Fortress, Minneapolis. Price: $14.95. ISBN 0 8006 3105 6)

Twenty-eight texts or collections of texts around a theme are presented in English translation with short introductions, notes, and suggestions for further reading. Written mainly from a Christian perspective, the book, the fruit of a collaborative Project on Ascetic Behaviour in Greco–Roman Antiquity connected with the Institute for Antiquity and Christianity, the Society for Biblical Literature, and the American Academy of Religion, celebrates the diversity of asceticism, even within Christianity, and the interesting connections and parallels between Christian and non-Christian manifestations of the ascetic urge (however that is to be defined). 'It should ... be a valuable resource for students and scholars of Greco–Roman antiquity who are not yet convinced that the complex religious self-understandings and orientations of the period have been adequately accounted for, much less critiqued, in terms of their decisive influence in the social, political, and religious history of the West' (from the editor's Introduction). Others, too, will find it an excellent way into the subject or even just a good read.

N. R. M. DE LANGE

10. PHILOLOGY AND GRAMMAR

ARNOLD, W.: *Das Neuwestaramäische* II. *Texte aus Ǧubbʿadīn* (Semitica Viva, 4/II). 1990. Pp. x, 454. (Harrassowitz, Wiesbaden. Price: DM 112.00. ISBN 3 447 03051 8; ISSN 0931 2811)

ARNOLD, W.: *Das Neuwestaramäische* III. *Volkskundliche Texte aus Maʿlūla* (Semitica Viva, 4/III). 1991. Pp. xii, 382. (Harrassowitz, Wiesbaden. Price: DM 112.00. ISBN 3 447 03166 2; ISSN 0931 2811)

ARNOLD, W.: *Das Neuwestaramäische* V. *Grammatik* (Semitica Viva 4/V). 1990. Pp. xxi, 410. (Harrassowitz, Wiesbaden. Price: DM 112.00. ISBN 3 447 03099 2; ISSN 0931 2811)

In these three large volumes Dr Werner Arnold continues the publication of his research on the modern Aramaic dialects spoken north of Damascus (see *B.L.* 1991, pp. 151–52, and for his *Lehrbuch des Neuwestaramäischen* see *B.L.* 1990, p. 145, to which notice we may add that the recorded cassette designed for use with the *Lehrbuch* and also published by Harrassowitz, is a valuable tool). Volume II contains transcribed texts collected in the Muslim village of Ǧubbʿadïn, which is briefly described in the introduction, while Volume III has 'folkloristic' texts from the predominantly Christian Maʿlūla. In Ǧubbʿadïn, Aramaic is clearly flourishing; in Maʿlūla there is strong outside influence, arising from tourism and the fact that many inhabitants earn their living far away. The texts, as in the earlier volume,

134 PHILOLOGY AND GRAMMAR

cover a wide variety of subjects ranging from village life to stories and poems. Readers of the *Book List* may be particularly interested in the Christian texts connected with various festivals published in the Ma'lūla volume. These include a Modern Western Aramaic version of the Lord's Prayer.

Volume v begins the work of synthesis, containing as it does a systematic grammar (phonology and morphology) of the three dialects in question. They differ somewhat from each other and forms in each are listed side by side. Apart from updating and expanding earlier works, notably A. Spitaler's *Grammatik des neuaramäischen Diakekts von Ma'lūla* (1938), this new grammar is characterized by a synchronic approach in which reference to earlier stages in the history of Aramaic plays no part. Spitaler is adjudged satisfactory on the diachronic side. The volume is provided with a brief introduction describing the villages concerned.

Remaining to be published are another volume of texts from Ma'lūla and, to complete the synthesis, a dictionary of modern western Aramaic.

J. F. HEALEY

CHARLESWORTH, J. H., with R. E. WHITAKER, L. G. HICKERSON, S. R. A. STARBUCK, and L. T. STUCKENBRUCK: *Graphic Concordance to the Dead Sea Scrolls*. 1991. Pp. xxxi, 529. (Mohr, Tübingen; Westminster/John Knox, Louisville KY. Price: DM 248.00. ISBN 3 16 145745 5; 0 664 21969 1)

Professor Charlesworth and his team at Princeton have performed a signal service to the academic community by producing this updated Concordance to the Qumran documents. Kuhn's *Konkordanz* of 1960 was an indispensable *vade mecum* for researchers while study of the Scrolls was centred on the early available large scrolls from Cave I, the Damascus Document, and the then published fragments from Cave IV. But it missed the larger scrolls and the hosts of fragments which have been published since 1960 in DJD and elsewhere, a process which is still going on though, if newspaper articles are anything to go by, not as quickly or as uncontroversially as most would like to see. This new *vade mecum* will make references to all the scrolls and fragments published up to 1990 readily checkable and remove the constant fear of scholars that they may be missing important allusions, especially from the fragments. Presumably, since a computer is involved, new fragments, including those we are told are being held back for doctrainire reasons, can easily be incorporated into a second edition. The Concordance has been carefully planned, and its sigla and procedures, sometimes quite complicated, for marking restorations, intralinear additions, uncertain letters, erasures and deletions etc., are clearly explained at the beginning. As in the case of Davies' edition of the Hebrew Inscriptions (see p. 29), there is every reason for trusting what we have been given, though Martin Hengel in his warm Preface reminds us that a Concordance, properly used, does not absolve us from studying the original manuscripts but rather gives us the means to study them more intensely. As also in the case of Davies' volume, the machine-readable texts on which the Concordance is based are soon to be made available to scholars and students in CD–ROM format. The recent burst of sensationalism discounted, there has perhaps been something of a falling-off in Qumran research in the last decade. This splendid volume should arrest it and lead to a renewal of interest in these remarkable documents which, as Hengel also reminds us, have revolutionized the study of the New Testament and the early Church, of the beginnings of Judaism, and of the history of the Hebrew language. It is a pity that, presumably for reasons of cost, the text entries are given in exceptionally small print. But buying a magnifying glass is a small price to pay for the benefits which this volume will bring to all who use it.

J. C. L. GIBSON

PHILOLOGY AND GRAMMAR 135

CONTI, G. (ed.): *Miscellanea Eblaitica*, 3 (Quaderni di Semitistica, 17). 1990. Pp. viii, 220. (Dipartimento di Linguistica, Università di Firenze)

These are four sources for the Sumerian–Eblaite bilinguals found at Ebla. The fourth of these is examined in the present work because it is the only source supported by a nearly complete set of photographs and because it has certain idiosyncracies with respect to the other three sources. Conti's first task is to describe the syllabary used in these documents. This takes up fifty-five pages. In the remainder of the book C. sets out a glossary of nearly five hundred entries and their Semitic equivalents for many of which he provides discussion, occasionally at length. There are ample indices. While not directly relevant to biblical studies there is much here of interest for comparative Semitics, for example, the root *rdm* previously known only in Hebrew where in the niphal it means 'to be in a deep sleep'.

W. G. E. WATSON

FOHRER, G. (ed.), with the co-operation of H. W. Hoffmann, F. Huber, J. Vollmer, and G. Wanke: *Hebräisch und aramäisches Wörterbuch zum Alten Testament*, 2, durchgesehene Auflage. 1989. Pp. xi, 331. (De Gruyter, Berlin, New York. Price: DM 48.00. ISBN 3 11 012112 3)

The new edition contains precisely the same number of pages as the old (for which see *B.L.* 1972, p. 78) but with change of paper and reduction of margins it is now a genuine pocket-dictionary. Opportunity has been taken mostly within the plates to adjust about 80 out of 11,000 or so entries in the Hebrew section (e.g. *hištaḥ^awāh* is now listed under *ḥwh* II) and correct the occasional misprint. Some characteristic renderings remain (e.g. *b^erit* as 'promise, obligation', *šelem* as 'concluding sacrifice'). The Aramaic section is unchanged.

W. JOHNSTONE

FRONZAROLI, P. (ed.): *Miscellanea Eblaitica*, 2 (Quaderni di Semitistica, 16). 1989. Pp. vi, 201. (Dipartimento di Linguistica, Università di Firenze)

Of the seven studies collected here, all except one in Italian, only three will be meaningful for readers of the *Book List*. Two of these are religious in character. Fronzaroli provides a translation of a difficult text, preserved on two tablets, which describes rituals to be performed in various circumstances of a military nature. Offerings are made four times a day: at dawn, at dusk and at two other unspecified times. He also identifies on an exercise tablet part of the treaty referred to in this text. From the administrative texts M. Bonechi isolates lists of ritual clothing for various officiants and shows them to be indicative of a ceremonial performed at Ebla although the actual details remain uncertain as yet. The third study, with the title 'L'assemblée en Syrie à l'époque pré-amorite', is by J.-M. Durand. He identifies a previously unknown term for 'assembly' used in the tablets from Ebla, Mari, and El Amarna; and the implications may be significant. The other contributions are very technical but G. Conti's presentation of the sources for the bilinguals from Ebla (pp. 45–78) is of importance for his own book reviewed above.

W. G. E. WATSON

136 PHILOLOGY AND GRAMMAR

HECKER, K.: *Rückläufiges Wörterbuch der Akkadischen* (Santag. Arbeiten und Untersuchungen zur Keilschriftkunde 1). 1990. Pp. xii, 316. (Harrassowitz, Wiesbaden. Price: DM 112.00. ISBN 3 447 02868 8)

Of the recent Akkadian lexica W. von Soden's *Akkadisches Handwörterbuch* is complete, and much of the *Chicago Assyrian Dictionary*. This reverse index is based mainly on the former. It is meant to aid scholars working on small fragments of texts. When only the beginnings of words are preserved one turns to the lexica to consider which of the possible endings from the words presented is most likely. But when only the endings of words remain recourse to the lexica is unhelpful. Thus a special alphabetically arranged index starting from the ends of words is needed. This one offers separate lists of roots, forms, endings, logograms, and words. No meaning or single passage is cited because these can be found in the lexica. This is meant for serious cuneiform scholars, not for Hebraists wanting to know the meanings of Akkadian words.

W. G. LAMBERT

KOEHLER, L. and BAUMGARTNER, W.: *Hebräisches und Aramäisches Lexikon zum Alten Testament*. IV Lieferung: *r'h-ts'*. 3rd Edition, edited by J. J. Stamm. 1990. Pp. x, 1081–1659. (Brill, Leiden. Price: fl. 300.00. ISBN 90 04 09256 0)

The first three parts of the third edition of this lexicon were reviewed in *B.L.* 1969, p. 65 (*Bible Bibliog.*, p. 191), 1975, pp. 114, and 1984, p. 144. The new fascicle completes the Hebrew part of the dictionary. It exhibits once again the careful and thorough, and also cautious, approach of Professor Stamm and his colleagues, and greater space is given than in the past to the discussion of debatable questions. On pp. 1267–68, for example, the entry on seraphim notes that the Hebrew word can be used of snakes and that some scholars think that the beings mentioned in Isaiah 6 were in the form of snakes; but the conclusion is preferred that the seraphim seen by Isaiah were in human form. The editor and publisher are to be congratulated on the completion of this invaluable aid to the study of the Hebrew Bible.

J. A. EMERTON

KOTTSIEPER, I.: *Die Sprache der Ahiqarsprüche* (Beihefte zur Zeitschrift für die alttestamentliche Wissenschaft 194). 1990. Pp. xi, 302. (De Gruyter, Berlin. Price: DM 124.00. ISBN 3 11 012331 2; ISSN 0934 2575)

The central, and by far the largest, section within this volume consists of a grammar of the dialect of the Ahiqar sayings. This is preceded by a presentation of the text in transliteration accompanied by a translation into German. There is also a glossary and, in folding pages at the back of the volume, there are reproductions of the nine columns of the Ahiqar text. On mainly morphological, but partly also orthographical and phonological, grounds the sayings are dated to the period 750–650 BC. A provenance in southern Syria is favoured, with the absence of Akkadian influence being taken to support this view. It may be noted that the translation of *ʿryh* by 'nackt' (XII 8; pp. 21, 225) overlooks the comments of two or three writers who have offered good grounds for translating by 'cold'. This is a substantial contribution to the study of early Aramaic, not least in the way in which it relates the language of the proverbs to other dialects and phases of Aramaic.

R. P. GORDON

PHILOLOGY AND GRAMMAR

MURTONEN, A.: *Hebrew in its West Semitic Setting*. Part One: *A Comparative Lexicon. Section Ba: Root System — Hebrew Material* (Studies in Semitic Languages and Linguistics XIII). 1988. Pp. xiv, 473. (Brill, Leiden. Price: fl. 186.00. ISBN 90 04 08064 3; ISSN 0081 8461)

MURTONEN, A.: *Hebrew in its West Semitic Setting*. Part One: *A Comparative Lexicon. Section Bb: Root System — Comparative Material and Discussion*. Sections C, D and E: *Numerals under 100, Pronouns, Particles* (Studies in Semitic Languages and Linguistics XIII). 1989. Pp. x, 516. (Brill, Leiden. Price: fl. 295.00. ISBN 90 04 08899 7; ISSN 0081 8461)

MURTONEN, A.: *Hebrew in its West Semitic Setting. A Comparative Survey of Non-Masoretic Hebrew Dialects and Traditions*. Part Two: *Phonetics and Phonology*. Part Three: *Morphosyntactics* (Studies in Semitic Languages and Linguistics XVI). 1990. Pp. xii, 178 and 8 spectograms; xxxix, 172; with 19 pp. of comprehensive synopsis and appendices of 105* pp. and 8 plates. (Brill, Leiden. Price: fl. 265.00; ca $135.00. ISBN 90 04 09309 5; ISSN 0081 8461)

The scope of Professor Murtonen's remarkable *magnum opus* was indicated in the review of Part One, Sect. A in *B.L.* 1988, pp. 149–50. It is a pleasure to be able to report its completion with these three volumes in spite of the author's failing health and a number of other factors, chiefly financial, which have led to a considerable reduction in its projected size. Instead of a planned six volumes we now have (a) in the first two volumes full lists of the surviving proper names and inflected roots in all the non-Tiberian varieties of classical or biblical Hebrew; (b) in the third volume a similar full list of such of these roots as are represented in the languages to which classical Hebrew is related, including not only the languages of the West Semitic group in which it is usually placed but the languages of East and South Semitic and of the Hamitic family with which its links become increasingly tenuous; (c) at the end of the third volume shorter lists of partially or non-inflected roots like numerals, pronouns, and particles, as these are represented both within the Hebrew sources and in the aforementioned related languages; and (d) in the fourth volume extended discussions of what may be culled from these lists with regard to phonological and morphosyntactical phenomena at the various stages of the transmission of classical Hebrew and, in general, of where classical Hebrew lies on the broader Semito–Hamitic spectrum. Of the value of the vast materials which Murtonen has gathered and organized in his *Lexicon* (vols 1–3) there can be no question. I am less confident that the methods he uses in his discussions, both linguistic and (often difficult to follow) statistical, will meet with widespread approval from his peers. But let that be for the future to decide. In the meantime we congratulate him most warmly on the appearance of these formidable volumes to crown a lifetime of selfless labour.

J. C. L. GIBSON

NICCACCI, A.: *Lettura Sintattica della Prosa Ebraico-Biblica. Principi e applicazioni* (Studium Biblicum Franciscanum Analecta N.31). 1991. Pp. xi, 264. (Franciscan Printing Press, Jerusalem. Price: $15.00)

In essence these readings comprise a class workbook prepared for use in conjunction with the author's *The Syntax of the Verb in Classical Hebrew Prose* (see *B.L.* 1991, p. 154). Since Niccacci has provided an outline of the companion volume in the introductory pages, *Lettura sintattica* can also be studied on its own.

The topics covered in part one are text linguistics as applied to Hebrew, the difference between verbal and nominal clauses, what is meant by 'text' and the principal constructions used in narrative and discourse. The concluding section, on the verbal system, incorporates an evaluation of M. Eskhult's

138 PHILOLOGY AND GRAMMAR

recent work on the verb (reviewed in *B.L.* 1991, p. 152). Clear tables throughout make the opening summary easy to follow.

In part two the following passages are analysed: Josh. 1–6; Judges 1–8; 2 Sam. 5 // 1 Chron. 11 and 14; 2 Sam. 6 // 1 Chron. 13 and 15–16; 2 Sam. 7 // 1 Chron. 17. Each passage is set out clause by clause and indentation is used to show (i) the main narrative line, (ii) background and antecedent material and (iii) direct speech. In this way the syntactic structure is evident at a glance. Comment on each verse is followed by remarks on the syntax of the passage as a whole with reference to neighbouring chapters (macrosyntax). N. is particularly interested in the parallel passages from the books of Samuel and Chronicles which show how the same matter can be expressed in different ways. The final section deals with the use of *way'hî* in Exod. 1–14. There are indices and a bibliography.

This workbook should encourage us, teachers and students alike, to analyse Hebrew not as isolated words or even sentences but as a set of cohesive texts with their own inner dynamics which, as the author shows, become apparent through correctly understanding the syntax of the verb.

W. G. E. WATSON

RENDSBURG, G. A: *Linguistic Evidence for the Northern Origin of Selected Psalms* (SBL Monograph Series, 43). 1990. Pp. xiii, 143. (Scholars Press, Atlanta GA. Price: $24.95 (member price: $14.95); paperback price: $14.95 (member price: $9.95). ISBN 1 55540 565 7; 1 55540 566 5 (pbk))

The question of dialect in biblical Hebrew (BH) is a difficult one. R. continues his efforts from previous studies to develop and apply criteria for identifying an 'Israelian Hebrew' (IH), as opposed to 'Judahite Hebrew'. His working procedure is to identify 'Israelian' texts and then isolate their characteristics. The texts include Qohelet, Proverbs, Job, Hosea, Song of Songs, and individual chapters of other books. The features isolated include *–ôt* as fem. sg.; *–kî*, 2 fem. sg.; *zeh/zû* and *še–* as relative pronouns; reduplicatory plurals of geminate nouns; *bal* as negative particle; *b–/l–* meaning 'from'; and a variety of vocabulary items.

There are a number of weaknesses in R.'s methodology. For example, he considers speeches in the mouths of Israelian figures as examples of Israelian speech even if in a text composed in Judah; likewise with Judean prophetic speeches against foreign nations. While such 'style-switching' is possible, it is difficult to control. Similarly, any linguistic feature found in Aramaic, Moabite, and Ammonite which is not standard BH is considered evidence of IH. Identification of Aramaisms has always been problematic, but R.'s procedure seems as doubtful as some attempts to find direct Aramaic influence. Although cautious, R. still accepts some of Dahood's somewhat dubious interpretations: e.g. *b–/l–* in the sense of 'from', yet apparently without knowing of Pardee's important study on Ugaritic prepositions.

R.'s study is very welcome, despite some problems. Hebrew dialect is a difficult field and any attempts to advance the study of it can only be applauded.

L. L. GRABBE

RETSÖ, J.: *Diathesis in the Semitic Languages. A Comparative Morphological Study* (Studies in Semitic Languages and Linguistics xiv). 1989. Pp. xvii, 254. (Brill, Leiden. Price: fl. 96.00. ISBN 90 04 08818 0; ISSN 0081 8461)

What, readers will demand, is diathesis? In the semantic relations between the verbal kernel of a sentence and its nominal elements, it is a covering term for these semantic relations and their morpho-syntactic representation. The book deals principally with two types of diathesis, the

PHILOLOGY AND GRAMMAR 139

passive and the causative. Perhaps surprisingly for most readers, these are closely linked (p. 48). There never was any common-Semitic passive or causative conjugation (pp. 88, 203). Elements like *yaqtil*, *yuqtal*, are 'an original G-stem reemployed as' causative conjugation (p. 140). The perfects like *hiqtil* come from noun elements: they are 'conjugated nouns' (p. 170). This theme is pursued across the full range of Semitic and into Afro–Asiatic, but the main evidence comes from Akkadian, Biblical Hebrew, and Vernacular Arabic. Parts of ch. 5, on the Arabic evidence, may well be skipped by many Old Testament scholars; but the effect of the argument on Arabic linguistics may be very powerful. According to it, many vernacular features have a diachronic ancestry anterior to 'High Arabic'. The Hebrew evidence is also very central, and includes apparent anomalies like 'passive qal', verbs in which the hiphil means the same as the qal or even has a passive meaning, and verbs in which imperfect hiphil has the same form as the qal. Or put it this way: the approach begins mainly from the imperfect, and one can say that one imperfect, *ya^caleh*, has two perfects (traditionally 'qal' and 'hiphil'), depending on meaning (p. 61). The Masoretic text is 'a veritable linguistic museum' giving evidence of many centuries of diachronic change (p. 73).

Thus diathesis, as it turns out, is no marginal phenomenon but leads on to a very radical reorganization of diachronic Semitic linguistics; here sympathy is shown for Garbini's scheme (p. 202f.) as against the traditional *Stammbaum* approach. There are some difficult abbreviations and terms: for *apophonic*, *apothematic* and *thematic*, which follows Rundgren's usage, see pp. 4f, 87. But the book is widely researched, densely and powerfully argued, and is an intellectual achievement of major importance, which will have deep eventual repercussions in exegesis. Incidentally, it completely dismisses Jenni's view of the piel (pp. 51, 142 nn.). One strange slip is in the discussion of hiphils with passive meaning on p. 185, since Isa 48:8, there quoted, contains no hiphil.

J. BARR

REYMOND, P.: *Dictionnaire d'Hébreu et d'Araméen Bibliques*. 1991. Pp. 449. (Cerf, Paris; Société Biblique Française. Price: Fr 290.00. ISBN 2 204 04463 6 (Cerf); ISBN 2 85300 713 8 (SBF))

The author, who is experienced in Hebrew lexicography as a result of helping to edit the third edition of the *Lexikon* (*HAL*) of L. Koehler and W. Baumgartner, notes that the only French dictionary in use for the Old Testament was written in the middle of the last century, and the present work provides a modern replacement for it. Since Reymond has sought to keep the price from being too high, his dictionary is concise and not intended to be a full-length work. The need for relative brevity has led to the regrettable, but understandable, omission of cognates from other Semitic languages, and no relevant scholarly literature other than *HAL* is mentioned. Words are recorded in alphabetical order without mention of roots, and usually only a selection of biblical references is given. In general, the dictionary is characterized by sober and dependable caution. It is perhaps the aim at conciseness that explains the failure to list all relevant meanings (e.g. the only meaning given for *dôr* is 'génération'; and 'to miss' is not recorded for the *qal* of *ḥāṭā*'). Reymond is aware of uncertainties in the state of the Hebrew text and in our understanding of many words, and he frequently mentions emendations, puts a question mark against a rendering or notes that it is traditional (and so presumably doubtful), or refers the reader to commentaries, grammars or *HAL* for further information. His attitude to new theories about lexicography is generally commendably cautious, even if it sometimes leads to improbable explanations, such as adherence to the view that *b^eliyya^cal* means 'sans valeur'. Occasionally, however, he can accept even such improbable theories as the view that *da^cat* in Isa. 53:11 means 'sueur' or that *derek* can mean

140   PHILOLOGY AND GRAMMAR

'puissance' (though he records that some explain the former differently and puts a question mark against the latter); and his acceptance of the derivation of *hištaḥ^awâ* from *ḥwh* says that the theory is based on Ugaritic (here he does mention a cognate language), but it is not noted that the analysis of the relevant Ugaritic verb is itself disputed. Apart from such occasional questionable statements, the greater part of this dictionary is sensible and reliable.

J. A. EMERTON

SIEBESMA, P. A.: *The function of the niph'al in Biblical Hebrew in relationship to other passive–reflective verbal stems and to the pu'al and hoph'al in particular* (Studia Semitica Neerlandica). 1991. Pp. ix, 207. (Van Gorcum, Assen/Maastricht. Price: fl. 49.50. ISBN 90 232 25945)

As the title suggests, this revision and translation of a 1988 doctoral thesis endeavours to examine the niphal verbal stem in comparison with other similar stems in Biblical Hebrew. Siebesma's detailed review of Jenni's study of the piel stem summarizes the difference in their methods; Jenni saw the niphal only in opposition to the qal but not in relation to other stems; Siebesma considers the niphal in relation to the other verbal stems as well. Using the concordance of Mandelkern and various dictionaries and lexicons, Siebesma finds 4143 niphal forms in the Hebrew Bible. His Hebrew epigraphic survey (pre–200 BC) finds six more. However, the two examples from the Siloam inscription are reconstructions and the Lachish ostracon 9 line 3 example is disputed. Siebesma generates numerous charts and statistics, identifying all niphal forms in the Bible and then observing their occurrences according to Biblical book, genre (prose, poetry, and prophecy, though it is not clear why two formal and one functional division should be used together), and whether the occurrence is perfect, imperfect, participal, infinitive, or imperative. He does the same for the passive qal, pual, hophal, and hithpael stems, noting roots which occur in different stems and whether they change their 'meaning'. Any future work on these stems will want to refer to this research.

Siebesma argues for a complex relationship between niphal, pual, hophal, and hithpael stems in their relationship to the 'active' stems. Thus it is not possible to conclude that each 'active' stem has a corresponding reflexive–passive stem, exclusive of other stems. For example, Siebesma finds that where niphal and pual forms of a root exist and the niphal occurs in semantic relationship to the qal, puals often form the perfect and niphals the imperfect of the reflexive–passive correspondent. On the other hand, when the niphal is in semantic relationship to the piel of the same root, pual perfects do not occur. Siebesma appears to favour the view that passive qals exist and became vocalized as puals and hophals, however he is cautious. Consideration of earlier verbal forms in proper names as well as second millennium West Semitic would appear to be of value in such diachronic questions.

R. S. HESS

SOKOLOFF, M.: *A Dictionary of Jewish Palestinian Aramaic of the Byzantine Period* (Dictionaries of Talmud, Midrash and Targum, II). 1990. Pp. 823. (Bar Ilan University Press, Ramat-Gan. Price: $99.00. ISBN 965 226 101 7)

This is a landmark volume in Aramaic studies and for several reasons. It is the first attempt to represent comprehensively an individual dialect from within the rabbinic literary corpus, in this case covering the period from the third century CE to the Arab Conquest. It has two major advantages over earlier lexical undertakings, first in that many new manuscripts have become

PHILOLOGY AND GRAMMAR

available in the present century, and secondly because the possibility of creating KWIC (Key Word in Context) concordances for all the sources used in the dictionary means that the entries are based on a complete lexical trawl. Furthermore, because the dictionary is dialect-specific the familiar problems encountered in older works (incomplete citation for individual dialects, uniform meaning despite dialectal variation) are overcome. Ten groups of sources are identified and used: Palestinian synagogal inscriptions, Palestinian Targums, Palestinian Midrashim, Palestinian Talmud, gaonic literature, poetry, fifth century papyri from Egypt, amulets, ketubboth, and Tiberian Massora. The standard Targums to the Pentateuch and Prophets are not cited, as originating in the Tannaitic period, nor is Pseudo–Jonathan (for two or three good reasons, to which the question of dating might be added). Aramaic loan-words in Hebrew contexts are left out, as are personal and geographical names. A full entry consists of lemma, parts of speech, English gloss, etymological information, semantic section giving various morphological forms and semantic features of the lexeme (phrases cited in Aramaic are also given in English translation), and, where appropriate, bibliographical information principally on form and meaning. There are over two hundred pages of indices detailing occurrences of words cited according to source. The volume is beautifully produced and the information is presented with exemplary clarity and consistency.

R. P. Gordon

Verheij, A. J.: *Verbs and Numbers. A Study of the Frequencies of the Hebrew Verbal Tense Forms in the Books of Samuel, Kings, and Chronicles* (Studia Semitica Neerlandica 28). 1990. Pp. iv, 135. (Van Gorcum, Assen/Maastricht. Price: fl. 35.00. ISBN 90 232 2572 4)

The research here published 'is a computer-assisted comparison of the books of Samuel, Kings, and Chronicles with respect to the absolute and relative frequencies of the Hebrew tense forms'. It is interested in the question whether Late Biblical Hebrew (exemplified in Chronicles) can be clearly distinguished from Early Biblical Hebrew. The methodological advance made is that material is gathered not on an *ad hoc* basis and not through exegesis, but through a clearly defined mathematical scheme. One striking result is that, though Chronicles is different from the other two books, the other two books are also substantially different from one another. Explanations are clear and powerful and the work is likely to provide a pattern for much future research.

J. Barr

Xella, P. (ed.): *Studi epigrafici e linguistici sul Vicino Oriente antico*, 8. 1991. Pp. 244. (Essedue edizioni, Verona. Price: Lire 40,000. ISBN 88 85697 37 2)

All fifteen contributions to the latest issue of this annual, fittingly dedicated to J. J. Stamm who was 80 last year, are on the topic of personal names (hence the subtitle *Onomata*). (Subscribers will note that while the price has remained unaltered the quality of printing has improved and there are nearly one hundred more pages than in the previous issue.) Readers of the *Book List* will turn first to F. Israel's notes on Hebrew and Philistine names (pp. 119–40), for which a sequel is promised on names from the Transjordan. Next, they will look at S. Ribichini and P. Xella's joint article listing the gods in theophoric names from Ugarit (pp. 149–70) and at M. G. Amadasi Guzzo and C. Bonnet's survey of equivalences between Greek and Phoenician names (pp. 1–21). Of interest, too, is F. M. Fales on West Semitic names in the Assyrian Empire. The other languages/areas covered are Abu Salabikh (F. Pomponio), Ebla (M. Bonechi), Egyptian (A. Roccati), Elamite

142 PHILOLOGY AND GRAMMAR

(R. Zadok), Emar (D. Arnaud), Hurrian (M. Salvini), Mari (J.-M. Durand), Middle Assyrian (C. Saporetti — A. Ghiroldi), Old Babylonian (M. Stol), Palmyrene (J. Teixidor), and pre-Islamic South Arabic (A. Avanzini).

W. G. E. Watson

ADDENDUM

Mori, A.: *Seisho no Shuchukozo (jo) Kyuyaku hen (Concentric Structure in the Bible*: (1) *Old Testament)*. 1991. Pp. 186. (Yorudansha, Tokyo. Price: ¥ 2300)

This is the first volume of the author's two-volume work on concentric structure in the Bible. Before giving various examples, he defines 'structure' and 'concentric structure' and, basing himself on Ezekiel 34:1–16, explains how to observe concentric structure in a biblical text. The major portion of this book is Chapter IV in which he lists forty-two examples of this structure. As an appendix the author presents a short study of the structure of the book of Jonah.

D. T. Tsumura

BOOKS RECEIVED 143

Books Received too Late for Notice in 1992

The books in the following list will be reviewed in the *Book List* for 1993.

ANDERSON, G. A. and OLYAN. S. M.: *Priesthood and Cult in Ancient Israel* (Journal for the Study of the Old Testament Supplement Series 125). 1991. (JSOT Press, Sheffield. ISBN 1 85075 322 9)

BAILEY, J. L. and BROEK, L. D.: *Literary Forms in the New Testament. A Handbook.* 1992. (Westminster/John Knox, Louisville KY. ISBN 0 664 25154 4)

BREWER, D. I.: *Techniques and Assumptions in Jewish Exegesis before 70 CE* (Texte und Studien zum Antiken Judentum 30). 1992. (Mohr, Tübingen. ISBN 3 16 145803 6; ISSN 0721 8753)

BROWN, S.: *Late Carthaginian Child Sacrifice and Sacrificial Monuments in their Mediterranean Context* (JSOT/ASOR Monograph Series 3). 1991. (JSOT Press, Sheffield. ISBN 1 85075 240 0; ISSN 0267 5684)

BRUEGGEMANN, W.: *To Build, to Plant. A Commentary on Jeremiah 26–52* (International Theological Commentary). 1991. (Eerdmans, Grand Rapids MI. ISBN 0 8028 0600 7)

BURROWS, M. S. and ROREM, P. (eds.): *Biblical Hermeneutics in Historical Perspective. Studies in Honor of Karlfried Froehlich on his Sixtieth Birthday.* 1991. (Eerdmans, Grand Rapids MI. ISBN 0 8028 3693 3)

DE CAEN, V. J.: *Newsletter for Targumic & Cognate Studies. A Revised Bibliography for the Samalian Dialect of Old Aramaic.* December 1991. (Department of Near Eastern Studies, University of Toronto, Ontario)

CARROLL, M. D.: *Contexts for Amos. Prophetic Poetics in Latin American Perspective* (Journal for the Study of the Old Testament Series 132). 1992. (JSOT Press, Sheffield. ISBN 1 85075 297 4; ISSN 0309 0787)

CLARKE, E. G. (ed.): *Newsletter for Targumic & Cognate Studies.* 1992. (Department of Near Eastern Studies, University of Toronto, Ontario. ISSN 0704 59005)

COLLINS, J. J. and CHARLESWORTH, J. H. (eds.): *Mysteries and Revelations. Apocalyptic Studies since the Uppsala Colloquium* (Journal for the Study of the Pseudepigrapha Supplement Series 9). 1991. (JSOT Press, Sheffield. ISBN 1 85075 299 0)

EDELMAN, D. V. (ed.): *The Fabric of History. Text, Artifact and Israel's Past* (Journal for the Study of the Old Testament Supplement Series 127). 1991. (Sheffield Academic Press. ISBN 1 85075 324 5; ISSN 0309 0787)

EMERTON, J. A. (ed.): *Congress Volume Leuven 1989* (Supplements to Vetus Testamentum XLIII). 1991. (Brill, Leiden. ISBN 90 04 09398 2; ISSN 0083 5889)

FAHR, H. and GLESSMER, U.: *Jordandurchzug und Beschneidung als Zurechtweisung in einem Targum zu Josua 5. Edition de Ms T.-S. B 13, 12* (Orientalia Biblica et Christiana 3). 1991. (J. J. Augustin, Glückstadt. ISBN 3 87030 152 X)

FLESHER, P. V. (ed): *New Perspectives on Ancient Judaism.* Volume 5: *Society and Literature in Analysis* (Studies in Judaism 5). 1990. (University Press of America, Lanham, New York and London. ISBN 0 8191 7614 1)

FOHRER, G.: *Erzähler und Propheten im Alten Testament. Geschichte der israelitischen und frühjüdischen Literatur* (Uni-Taschenbücher 1547). 1989. (Quelle & Meyer, Heidelberg. ISBN 3 494 02169 4)

FOHRER, G., HOFFMANN, H. W., HUBER, F., MARKERT, L. and WANKE, G.: *Exegese des Alten Testaments Einführung in die Methodik* (Uni-Taschenbücher 267). 1989. (Quelle & Meyer, Heidelberg. ISBN 3 494 02165 1)

144 BOOKS RECEIVED

Fox, R. L.: *The Unauthorized Version. Truth and Fiction in the Bible*. 1991. (Viking, London. ISBN 0 670 82412 7)

HAAK, R. D.: *Habakkuk* (Supplements to Vetus Testamentum XLIV). 1992. (Brill, Leiden. ISBN 90 04 09506 3; ISSN 0083 5889)

HALPERN, B. and HOBSON, D. W. (eds.): *Law and Ideology in Monarchic Israel* (Journal for the Study of the Old Testament Supplement Series 124). 1991. (Sheffield Academic Press. ISBN 1 85075 323 7)

HOLDEN, L.: *Forms of Deformity* (Journal for the Study of the Old Testament Supplement Series 131). 1991. (Sheffield Academic Press. ISBN 1 85075 327 X)

HOUTEN, C. VAN: *The Alien in Israelite Law* (Journal for the Study of the Old Testament Supplement Series 107). 1991. (Sheffield Academic Press. ISBN 1 85075 317 2)

JACOBS, L.: *Structure and form in the Babylonian Talmud*. 1991. (Cambridge University Press. ISBN 0 521 40345 6)

JONGELING, K., MURRE-VAN DEN BERG, H. L. and VAN ROMPEY, L. (eds.): *Studies in Hebrew and Aramaic Syntax presented to Professor J. Hoftijzer on the occasion of his sixty-fifth birthday* (Studies in Semitic Languages and Linguistics xvii). 1991. (Brill, Leiden. ISBN 90 04 09520 9; ISSN 0881 8461)

KARPP, H.: *Schrift, Geist und Wort Gottes. Geltung und Wirkung der Bibel in der Geschichte der Kirche. Von der Alten Kirche bis zum Ausgang der Reformationszeit*. 1992. (Wissenschaftliche Buchgesellschaft, Darmstadt. ISBN 3 534 10862 0)

KREUZER, S. and LÜTHI, K. (eds.): *Zur Aktualität des Alten Testaments. Festschrift für Georg Sauer zum 65. Geburtstag*. 1992. (Lang, Frankfurt (Main)–Bern–New York–Paris. ISBN 3 631 44045 6)

KÜNG, H.: *Judaism*. 1992. (SCM Press, London. ISBN 0 334 02524 9)

LIWAK, R. and WAGNER, S. (eds.): *Prophetie und leschichtliche Wirklichkeit im alten Israel. Festschrift für Siegfried Herrmann zum 65. Geburtstag*. 1991. (Kohlhammer, Stuttgart. ISBN 3 17 011314 3)

LOHFINK, N.: *Die Väter Israels im Deuteronomium Mit einer Stellungnahme von Thomas Römer* (Orbis Biblicus et Orientalis 111). 1991. (Universitätsverlag, Freiburg (CH); Vandenhoeck & Ruprecht, Göttingen. ISBN 3 7278 0778 4 (Universitätsverlag); ISBN 3 525 53744 1 (Vandenhoeck & Ruprecht))

LOWERY, R. H.: *The Reforming Kings. Cult and Society in First Temple Judah* (Journal for the Study of the Old Testament Supplement Series 120). 1991. (JSOT Press, Sheffield. ISBN 1 85075 318 0)

MASSON, M.: *Élie, ou l'appel du silence* (Parole présente). 1992. (Cerf, Paris. ISBN 2 204 04379 6; ISSN 0986 0126)

McCREESH, T. P.: *Biblical Sound and Sense. Poetic Sound Patterns in Proverbs 10–29* (Journal for the Study of the Old Testament Supplement Series 128). 1991. (Sheffield Academic Press. ISBN 1 85075 326 1)

McCREESH, T. P. (ed.): *Old Testament Abstracts. Vol. 14, No. 3* (Liturgical Press, Collegeville MN. ISSN 0364 8591)

McLAREN, J. S.: *Power and Politics in Palestine. The Jews and the Governing of their Land 100 BC–AD 70* (Journal for the Study of the New Testament Supplement Series 63). 1991. (JSOT Press, Sheffield. ISBN 1 85075 319 9)

METZGER, B. M., DENTAN, R. C. and HARRELSON, W.: *The Making of the New Revised Standard Version of the Bible*. 1991. (Eerdmans, Grand Rapids MI. ISBN 8 80283 0620 1)

The Midrash on Proverbs, translated from the Hebrew with an Introduction and Annotations by B. L. Visotzky (Yale Judaica Series, XXVII). 1992. (Yale University Press, New Haven and London. ISBN 0 300 05107 7)

BOOKS RECEIVED 145

MILETTO, G.: *L'Antico Testamento ebraico nella tradizione babilonese I frammenti della Genizah* (Quaderni di Henoch 3). 1992. (Silvio Zamorani Editore, Torino. ISBN 88 7158 0133)

MINETTE DE TILLESSE, C. (ed.): *Revista Biblica Brasileira. Ano 8, 4.* 1991. (Nova Jerusalém, Fortaleza CE. Brazil)

MURRAY, R.: *The Cosmic Covenant. Biblical Themes of Justice, Peace and the Integrity of Creation.* 1992. (Sheed & Ward, London. ISBN 0 7220 2750 8)

NEUSNER, J.: *An Introduction to Judaism; a Textbook and Reader.* 1991. (Westminster/John Knox, Louisville KY. ISBN 0 664 25348 2)

NEUSNER, J.: *Judaism without Christianity. An introduction to the System of the Misnah.* 1991. (Ktav Publishing House, Hoboken NJ. ISBN 0 88125 333 2)

OLLENBURGER, B. C., MARTENS, E. A. and HASEL, B. F. (eds): *The Flowering of Old Testament Theology. A Reader in Twentieth-Century Old Testament Theology, 1930–1990* (Sources for Biblical and Theological Study 1). 1992. (Eisenbrauns, Winona Lake IN. ISBN 0 931464 62 5)

ORLINSKY, H. M. and BRATCHER, R. G.: *A History of Bible Translation and the North American Contribution* (Society of Biblical Literature. Biblical Scholarship in North America). 1991. (Scholars Press, Atlanta GA. ISBN 1 55540 571 1 (cloth); ISBN 1 55540 572 X (paper))

PELTENBURG, E.: *The Burrell Collection Western Asiatic Antiquities.* 1991. (Edinburgh University Press [for] The Burrell Collection Glasgow Museums. ISBN 0 7486 0224 0)

PETROTTA, A. J.: *Lexis Ludens. Wordplay and the Book of Micah* (American University Studies Series VII Theology and Religion 105). 1991. (Lang, New York. ISBN 0 8204 1539 1; ISSN 0740 0446)

PETTEY, R. J.: *Asherah Goddess of Israel* (American University Studies Series VII Theology and Religion 74). 1990. (Lang, New York. ISBN 0 8204 1306 2; ISSN 0740 0446)

PILCH, J. J.: *Introducing the Cultural Context of the Old Testament. Hear the Word!* Volume I. 1991. (Paulist Press, New York. ISBN 0 8091 3271 0)

RASHKOW, I. N.: *Upon the Dark Places. Anti-Semitism and Sexism in English Renaissance Biblical Translation* (Bible and Literature Series 28). 1990. (Almond Press, Sheffield. ISBN 1 85075 251 6; ISSN 0260 4493)

RODD, C. S.: *The Book of Job* (Epworth Communications). 1990. (Epworth Press, London. ISBN 0 7162 0468 1)

ROGERSON, J. W.: *W. M. L. de Wette, Founder of Modern Biblical Criticism. An Intellectual Biography* (Journal for the Study of the Old Testament Supplement Series 126). 1992. (JSOT Press, Sheffield. ISBN 1 85075 330 X)

ROOF, E. F.: *Let the Rivers run. Stewardship and the Biblical Story* (Library of Christian Stewardship). 1992. (Eerdmans, Grand Rapids MI. ISBN 0 8028 0609 0)

SANDERS, E. P.: *Judaism Practice and Belief 63 BCE–66 CE.* 1992. (SCM Press, London; Trinity Press International, Philadelphia. ISBN 0 334 02470 6; ISSN 1 56338 015 3)

SCHÄFER, P. and BECKER, H.-J. (eds.): *Synopse zum Talmud Yerushalmi.* Band I/1–2 *Ordnung Zera'im: Berakhot und Pe'a,* in Zusammenarbeit mit G. Reeg und unter Mitwirkung von A. Engel, K. Ipta, U. Lohmann, M. Urban und G. Wildensee (Texte und Studien zum Antiken Judentum 31). 1991. (Mohr, Tübingen. ISBN 3 16 14849 4; ISSN 0721 8753)

146 BOOKS RECEIVED

SCHWARTZ, D. R.: *Studies in the Jewish Background of Christianity* (Wissenschaftliche Untersuchungen zum Neuen Testament 60). 1992. (Mohr (Paul Siebeck), Tübingen. ISBN 3 16 145789 6; ISSN 0512 1604)

SEGAL, B.-Z. (ed.): *The Ten Commandments in History and Tradition. English version edited by B. Levi.* 1990. (Magnes, Jerusalem. ISBN 965 223 724 8)

SILVA, M.: *God, Language and Scripture. Reading the Bible in the light of general linguistics* (Foundations of Contemporary Interpretation, 4). 1990. (Zondervan, Grand Rapids MI. ISBN 0 310 40951 9)

SOHN, S.-T.: *The Divine Election of Israel.* 1991. (Eerdmans, Grand Rapids MI. ISBN 0 8028 0545 0)

STAUBLI, T.: *Das Image der Nomaden im Alten Israel und in der Ikonographie seiner sesshaften Nachbarn* (Orbis Biblicus et Orientalis 107). 1991. (Universitätsverlag, Freiburg (CH); Vandenhoeck & Ruprecht, Göttingen. ISBN 3 7278 0769 5 (Universitätsverlag); ISBN 3 525 53740 9 (Vandenhoeck & Ruprecht))

SWARTZ, M .D: *Mystical Prayer in Ancient Judaism. An Analysis of Ma'aseh Merkavah* (Texte und Studien zum Antiken Judentum 28). 1992. (Mohr, Tübingen. ISBN 3 16 145679 3)

THIBAUT, A.: *L'Infidélité du Peuple Élu: 'APEITHO entre la Bible Hébraïque et la Bible Latine* (Collectanea Biblica Latina XVII). 1988. (San Girolamo, Rome)

THRONTVEIT, M. A.: *Ezra-Nehemiah* (Interpretation A Bible Commentary for Teaching and Preaching). 1992. (John Knox, Louisville, KY. ISBN 0 8042 3111 7)

TOURNAY, R. J.: *Seeing and Hearing God with the Psalms. The Prophetic Liturgy of the Second Temple in Jerusalem.* Translated by J. Edward Crowley (Journal for the Study of the Old Testament Supplement Series 118). 1991. (Sheffield Academic Press. ISBN 1 85075 313 X)

TRIBLE, P.: *God and the Rhetoric of Sexuality.* 1991. (SCM Press, London. ISBN 0 334 02529 X)

TRIBLE, P.: *Texts of Terror. Literary–Feminist Readings of Biblical Narratives.* 1992. (SCM Press, London. ISBN 0 334 02530 3)

VANDERKAM, J. C. (ed.): *'No One Spoke Ill of Her'. Essays on Judith* (Society of Biblical Literature: Early Judaism and its Literature 02). 1992. (Scholars Press, Atlanta GA. ISBN 1 55540 672 6)

Vetus Latina. Die Reste der altlateinischen Bibel nach Petrus Sabatier neu gesammelt und herausgegeben von der Erzabtei Beuron. 11/2: Sirach (Ecclesiasticus). Herausgegeben von W. Thiele. 4. Lieferung: *Sir, 3, 31–7, 30.* 1992. (Herder, Freiburg. ISBN 3 451 00427 5; ISSN 0571 9070)

Vetus Latina. Die Reste der altlateinischen Bibel nach Petrus Sabatier neu gesammelt und herausgegeben von der Erzabtei Beuron. 12: Esaias. Herausgegeben von R. Gryson. 8. Lieferung: *Is. 26, 20–30, 15.* 1991. (Herder, Freiburg. ISBN 3 451 00476 3; ISSN 0571 9070)

WESTBROOK, R.: *Property and the Family in Biblical Law* (Journal for the Study of the Old Testament Supplement Series 113). 1991. (JSOT Press, Sheffield. ISBN 1 85075271 0)

YOUNG, G. D. (ed.): *Mari in Retrospect. Fifty Years of Mari and Mari Studies.* 1992. (Eisenbrauns, Winona Lake IN. ISBN 0 931 46428 5)

Index of Authors

(N.B. — Names occurring more than once in the same review or on the same page are listed on their first occurrence only)

	PAGE		PAGE
AALEN, S.	122	BEAUCAMP, É.	48
AARFLOT, A.	8	BECK, P.	12
ABELA, A.	8	BECKER, H.-J.	145
Abr-Nahrain	19	BECKER, U.	62
ACHENBACH, R.	97	BECKING, B.	65
ACKROYD, P. R.	60	BECKMAN, G. M.	117
ADDINALL, P.	98	BEIT-ARIEH, I.	32
AEJMELAEUS, A.	45	BELLEVILLE, L. L.	123
ALEXANDER, L.	122	BEN ZVI, E.	62
ALONSO SCHÖKEL, L.	98	BEN-TOR, A.	11
ALTMAN, A.	118	BENJAMIN, D. C.	119
AMADASI GUZZO, M. G.	141	BERNAL, M.	26
AMARE, M.	73	BEUKEN, W. A. M.	13
AMUNDSEN, A. B.	8	*Bibelen i Norge*	8
ANBAR, M.	40	*Bibelkommissionen*	59
ANDERSON, G. A.	143	BIENKOWSKI, P.	26
ANNANDALE-POTTGIETER, J.	45	BIETAK, M.	12
ARICHAE, D. C.	57	BIRAN, A.	12, 32
ARNAUD, D.	142	BLENKINSOPP, J.	11, 102
ARNOLD, W.	133	BLIDSTEIN, G. J.	131
ARTOLA, A. M.	98	BLOK, H.	27
ARTZI, P.	117	BLUM, E.	12
VON ARX, U.	40	BOCCACCINI, G.	25
ASALI, K. J.	41	BODI, D.	32, 63
ASSMANN, J.	99, 115, 120	DE BOER, P. A.	64
ATTIAS, J.-C.	123	BOFF, C.	112
ATTRIDGE, H. W.	7	BOGAERT, P.-M.	46
AUFRECHT, W. E.	25	BONECHI, M.	135
AVANZINI,Z A.	142	BONFIL, R.	12
AVIRAM, J.	7	BONNET, C.	141
		BORBONE, P. G.	25, 87
		BORG, V.	8
BAILEY, J. L.	143	BORI, P. C.	101
BAILLET, M.	9	BORRET, M.	49
BAJARD, J.	45	BOTTERWECK, G. J.	9
BAK, D. H.	61	BOURRIAU, J.	12
BARBIERO, G.	99	BOZAK, B. A.	64
BARKAY, G.	12	BRATCHER, R. G.	49, 145
BARKER, M.	100	BREKELMANS, C.	65
BARNES, R.	85	BRÉSARD, L.	49
BARSTAD, H.	12	BRETT, M. G.	101
BARTELMUS, R.	13	BREWER, D. I.	143
BARTH, C.	100	BRIEND, J.	9
BARTON, J.	61	BRODBECK, A.	121
BATALDEN, S.	57	BROEK, L. D.	143
BAUMGARTEN, J. M.	131	BROOKE, G. J.	122
BAUMGARTNER, W.	136	BROOKS, R.	102–03

148 INDEX

	PAGE		PAGE
BROOTEN, B. J.	7	DARR, K. P.	104
BROWN, S.	143	DAVIES, G. I.	29, 33, 39
BRUEGGEMANN, W.	103, 143	DAVIES, P. R.	11, 122
Bulletin of the Anglo-Israel		DAVILA, J. R.	7
Archaeological Society	31	DAVIS, RABBI A.	53
BUNIMOWITZ, S.	12	DAWN, M. J.	43
BUNNENS, G.	27	DEISSLER, A.	104
BURKE, D.	103	DELL'AVERSANO, C.	25
BURROWS, M. S.	143	DELL, K. J.	66
BUSTO SAIZ, J. R.	45	DELSMAN, W. C.	115, 120
BUTTERWECK, C.	115	DEMSKY, A.	117
		DENNIS, T.	67
		DENTAN, R. C.	144
CACQUOT, A.	9	DERFLER, S. L.	42
DE CAEN, V. J.	143	DEVER, W. G.	30, 32
CARDENAL, E.	112	DIAKONOFF, I. M.	10
CARR, D. M.	65	DIETRICH, M.	115, 120
CARROLL, M. D.	143	DIEZ MERINO, L.	46
CARROLL, R. P.	11, 103	DIJKSTRA, M.	33
CASPARI, W.	72	DIMANT, D.	131
CASSIODORUS	49	DOHMEN, C.	12
CATHCART, K. J.	44	DOORLY, W. J.	67
CHARLESWORTH, J. H.	7, 131, 134,	DORAN, R.	7
143		DORIVAL, J.	46
CHRISTIE, S.	8	DORSEY, D. A.	30
CLARKE, E. G.	45, 143	DOTHAN, M.	32, 43
CLEMENTS, R. E.	10, 13	DOTHAN, T.	32
COGAN, M.	10	DRAZIN, I.	45
COGGINS, R. J.	65	VAN DUIN, C.	64
COHN-SHERBOK, D.	10	DUKE, R. K.	68
COLLESS, B. E.	19	DURAND, J.-M.	135, 142
COLLINS, A. Y.	7, 103	DUS, J.	43
COLLINS, J. J.	7, 22, 102, 143		
CONRAD, D.	120		
CONROY, C.	65	EBACH, J.	104
CONTI, G.	135	EDELMAN, D. V.	65, 68, 143
COOGAN, M. D.	22, 29	EITAM, D.	43
COOK, J.	45	EITAN, A.	11
COOTE, R. B.	42	ELAT, M.	10
CORTESE, E.	65	*Elenchus of Biblica 1988*	21
COTHENET, E.	9	ELLINGTON, J.	55
COWE, S. P.	45	ELLIS, E. E.	68, 123
COX, C. E.	45	ELLUL, J.	69
CRAWFORD, H.	116	EMERTON, J. A.	143
CRIBB, R.	27	ENGELSTAD, C. F.	8
CROUZEL, H.	49	EPHʿAL, I.	10
CUNCHILLOS, J.-L.	28	ERIKSEN, E. O.	12
CUNNINGHAM, A.	10	ESCOBAR, S.	57
		EVANS, C. A.	69
		EYNIKEL, E.	65
DAHLBERG, B. T.	29		
DAHMEN, U.	13		
DANBOLT, G.	8	FABRY, H.-J.	12
DANIELS, D. R.	66	FAHR, H.	143
DAR, S.	31	FALES, F. M.	10, 141

INDEX

149

	PAGE
FARMER, K. A.	70
FELDMAN, L. H.	128
FERNANDEZ-MARCOS, N.	45
FICK, U.	57
FLEISHMAN, J.	118
FLESHER, P. V.	143
FLINT, P. W.	45
FLORENTIN, M.	19
FOHRER, G.	13, 135, 143
FOKKELMAN, J. P.	70
FORD, J. M.	102
FOX, M. V.	70
FOX, R. L.	144
FRANKEN, H. J.	27, 33, 41
FRANKISH, J.	34
FREEDMAN, D. N.	22
FRETHEIM, T. E.	50
FRITZ, V.	18
FRONZAROLI, P.	135
FUHS, H. F.	12
FULLER, R.	7
GABEL, J. B.	71
GAEBELEIN, F. E.	50
GAGER, J. G.	7
GALEY, J.-C.	105
GAMMIE, J. G.	13
GARCIA MARTINEZ, F.	25
GARFINKEL, Y.	12
GARR, W. R.	22
GARRONE, D.	13
GARSIEL, M.	71
GERHARDSSON, B.	22
GESE, H.	14
GHIROLDI, A.	142
GIBSON, S.	31
GILBERT, M.	20, 131
GITAY, Y.	71
GITIN, S.	32
GLASSNER, G.	51
GLESSMER, U.	143
GOLKA, F. W.	51
GOODRICK, E. W.	14
GOPHNA, R.	11
GORDON, C. W.	19
GORDON, R. P.	44
GÖRG, M.	51
GOVRIN, Y.	11
GRABBE, L. L.	11
GREEN, D. E.	9
GREENBERG, M.	10
GREENFIELD, J. C.	7, 33
GREENGUS, S.	128
GREENSPOON, L.	45

	PAGE
GREISCH, J.	15
GRESSMANN, H.	72
GRIFFITHS, J. G.	116
GRYSON, R.	48
GUINAN, M. D.	72
GUTEKUNST, W. C.	115
GUTIERREZ, G.	113
HAAK, R. D.	144
HAAVIK, Å.	8
HACKETT, J. A.	33
HACKETT, P.	71
HAHN, J.	18
HAIK-VANTOURA, S.	16
HAILE, G.	73
HALLIGAN, J. M.	11
HALLO, W. W.	10
HALPERN, B.	22, 144
HAMILTON, V. P.	52
HANKS, J. M.	69
HARALDSØ, B.	8
HARDING, G.	59
HARL, M.	45–46
HARPER, P. O.	12
HARRELSON, W.	144
HARRINGTON, D. J.	7
HASEL, G. F.	73, 105, 145
HAYWARD, R.	113
HAUGE, I.	8
Hebrew Union College Annual	128
HECKER, K.	120, 136
HEILIGENTHAL, R.	18
HEINTZ, J.-G.	32
HELTZER, M.	43
HERRMANN, S.	74
HERZOG, Z.	33
HEYMEL, M.	106
HICKÉRSON, L. G.	134
HILDEBRAND, K.-G.	59
HILL, A. E.	74
HO, A.	106
HOBSON, D. W.	144
HODNE, Ø.	8
HOFFMANN, H. W.	135, 143
HOFFNER, H. A.	117
HOFTIJZER, J.	33
HOGLAND, K.	11
HOLDEN, L.	144
HOLTER, Å.	8
HONIGWACHS, Y.	74
HOPPE, L. J.	94
HORSLEY, R. A.	11
VAN HOUTEN, C.	144
HOUTMAN, C.	106

150   INDEX

	Page
Huber, F.	135, 143
Huehnergard, J.	33
Hulmes, E.	113
Hultgren, A. J.	22
Husser, J.-M.	33
Hvidberg-Hansen, F. O.	33
Ibrahim, M. M.	33
Idinopulos, T. A.	131
Imhof, P.	17
Internationale Zeitschriftenschau (IZBG)	17
Ishida, T.	10
Israel, F.	13, 33, 141
Jacobs, L.	144
Jacobson, D. M.	31
Jagersma, H.	74
James, P.	34
Jamieson, A.	27
Jamieson-Drake, D. W.	34
Jenkins, R. G.	45
Jensen, O.	8
Jobling, D.	11
Jones, D. R.	113
de Jonge, M.	123
Jongeling, K.	144
Kaiser, W. C.	107
Kallai, Z.	65
Kannengiesser, C.	103
Karpp, H.	144
Karrer, M.	75
Kasher, R.	128
Kausen, E.	115
Kawar, W.	27
Kearney, R.	15
Keel, O.	35
Kevers, P.	65
Kinlaw, D. F.	51
Kinzig, W.	75
Klein, H.	107
Klein, J.	117
Klein, M. L.	128
Kleinkaufmann, Rabbi A.	53
Klinghardt, M.	99
Knirck, C.-M.	108
Koch, R.	107
Kochavi, M.	11
Koehler, L.	136
Kohlenberger, J. R. iii	14
Kokkinos, N.	34

	Page
van der Kooij, A.	33, 45–46
Kottsieper, I.	136
Koucky, F. L.	29
Koyma, K.	57
Kraft, R. A.	7
Kramer, S. N.	10, 117
Krasovec, J.	65
Kratz, R. G.	6
Kraus Reggiani, C.	25
Kreuzer, S.	144
Kronholm, T.	13
Kugel, J. L.	22, 103
Kullerud, D.	8
Küng, H.	144
Kutscher, R.	117
Kvarme, O.Chr.M.	8
Laberge, L.	65
Lagrange, M.-J., op	20
Lang, B.	17
Lauer, S.	18
Lawton, D.	17
Lefebvre, P.	45
Lemaire, A.	9, 33, 65
Levenson, D.	7, 102
Levenson, J. D.	102
Levine, B. A.	33
Ling-Israel, P.	118
Lipinski, E.	43
Liverani, M.	10
Liwak, R.	13, 144
Lloyd Jones, G.	17
Loader, J. A.	76
Lohfink, N.	17, 65, 77, 108, 144
Longacre, R. E.	77
Longenecker, R. W.	124
Longman, T. iii	18, 118
van Loopik, M.	124
Loretz, O.	115, 120
Lowery, R. H.	144
Lubsczyk, H.	65
Lundbom, J. R.	22
Lust, J.	45–46, 65
Luther, K.	72
Lüthi, K.	144
Luzbetak, L. J.	57
McCarter, P. K.	33
McCarthy, C.	46
McCreesh, T. P.	18, 144
McEvenue, S.	78
McKenzie, S. L.	78

INDEX

151

	Page
McKnight, S.	125
McLaren, J. S.	144
McNutt, P. M.	36
McVey, K. E.	7
Maarsingh, B.	52
Macuch, R.	19
Magonet, J.	10, 126
Magrill, P.	31
Maier, J.	25, 114
Margain, J.	9
Markert, L.	143
Marquardt, F.-W.	104
Marquis, G.	45
Martens, E. A.	145
Martin, R.	45
Mason, R.	80
Mason, S.	126
Masson, M.	144
Matthers, J. M.	29
Matthews, D. M.	118
Matthews, V. H.	119
Matties, G. H.	80
Mazar, A.	12, 43
Meeks, W. A.	22
Meinhold, A.	53
Mendenhall, G. E.	41
Mershen, B.	27
The Metsudah Chumash/Rashi	53
Metzger, B. M.	144
Meyers, C. L.	36
Meyers, E. M.	36
The Midrash on Proverbs	144
Miletto, G.	25, 145
Milgrom, J.	13, 54, 131
Millard, A. R.	10, 27
Millot, L.	32
Minette de Tillesse, C.	145
Mollenkott, V. R.	108
Momigliano, A.	126
Moorey, P. R.	37
Mori, A.	81, 142
Morkot, R.	34
Mosala, I.	112
Moscati, S.	13
Mowvley, H.	81
Müller, G.	18
Müller, H.-P.	19, 33
Müller, W. W.	115
Muraoka, T.	19–20, 45
Murphy, F. J.	7
Murphy, R. E.	102
Murphy-O'Connor, J.	20
Murray, R.	145
Murre-van den Berg, H. L.	144
Murtonen, A.	137

	Page
Myhren, D. G.	8
Na'aman, N.	10
Nakazawa, K.	54
Naumann, T.	81
Negbi, O.	12, 33
Neusner, J.	127–28, 145
Newsom, C. A.	7, 22
Niccacci, A.	137
Nickelsburg, G. W. E.	7
Nida, E. A.	46
Niehr, H.	108
Nielsen, K.	81
The NIV Exhaustive Concordance	14
Nobile, M.	65
North, R.	21
Norton, G. J.	46
The NRSV Concordance Unabridged	14
O'Brien, J. M.	82
O'Connell, K. G.	29
O'Neill, J. C.	21
Oded, B.	10
Ognibeni, B.	46
Old Testament Abstracts	18, 144
Ollenburger, B. C.	43, 145
Olyan, S. M.	143
Oren, E.	12
Orlinsky, H. M.	145
Osumi, Y.	82
Otto, E.	21
Ottosson, M.	22, 83
Paper, H. H.	128
Pardee, D.	33
Parente, F.	25
Patrich, J.	119
Paul, M. J.	65
Paul, S. M.	84
Pauly, D.	104
Peek-Horn, M.	114
Pelletier, A.-M.	16
Peltenburg, E.	145
Perdue, L. G.	13, 109
Peshitta	46
Péter-Contesse, R.	55
Peterca, V.	65
Petersen, D. L.	11
Petrotta, A. J.	145
Pettey, R. J.	145
Pettinato, G.	37
Philip, G.	27

INDEX

	Page		Page
Piccirillo, M.	27	Rubin, R.	8
Pietersma, A.	46	Rüger, H. P.	88
Pilch, J. J.	145		
Pinero, A.	25		
Pisano, S.	46	Sacchi, P.	88
van der Ploeg, J. P. M.	47	Saebø, M.	8, 13
Pomponio, F.	141	Salvesen, A.	47
Poswick, R.-F.	45	Salvini, M.	142
Preuss, H. D.	13, 109	Sameh, L.	57
Prewitt, T. J.	85	Sanders, E. P.	145
Prickett, S.	85	Sanders, J. A.	46, 102
Propp, W. H.	22–23	Saporetti, C.	142
Provan, I. W.	55	Sass, B.	38
Puech, E.	7, 33	Saydon, P. P.	56
		Schäfer, P.	129, 145
Raabe, P. R.	86	Schäfer-Lichtenberger, C.	65
Raban, A.	43	Scharbert, J.	18
von Rad, G.	43	Schellong, D.	104
Rainey, A. F.	117	Schenker, A.	46, 65, 111
Rajak, T.	122	Schiffman, L. H.	129, 131
Rapp, G., Jr	33	Schlögl, H. A.	121
Rappaport, U.	131	Schmid, H.	89
Rashkow, I. N.	145	Schmidt, W. H.	89
Rattray, S.	13	Schneider, M.	16
Reade, J.	38	Schrey, H.-H.	18
Redford, P. R.	11	Schuller, E.	7
de Regt, L. J.	86	Schulz, A.	72
Reiterer, F. V.	110	Schumacher, J.	8
Renaud, B.	86	Schüssler Fiorenza, E.	111
Rendsburg, G. A.	138	Schwartz, D. R.	146
Rendtorff, R.	99, 102	Schwartz, S.	129
Retsö, J.	138	Schwienhorst-Schönberger, L.	
Reventlow, H. Graf	23		89
Revista Bíblica Brasileira	24, 145	Scullion, J. J.	108
Reviv, H.	44	Seebass, H.	18
Reyburn, W. D.	49	Sefati, Y.	117
Reymond, P.	139	Segal, B.-Z.	146
Ribichini, S.	141	Seybold, K.	90
Rice, G.	55	Shachar, A.	7
Richter, W.	56	Shatzman, I.	130
Ricoeur, P.	16	Shavitsky, Z.	20
Ringgren, H.	9, 12, 111	Sherwood, S. K.	91
Robertson, E.	23	Shiloh, Y.	32
Roccati, A.	141	Shuval, M.	35
Rodd, C. S.	145	Siebesma, P. A.	140
Rofé, A.	25, 87	Silva, M.	146
Rogerson, J. W.	87, 145	Simon, U.	91
Römer, W. H. P.	120	Singer, I.	43
van Rompey, L.	144	Sipila, S.	45
Roobaert, A.	27	Skaist, A.	117
Roof, E. F.	145	Sklba, R. J.	91
Rorem, P.	143	Smelik, K. A. D.	39, 65
Rosati, G.	120	Smend, R.	23
Ross, A. P.	51	Smith, D. L.	11
Rosso Ubigli, L.	25	Smith, M. S.	92, 112

INDEX

153

	PAGE		PAGE
SOGGIN, J. A.	18, 25	TOBIN, T. H.	7
SOHN, S.-T.	146	TÖKEI, F.	24
SOKOLOFF, M.	140	TOOMBS, L. E.	29
SOLL, W.	92	TOURNAY, R. J.	146
SOLLAMO, R.	45	TOV, E.	7, 45–46, 131
SØRBØ, J. I.	8	TOWNSEND, J. J.	58
SPERLING, U.	92	TREBILCO, P. R.	132
SPOTTORNO, V.	45	TREBOLLE, J.	45
STARBUCK, S. R. A.	134	TREVES, M.	24
STAUBLI, T.	146	TRIBLE, P.	146
STEGEMANN, H.	131	TSCHUGGNALL, P.	113
STEIBLE, H.	121		
STEINER, M.	27		
STEMBERGER, G.	25, 130	ÜBELACKER, W.	22
STERN, E.	32	UEHLINGER, C.	35, 93
STERNBERG-HOTABI, H.	115	UHLIG, S.	21
STINE, P. C.	57	ULRICH, E. C.	7, 102
STOL, M.	142	ÜNAL, A.	120
STONE, M. E.	7, 57	URMAN, D.	31
STRACK, H. L.	130	USSISHKIN, D.	12
STRANGE, J. F.	36		
STRÜBIND, K.	93		
STRUGNELL, J.	131	VANDERKAM, J. C.	6–7, 23, 146
STRUCKENBRUCK, L. T.	134	VANGEMEREN, W. A.	51
STUDIUM BIBLICUM FRANCISCANUM		VARGON, S.	118
	58	VAWTER, B.	94
SUCUPIRA, L.	24	VERBRUGGE, V. D.	15
SUGIRTHARAJAH, R. S.	112	VERHEIJ, A. J.	141
SUNDERMEIER, T.	99	VERMEYLEN, J.	65
SUNDSTRÖM, G.-B.	59	VERVENNE, M.	65
Supplément au Dictionnaire de la		VESCO, J.-L.	20
Bible	9	Vetus Latina	48, 146
SUSSMAN, V.	12	VIAL, F.	101
Svensk exegetisk årsbok	22	VIVIAN, A.	25
SWARTZ, M. D.	146	VOITILA, A.	45
SYKES, S. W.	113	VOLLMER, J.	135, 144
SZYSZMAN, S.	46		
		DE WAARD, J.	46
TALMON, SH.	131–32	WAGNER, S.	144
TARADACH, M.	132	WALLIS, G.	13
TAYLOR, J.	20	WALLS, A.	57
TAYLOR, J. E.	31	WALSH, P. G.	49
TEIXIDOR, J.	142	WALTON, J. H.	51, 74
TENGSTRÖM, S.	12	WANKE, G.	135, 143
THEISSEN, G.	113	WEINFELD, M.	43, 59
Theological Dictionary of the Old		WEINRICH, M.	104
Testament	9	WEIPPERT, M.	33
Theologische Realenzyklopädie		WEIS, R. D.	46
(TRE)	18	WERBICK, J.	114
Theologisches Wörterbuch zum		WERNER, R.	121
Alten Testament	12	WESSELIUS, J. W.	120
THIBAUT, A.	146	WESTBROOK, R.	146
THORPE, I. J.	34	WESTERMANN, C.	95
THRONTVEIT, M. A.	146	WEVERS, J. W.	45–46

INDEX

	Page		Page
Wewers, G. A.	18	Xella, P.	141
Wheeler, C. B.	71		
Whitaker, R. E.	134		
White, H. C.	95		
White, S. A.	7	Yikutieli, Y.	12
Whiteman, D. L.	57	Young, G. D.	146
Wightman, G.	27		
Wightman, J. G.	31		
Wills, L. M.	7	Zadok, R.	142
Wimbush, V. L.	133	Zakovitch, Y.	60
van Wolde, E. J.	65, 96	Zatelli, I.	25
Wöller, H.	114	Zayadine, F.	27
Wolters, A.	33	Zertal, A.	43
Wood, B. G.	39	Zevulun, U.	12
Wright,. C. J. H.	115	Zimhoni, O.	12
Wright, J. S.	51	Zuckerman, B.	97

The Society for Old Testament Study is a British Society for Old Testament scholars. Candidates for membership, which is not confined to British subjects, must be nominated by two members of the Society. Residents of the British Isles are normally admitted to ordinary membership and non-residents to associate membership. All correspondence concerning domestic affairs of the Society should be sent to:

Dr P. M. Joyce
Department of Theology
University of Birmingham
P.O. Box 363
Birmingham B15 2TT
England